T0268886

POLISH
DICTIONARY
&
PHRASEBOOK

POLISH
DICTIONARY
&
PHRASEBOOK

Hippocrene Books, Inc.
New York

Copyright © 2011 Hippocrene Books

All rights reserved.

For information, address:
HIPPOCRENE BOOKS, INC.
171 Madison Avenue
New York, NY 10016
www.hippocrenebooks.com

Library of Congress Cataloging-in-Publication Data

Polish-English/English-Polish dictionary & phrasebook /
editors of Hippocrene Books.
    p. cm.
 ISBN-13: 978-0-7818-1259-7 (pbk.)
 ISBN-10: 0-7818-1259-3 (pbk.)
1. Polish language--Dictionaries--English. 2. English
language--Dictionaries--Polish. 3. Polish language--Con-
versation and phrasebooks--English. I. Hippocrene Books
(Firm) II. Title: Polish-English/English-Polish dictionary
and phrasebook.

 PG6640.P66 2011
 491.8'5321--dc23

                       2011022448

CONTENTS

INTRODUCTION

Polish belongs to the West Slavic branch of the Indo-European family of languages and, together with Russian and Ukrainian, numbers among the most widely-spoken Slavic languages in the world. The total number of Polish speakers amounts to some 50 million, approximately 40 million of which are inhabitants of Poland. The remaining 10 million speakers are Poles living outside of Poland — Polish emigrants all over the world as well as descendents of Poles who, as a result of frontier changes after World War II, were left outside the territory of their fatherland. While the former are to be found mainly in the Americas, Western Europe and Australia, the latter constitute significant minorities in Lithuania, Belarus, Ukraine, and Russia.

The beginnings of Polish as an independent language date back to the 10th century and are linked to the establishment and growth of the Polish state. The oldest records of written Polish come from 1136, even though Polish names of tribes, sovereigns, rivers and settlements appeared in much earlier Latin documents. Until the 14th century, Polish existed mainly in regional spoken forms. Yet a long-time tradition of using the vernacular at princely and ducal courts, in state administration, and in religious as well as secular rhetoric facilitated the creation of a common, national language. This supra-regional language had emerged by the 15th century and became established in the 16th, mainly as a result of the expansion of Renaissance writing and the conscious efforts on the part of authors and printers of the time. The invention and popularization of print contributed to the spread of Polish literary language and its cultivation, and thus the second half of the 16th century is considered the "golden age" of Polish culture.

The 18th century witnessed a revival of Polish, after a period of extended influence of Latin and French. Under the influence of the great Romantic poets (such as Adam Mickiewicz), a new type of written Polish arose: closer to the conversational language and permeated with folk and regional elements. During the Partitions Period (1795-1918), the territory of Poland was subjected to intensive Russification and Germanization by Russian, Prussian and Austrian perpetrators, aiming to obliterate Polish language and identity. These attempts failed due to the consistent resistance on the part of Polish society, for whom the preservation of its language and culture became a patriotic duty. After Poland regained its independence, Polish was re-introduced to schools and all public institutions.

A BRIEF GRAMMAR

Polish is an inflectional language with 3 tenses, 7 cases (Nominative, Genitive, Dative, Accusative, Instrumental, Locative, and Vocative), 2 numbers (singular and plural), and 3 genders (masculine, feminine and neuter). There are relatively few vowels (a, e, o, u i, y, ę, ą), but numerous consonants and consonant clusters. Words are usually multi-syllable, with stress falling on the penultimate syllable.

Polish is definitely a complex language, but it is not necessary to master all the nuances of its grammar and vocabulary to be understood. The language contained in this *Phrasebook* should be absolutely sufficient for any English speaker to get by on his or her trip. No one expects a guest from abroad to speak this difficult language flawlessly, and the very fact of a foreigner trying to communicate in Polish (even if it is broken Polish) is appreciated by most Poles, who undoubtedly will go to great lengths to understand their interlocutor and make sure that they are understood. Since Poles have a reputation as a friendly and hospitable nation, the whole experience is bound to be fun!

Articles and Genders

Unlike English, Polish does not have articles, so there are no direct equivalents of the English "a," "an," and "the," and a determination of a noun as definite or indefinite depends on the context. However, definiteness can be expressed by the pronouns *ten*, *ta*, *to* (functioning as definite articles) and *jakiś*, *jakaś*, *jakieś* (serving as indefinite articles, similar to the English "a"). The use of pronouns to convey definiteness of nouns is characteristic of colloquial Polish.

In Polish there are **three genders:** masculine, feminine and neuter. Gender plays an important role in grammatical agreement, i.e. nouns require an appropriate ending in the modifying adjectives, pronouns or numerals. For example, adjectives describing masculine nouns also need to have masculine endings, etc., as in:

masculine:	dobry ojciec	*a good father*
feminine:	dobra matka	*a good mother*
neuter:	dobre dziecko	*a good child*

In general, the names for living creatures correspond to the natural distinction in gender: names for males will be masculine in gender and names for females will be feminine. The gender of other nouns is usually a matter of custom.

The gender of a noun can be deduced from its nominative form. Masculine nouns usually end in a consonant (e.g. *ojciec* = father, *Polak* = Pole, *chłopiec* = boy, *nauczyciel* = teacher); feminine nouns usually end in –**a** (e.g. *matka* = mother, *Polka* = Pole, *dziewczyna*=girl, *nuczycielka* = teacher) or –**i** (e.g. *pani* = Madam, Miss, Ms., Mrs.*)*; and neuter nouns usually end in –**o** (e.g. *dziecko* = child, *okno* = window, *ucho* = ear), or – **e** (e.g. *śniadanie* = breakfast, *pranie* = laundry), or –**ę** (e.g. *imię* = name, *zwierzę* = animal).

Cases

Many Polish words, including nouns, are inflected by the cases. Case is reflected in a changed word form, according to its function in a sentence. Polish has **seven cases**, in both singular and plural:

Nominative – expresses the subject of a sentence, e.g. *Okno jest duże* = The window is big.

Genitive – expresses possession and almost all meanings of *of*, e.g. *Dziecko naszego nauczyciela* = Our teacher's child; *początek książki* = the beginning of the book; *szklanka wody* = a glass of water; *trochę masła* = a little butter

Dative – expresses indirect object (beneficiary of an action), e.g. *Pomagam mamie* = I'm helping my mom.

Accusative – expresses direct object, e.g. *Mam syna i córkę* = I have a son and a daughter; *Chcę kupić cukier i kawę* = I want to buy sugar and coffee.

Instrumental – expresses the means by which something is done, e.g. *Jedziemy pociągiem* = We're going by train, as well as predicate nouns (single nouns or noun phrases following a form of the verb "to be" or another linking verb), e.g. *Jan jest nauczycielem* = John is a teacher; *Adam Mickiewicz był wspaniałym poetą* = Adam Mickiewicz was a great poet.

Locative – used with certain prepositions: **w** (in), **na** (on, at), **po** (after), **przy** (near), **o** (about), e.g. *Dzieci są teraz w szkole* = The children are at school now.; *Co robisz po pracy?* = What are you doing after work?

Vocative – used in direct address, e.g. *Dzień dobry, panie doktorze!* = Good morning, doctor!

Pronouns

Personal Pronouns

Singular		*Plural*	
ja	I	**my**	we
ty	you (*sg.*)	**wy**	you (*pl.*)

on	he	**oni**	they (*masc. pers.;* *used for male and mixed male and female groups*)
ona	she	**one**	they (*non-masc. pers.;* *used for groups not containing any males*)
ono	it		

Pronouns of Formal Address

These pronouns are used to address strangers, superiors, or people of authority.

Singular
pan sir, you, Mr.
pani madam, you, Ms., Miss, Mrs.

Plural
panowie sirs, you (*masc. pl.*)
panie madams, you (*fem. pl.*)
państwo ladies and gentlemen, Mr. and Mrs. (e.g. **państwo Kowalscy** = Mr. and Mrs. Kowalski)

Possessive Pronouns

English	*Polish*
my, mine	**ja → mój** (*before masc. sg. nouns*), **moja** (*before fem. sg. nouns*), **moje** (*before neuter sg. nouns*), **moi** (*before masc. pers. pl. nouns*), **moje** (*before other pl. nouns*)
your, yours	**ty → twój, twoja, twoje** (*sg.*); **twoi, twoje** (*pl.*) (*usage as above*)
his	**on → jego** (*Gen.*)
her, hers	**ona → jej** (*Gen.*)
its	**ono → jego** (*Gen.*)
	pan →pana (*Gen.*)
	pani → pani (*Gen.*)

our, ours	**my** → **nasz** (*before masc. sg. nouns*),
	nasza (*before fem. sg. nouns*),
	nasze (*before neuter sg. nouns*);
	nasi (*before masc. pers. pl. nouns*),
	nasze (*before other pl. nouns*)
your, yours	**wy** → **wasz, wasza, wasze** (*sg.*);
	wasi, wasze (*pl.*) (*usage as above*)
their, theirs	**oni** → **ich** (*Gen.*)
their, theirs	**one** → **ich** (*Gen.*)
	państwo → **państwa** (*Gen.*)
	panie → **pań** (*Gen.*)
	panowie → **panów** (*Gen.*)

Adjectives

Adjectives agree with the nouns they modify in gender, number, and case. The masculine singular ending is –y or –i (*dobry* = good, *miły* = nice, *drogi* = expensive); the feminine singular ending is –a (*dobra, miła, droga*); the neuter singular ending is –e (*dobre, miłe, drogie*). For example:

dobry/miły chłopiec – a good/nice boy
dobra/miła dziewczyna – a good/nice girl
dobre/miłe dziecko – a good/nice child

drogi samochód – an expensive car
droga sukienka – an expensive dress
drogie biurko – an expensive desk

Adjectives usually precede nouns even though there are exceptions.

Adverbs

Many adverbs in Polish are formed by adding the ending –o or –e to the adjectives, as in the examples below:

English	Adjective	Adverb
good	dobry	dobrze
bad	zły	źle
pretty	ładny	ładnie
ugly	brzydki	brzydko
expensive	drogi	drogo
cheap	tani	tanio

Some examples of non-adjectival adverbs are:

always – **zawsze**

already – **już**

soon – **niedługo**

still – **jeszcze**

hardly ever – **rzadko kiedy**

often – **często**

usually – **zwykle**

Verbs and Tenses

The basic form of a verb is **infinitive**, the citation form listed in all dictionaries. A typical infinitive ending is **–ć**. Verbs **conjugate**, i.e. vary according to number, person and tense, based on patterns. These patterns, or classes, of verbs are called **conjugations** and are based on certain sets of present-tense endings. The forms of 1st person singular and 2nd person singular determine the class of a verb. Verbs are negated by placing the negative particle **"nie"** directly before them (e.g. *Nie chcę* = I don't want to; *Nie byliśmy tam* = We weren't there). Polish has three tenses: **present**, **past**, and **future**.

The following conjugations of the verbs **chcieć** (*to want*), **być** (*to be*), and **mieć** (*to have*) are given as examples:

CHCIEĆ (*to want*)

Present tense:

Singular

(ja)	chcę	I want
(ty)	chcesz	you want
on/pan		he wants
ona/pani	chce	she wants
ono/to		it wants

Plural

(my)	chcemy	we want
(wy)	chcecie	you want
oni/	chcą	they want
państwo/		
panowie		
one/panie	chcą	they want

Past tense:

Singular

(ja)	chciałem (*m*)	I wanted
	chciałam (*f*)	
(ty)	chciałeś (*m*)	you wanted
	chciałaś (*f*)	
on/pan	chciał	he wanted
ona/pani	chciała	she wanted
ono/to	chciało	it wanted

Plural

(my)	chcieliśmy (*m*)	we wanted
	chciałyśmy (*f*)	
(wy)	chcieliście (*m*)	you wanted
	chciałyście (*f*)	
oni/	chcieli	they wanted
państwo/		
panowie		
one/panie	chciały	they wanted

Future tense:

Singular

(ja)	**zechcę** *or*	I will want
	będę chciał (*m*)	
	będę chciała (*f*)	
(ty)	**zechcesz** *or*	you will want
	będziesz chciał (*m*)	
	będziesz chciała (*f*)	
on/pan	**zechce** *or*	he will want
	będzie chciał	
ona/pani	**zechce** *or*	she will want
	będzie chciała	
ono/to	**zechce** *or*	it will want
	będzie chciało	

Plural

(my)	**zechcemy** *or*	we will want
	będziemy chcieli (*m*)	
	będziemy chciały (*f*)	
(wy)	**zechcecie** *or*	you will want
	będziecie chcieli (m)	
	będziecie chciały (f)	
oni/	**zechcą** *or*	they will want
państwo/	**będą chcieli**	
panowie		
one/panie	**zechcą** *or*	they will want
	będą chciały	

BYĆ (*to be*)

Present tense:

Singular

(ja)	**jestem**	I am
(ty)	**jesteś**	you are
on/pan		he is
ona/pani	**jest**	she is
ono/to		it is

Plural

(my)	jesteśmy	we are
(wy)	jesteście	you are
oni/ państwo/ panowie	są	they are
one/panie	są	they are

Past tense:

Singular

(ja)	byłem (*m*) byłam (*f*)	I was
(ty)	byłeś (*m*) byłaś (*f*)	you were
on/pan	był	he was
ona/pani	była	she was
ono/to	było	it was

Plural

(my)	byliśmy (*m*) byłyśmy (*f*)	we were
(wy)	byliście (*m*) byłyście (*f*)	you were
oni/ państwo/ panowie	byli	they were
one/panie	były	they were

Future tense:

Singular

(ja)	będę	I will
(ty)	będziesz	you will
on/pan		he will
ona/pani	będzie	she will
ono/to		it will

Plural

| (my) | będziemy | we will |
| (wy) | będziecie | you will |

oni/	będą	they will
państwo/		
panowie		
one/panie	będą*	they will

*The future tense of other verbs is usually formed by adding the infinitive to the future tense of the verb **być** (e.g. *będę czytać* = I will read; *będą podróżować* = they will travel).

MIEĆ (*to have*)

Present tense:

Singular

(ja)	mam	I have
(ty)	masz	you have
on/pan		he has
ona/pani	ma	she has
ono/to		it has

Plural

(my)	mamy	we have
(wy)	macie	you have
one/panie	mają	they have
oni/	mają	they have
państwo/		
panowie		

Past tense:

Singular

(ja)	miałem (*m*)	I had
	miałam (*f*)	
(ty)	miałeś (*m*)	you had
	miałaś (*f*)	
on/pan	miał	he had
ona/pani	miała	she had
ono/to	miało	it had

Plural

(my)	mieliśmy (*m*) miałyśmy (*f*)	we had
(wy)	mieliście (*m*) miałyście (*f*)	you had
oni/ państwo/ panowie	mieli	they had
one/panie	miały	they had

Future tense:

Singular

(ja)	będę miał (*m*) bedę miała (*f*)	I will have
(ty)	będziesz miał (*m*) będziesz miała (*f*)	you will have
on/pan	będzie miał	he will have
ona/pani	będzie miała	she will have
ono/to	będzie miało	it will have

Plural

(my)	będziemy mieli (*m*) będziemy miały (*f*)	we will have
(wy)	będziecie mieli (*m*) będziecie miały (*f*)	you will read
oni/ państwo/ panowie	będą mieli	they will have
one/panie	będą miały	they will have

PRONUNCIATION

This book uses a simplified phonetic transcription to represent the sounds of Polish. Polish is a phonetic language, meaning that the sounds generally correspond to a word's spelling. Polish pronunciation is much more regular than that of English. The Polish alphabet consists of the following letters:

a, ą, b, c, ć, d, e, ę, f, g, h, i, j, k, l, ł, m, n, ń, o, ó, p, r, s, ś, t, u, w, y, z, ź, ż

Below are explanations of the pronunciation of Polish letters and letter combinations and corresponding sounds, using English examples wherever possible. Sounds have been divided into "vowels" and "consonants." To use the phonetics in this book, just read the pronunciation as if it were English.

Underlining indicates which syllable in a word should be stressed. In most Polish words, the next-to-last syllable is stressed: <u>je</u>den [<u>yeh</u>-dehn] (*one*), cho<u>ro</u>ba [hoh-<u>roh</u>-bah] (*illness*).

Soft sounds are marked with the apostrophe (') in phonetics. You will see this in such pairs as *n* and *n'*, where the *n'* sound is much softer than the regular *n*.

In some cases Polish phonetics will show letter combinations that appear in English words, but are pronounced differently in English than in Polish. In such examples an additional space or hyphen has been inserted to indicate that one should avoid blending the two sounds:

Polish: schody [<u>s-hoh</u>-dyh *or* <u>s hoh</u>-dyh]
English: stairs

In the example above '*s*' and '*h*' have been separated as they should not be pronounced as '*sh*', but as separate sounds.

Vowels

Polish letter	Pronunciation	Symbol	Example	Phonetic transcription & English meaning
a	like *a* in *start*	ah	pan	*pahn* sir, Mr.
i	like *ee* in *see*	ee	ile	*ee-leh* how much/many
e	like *e* in *pen*	eh	krem	*krehm* cream
			ten	*tehn* this *(for masc. nouns)*
o	like *o* in *north*	oh	sok	*sohk* juice
ó, u	like *u* in *push* or *oo* in *foot*, but slightly longer	uh	stół	*stuhw* table
			zupa	*zuh-pah* soup
y	like *i* in *sit* or *it*	yh	syn	*syhn* son
ą	*ohn* before a consonant (similar to *on* in *don't*)	ohn	piątek	*pyohn-tehk* Friday
	ohm before b and p	ohm	zastąpić	*zah-stohm-peech'* replace
	ohm at the end of a word (similar to French *bon, son, ton*)	ohm	ją	*yohm* her (Acc.)
			mają	*mah-yohm* (they) have
ę	like *en* in *bent* or *sense*, before a consonant	ehn	księgarnia	*ksh'yehn-gahr-n'yah* bookstore
			pięta	*pyehn-tah* heel
	ehm before b and p	ehm	sęp	*sehmp* vulture
	eh at the end of a word	eh	farbę	*fahr-beh* paint (Acc.)

Consonants & Consonant Clusters

Polish letter	Pronunciation	Symbol	Example	Phonetic transcription & English translation
c	like ts in tsunami	ts	koc	kohts blanket
ć, ci	like ch in cheap, but shorter and softer	ch'	ćma ciepły	ch'mah moth ch'yeh-pwyh warm
cz	like tch in match	ch	czarny	chahr-nyh black
dz	like ds in kids or Leeds	dz	dzbanek	dzbah-nehk jug, pitcher
dź, dzi	like j in jeep, but shorter and softer	dj'	dźwigać dziadek dziękuję	dj'vee-gahch' carry, lift dj'yah-dehk grandfather, grandpa dj'yehn-kuh-yeh thank you
drz, dż	like j in judge or jeans, or dg in edge	dj	drzewo dżem dżinsy	dieh-voh tree djehm jam dieen-syh jeans
h, ch	hard, like ch in Bach	h	hotel chata	hoh-tehl hotel hah-tah cottage, cabin
j	like y in yellow	y	jak	yahk how

ł	w	like w in wet or wow	koło ładny	*koh-woh* wheel *wah-dnyh* pretty
ń, ni	n'	like ny in canyon	styczeń pralnia	*styh-chehn'* January *prahl-n'yah* laundry (place)
r	r	slightly rolled and harder than English (like r in Spanish *arriba*)	rok	*rohk* year
ż, rz	zh	like s in *measure* and *vision*, but harder	żółty rzeka	*zhuhw-tyh* yellow *zheh-kah* river
ź, zi	zh'	like s in *measure* and *vision*, but softer, closer to the French	źrenica zielony	*zh'reh-n'ee-tsah* pupil (in eye) *zh'yeh-loh-nyh* green
ś, si	sh'	similar to *she*, but softer and shorter	środa się siedem	*sh'roh-dah* Wednesday *sh'yeh* oneself (*pron.*) *sh'yeh-dehm* seven
sz	sh	like *sh* in *sharp*	koszula	*koh-shuh-lah* shirt
w	v	like *v* in *vessel*	winda	*veen-dah* elevator

The consonants **b, d, f, g, k, l, m, n, p, s, t,** and **z** are pronounced very similar to English, as in the following examples:

b as in the English *boy* → Polish: **banan** (banana)

d as in the English *dog* → Polish: **dom** (house, home)

f as in the English *fan* → Polish: **farba** (paint)

g as in the English *goose* → Polish: **gra** (game), **noga** (leg, foot)

k as in the English *kite* → Polish: **rok** (year), **oko** (eye)

l as in the English **let** → Polish: *lody* (ice cream)

m as in the English *met* → Polish: **mama** (mom)

n as in the English *net* → Polish: **pan** (sir, Mr.)

p as in the English *pet* → Polish: **pan** (sir, Mr.), **kanapa** (couch, sofa)

s as in the English *safe* → Polish: **nos** (nose)

t as in the English *ten* → Polish: **kot** (cat)

z as in the English *zip* →Polish: **zupa** (soup)

Polish-English
Dictionary

A

academia *ah-kah-deh-myah* academy
administracja *ahd-mee-n'ee-strah-tsyah* administration
adres *ah-drehs* address (*n.*)
adwokat *ahd-voh-kaht* attorney
agencja *ah-gehn-tsyah* agency (*n.*)
agent *ah-gehnt* agent
AIDS *ehyts* AIDS
akcent *ahk-tsehnt* accent
akceptować *ahk-tsehp-toh-vahch'* accept
akr (0,4 hektara) *ahkr* acre (0.4 hectares)
akt urodzenia *ahkt uh-roh-dzeh-n'yah* birth certificate
aktor *ahk-tohr* actor
aktywista *ahk-tyh-vee-stah* activist
akumulator *ah-kuh-muh-lah-tohr* battery
alarm *ah-lahrm* alarm (warning signal)
alarm pożarowy *ah-lahrm poh-zhah-roh-vyh* fire alarm
albo *ahl-boh* or
ale *ah-leh* but (*conj*)
aleja *ah-leh-yah* avenue
alergia *ah-lehr-gyah* allergy
alkohol *ahl-koh-hohl* alcohol, liquor
ambasada *ahm-bah-sah-dah* embassy
ambasador *ahm-bah-sah-dohr* ambassador
anemiczny *ah-neh-mee-chnyh* anemic
antena satelitarna *ahn-teh-nah sah-teh-lee-tahr-nah* satellite
antybiotyki *ahn-tyh-byoh-tyh-kee* antibiotics
antyk *ahn-tyhk* antique
antykoncepcja *ahn-tyh-kohn-tsehp-tsyah* contraception
anulować *ah-nuh-loh-vahch'* cancel
aparat fotograficzny *ah-pah-raht foh-toh-grah-fee-chnyh* camera
apartament *ah-pahr-tah-mehnt* suite
apelować *ah-peh-loh-vahch'* appeal (*v.* – legal, in court)
apetyt *ah-peh-tyht* appetite
apteczka *ahp-tehch-kah* first-aid kit
apteka *ahp-teh-kah* pharmacy
architektura *ahr-hee-tehk-tuh-rah* architecture
aresztować *ah-reh-shtoh-vahch'* arrest (*v.*)
armia *ahr-myah* army
artretyzm *ahr-treh-tyhzm* arthritis

artykuły *ahr-tyh-kuh-wyh* goods
aspiryna *ah-spee-ryh-nah* aspirin
astma *ahst-mah* asthma
asystować *ah-syh-stoh-vahch'* assist (cooperate with)
atak *ah-tahk* assault, attack (*n.*)
atak serca *ah-tahk sehr-tsah* heart attack
atakować *ah-tah-koh-vahch'* assault (*v.*)
atakować *ah-tah-koh-vahch'* attack (*v.*)
atrament *ah-trah-mehnt* ink
auto *ahw-toh* car
autobus *ahw-toh-buhs* bus
automatyczna skrzynia biegów *ahw-toh-mah-tyhch-nah skshyh-n'yah byeh-guhf* automatic transmission
automatyczny *ahw-toh-mah-tyhch-nyh* automatic
autor *ahw-tohr* author
autorytet *ahw-toh-ryh-teht* authority (influence)
autostrada *ahw-toh-strah-dah* highway
awans *ah-vahns* promotion
azyl *ah-zyhl* refuge

B

babcia *bahp-ch'yah* grandmother
badać *bah-dahch'* examine, inspect
badać *bah-dahch'* inspect
badanie *bah-dah-n'yeh* test (medical)
bagaż *bah-gahzh* baggage, luggage
bagaż podręczny *bah-gahzh poh-drehn-chnyh* carry-on
bagażnik *bah-gahzh-n'eek* trunk (car)
bak *bahk* gas tank
balkon *bahl-kohn* balcony
banan *bah-nahn* banana
bandaż *bahn-dahzh* bandage
bank *bahnk* bank
bankomat *bahn-koh-maht* ATM
bar *bahr* bar, lounge (hotel)
baranek *bah-rah-nehk* lamb (animal)
baranina *bah-rah-n'ee-nah* lamb (food)
bardzo *bahr-dzoh* very (*adv.*)
bariera *bah-ryeh-rah* barrier
barierka *bah-ryehr-kah* rail (for protection, support)
bark *bahrk* shoulder
basen *bah-sehn* pool
bawełna *bah-vehw-nah* cotton

baza _bah-zah_ base
bąbel _bohm-behl_ blister
beczka _beh-chkah_ barrel
benzyna _behn-zyh-nah_ gasoline
benzyna _behn-zyh-nah_ petrol
beton (_building material_) _beh-tohn_ concrete (_n._)
bez _behs_ without
bezdomny _behz-dohm-nyh_ homeless
bezpieczeństwo _behs-pyeh-chehn'-stfoh_ safety
bezpieczeństwo _behs-pyeh-chehn'-stfoh_ security
bezpieczny _behs-pyeh-chnyh_ safe (_adj._)
bezpłatny _behz-pwaht-nyh_ free (without charge)
bezprzewodowy internet _behs-psheh-voh-doh-vyh een-tehr-neht_ wireless internet
biały _byah-wyh_ white
biblia _beeb-lyah_ bible
biblioteka _bee-blyoh-teh-kah_ library
biec _byehts_ run
bieda _byeh-dah_ poverty
bieg _byehg_ gear
biegać _byeh-gahch'_ run
biegunka _byeh-guhn-kah_ diarrhea
bielizna _byeh-leez-nah_ underwear
bilet _bee-leht_ ticket
bilet powrotny _bee-leht poh-vroh-tnyh_ round-trip ticket
bitwa _beet-fah_ battle (_n._)
biurko _byuhr-koh_ desk
biuro _byuh-roh_ office
biurokracja _byuh-roh-krah-tsyah_ bureaucracy
biznes _beez-nehs_ business (commerce)
biżuteria _bee-zhuh-teh-ryah_ jewelry
bliski _blees-kee_ intimate
blisko _blee-skoh_ close (_adv._)
blizna _blee-znah_ scar
bliźniak (_masc._)/**bliźniaczka** (_fem._) _bleezh'-n'yahk/bleezh'-n'yah-chkah_ twin
bluzka _bluhs-kah_ shirt (woman's)
błagać _bwah-gahch'_ appeal (_v._)
błędny _bwehn-dnyh_ incorrect
błogosławić _bwoh-goh-swah-veech'_ bless
błoto _bwoh-toh_ mud
bochenek (chleba) _boh-heh-nehk (hleh-bah)_ loaf
boisko _boh-yee-skoh_ field (sports)
bok _bohk_ side
boleć _boh-lehch'_ hurt

bolesny *boh-lehs-nyh* painful
bomba *bohm-bah* bomb
ból *buhl* pain; torture (*n.*)
ból ucha *buhl uh-hah* earache
ból zęba *buhl zehm-bah* toothache
brać *brahch'* take
brać ślub z (kimś) *brahch' sh'luhp z (keemsh')* marry
 (~ someone)
brat *braht* brother
bratanek *brah-tah-nehk* nephew (*brother's son*)
bratanica *brah-tah-n'ee-tsah* niece (*brother's daughter*)
brązowy *brohn-zoh-vyh* brown
broń *brohn'* gun
brud *bruhd* dirt (mess)
brudny *bruhd-nyh* dirty
brzeg *bzhehg* shore
brzoskwinia *bzhohs-kfee-n'yah* peach
brzuch *bzhuhh* stomach (belly)
budka telefoniczna *buht-kah teh-leh-foh-n'eech-nah*
 phone booth
budynek *buh-dyh-nehk* building
budzić (się) *buh-dj'eech' (sh'yeh)* wake (*v.*)
budzik *buh-dj'eek* alarm (alarm clock)
bunt *buhnt* rebellion
buntować się *buhn-toh-vahch' sh'yeh* rebel (*v.*)
buntownik *buhn-tohv-n'eek* rebel (*n.*)
burmistrz *buhr-meestsh* mayor
burza *buh-zhah* storm (*n.*)
but *buht* shoe, boot
butelka *buh-tehl-kah* bottle
być może *byhch' moh-zheh* possibly (*adv.*)
być w stanie *bych' fstah-n'yeh* able (*v.* – be able to)
bydło *byh-dwoh* cattle
byk *byhk* bull

C

całkowity *tsahw-koh-vee-tyh* total, entire
całować *tsah-woh-vahch'* kiss (*v.*)
cały *tsah-wyh* entire
cebula *tseh-buh-lah* onion
cegła *tseh-gwah* brick
cel *tsehl* purpose
cel podróży *tsehl poh-druh-zhyh* destination

cement *tseh-mehnt* cement
cena *tseh-nah* price
cena pokoju (za dzień / za dobę) *tseh-nah poh-koh-yuh (zah dj'yehn' / zah doh-beh)* room rate
cent *tsehnt* cent
centrum *tsehn-truhm* center
centrum handlowe *tsehn-truhm hahn-dloh-veh* shopping center
(w) centrum miasta *f tsehn-truhm myah-stah* downtown
ceramika *tseh-rah-mee-kah* pottery
chcieć *hch'yehch'* want
chirurg *hee-ruhrg* surgeon
chleb *hlehp* bread
chlebak *hleh-bahk* knapsack
chłopak *hwoh-pahk* boyfriend
chłopiec *hwoh-pyehts* boy
chodnik *hohd-n'eek* pavement
chodzić *hoh-dj'eech'* walk (*v.*)
choroba *hoh-roh-bah* disease, illness
choroba lokomocyjna *hoh-roh-bah loh-koh-moh-tsyhy-nah* motion sickness
chory *hoh-ryh* sick
chronić *hroh-n'eech'* protect
chudy *huh-dyh* thin
chusteczki do pielęgnacji niemowląt *huh-stehch-kee doh pyeh-lehn-gnah-tsyee n'yeh-mohv-lohnt* baby wipes
chwila *hfee-lah* moment
chwytac *hfyh-tahch'* catch (*v.*)
ciało *ch'yah-woh* body
ciastko *ch'yahst-koh* pastry
ciasto *ch'yah-stoh* dough; pie; cake
ciąć *ch'yohn'ch'* cut (*v.*)
ciągnąć *ch'yohng-nohnch'* pull
cichy *ch'ee-hyh* quiet
ciecierzyca *ch'yeh-ch'yeh-zhyh-tsah* chickpeas
ciemny *ch'yehm-nyh* dark
ciepły *ch'yeh-pwyh* warm
cierpieć na chorobę morską *ch'yehr-pyehch' nah hoh-roh-beh mohr-skohm* seasick (to be/feel ~)
cierpliwość *ch'yehr-plee-vohsh'ch'* patience
cięcie *ch'yehn'-ch'yeh* cut (*n.*)
ciężarówka *ch'yehn-zhah-ruhf-kah* truck
ciężki *ch'yehn-zhkee* hard (difficult); heavy
cisza nocna *ch'ee-shah nohts-nah* curfew (hotel)

cło *tswoh* customs duty
cmentarz *tsmehn-tahzh* cemetery
co *tsoh* what
coś *tsohsh'* something
córka *tsuhr-kah* daughter
cukier *tsuh-kyehr* sugar
cukierek miętowy *tsuh-kyeh-rehk myehn-toh-vyh* mint (candy)
cukierek *tsuh-kyeh-rehk* candy
cukrzyk *tsuh-kshyhk* diabetic (*n.*)
CV *see vee* resume (*n.*)
cynamon *tsyh-nah-mohn* cinnamon
cytryna *tsyh-tryh-nah* lemon
cywil (*colloquial*) *tsyh-veel* civilian (*n.*)
czajnik *chahy-n'eek* kettle
czarny *chahr-nyh* black
czas *chahs* time
czasownik *chah-sohv-n'eek* verb
czaszka *chahsh-kah* skull
czek *chehk* check (bank)
czekać *cheh-kahch'* wait (*v.*)
czekolada *cheh-koh-lah-dah* chocolate
czerwiec *chehr-vyehts* June
czerwony *chehr-voh-nyh* red
często *chehn-stoh* often (*adv.*)
część *chehnsh'ch'* section
część zapasowa *chehn'sh'ch' zah-pah-soh-vah* spare part
członek *chwoh-nehk* member
członek (*pl.* **członkowie**) **rodziny królewskiej** *chwoh-nehk* (*pl.* *chwohn-koh-vyeh*) *roh-dj'ee-nyh kruh-lehf-skyehy* royalty
człowiek *chwoh-vyehk* human (*n.*)
czoło *choh-woh* forehead
czterdzieści *chtehr-dj'yehsh'-ch'ee* forty
czternaście *chtehr-nahsh'-ch'yeh* fourteen
cztery *chteh-ryh* four
czuć (się) *chuhch' (sh'yeh)* feel
czwartek *chfahr-tehk* Thursday
czy *chyh* if
czynność *chyhn-nohsh'ch'* activity
czysty *chyh-styh* clean, pure
czytać *chyh-tahch'* read

Ć

ćwierć *ch'fyehrch'* quarter

D

dach *dahh* roof
daleki *dah-leh-kee* far (*adj.*)
daleko *dah-leh-koh* far (*adv.*)
daleko od *dah-leh-koh ohd* away
danie *dah-n'yeh* dish (food)
data *dah-tah* date (*n.*)
data urodzenia *dah-tah uh-roh-dzeh-n'yah* date of birth
data ważności *dah-tah vahzh-nohsh'-ch'ee* expiration
   date
dawać *dah-vahch'* give
decydować *deh-tsyh-doh-vahch'* decide
decyzja *deh-tsyh-zyah* decision
dekada *deh-kah-dah* decade
deklaracja celna *deh-klah-rah-tsyah tsehl-nah* customs
   declaration
demokracja *deh-moh-krah-tsyah* democracy (system)
dentysta *dehn-tyhs-tah* dentist
deprawować *deh-prah-voh-vahch'* corrupt (deprave) (*v.*)
deser *deh-sehr* dessert
deszcz *dehshch* rain (*n.*)
detergent *deh-tehr-gehnt* detergent
dezodorant *deh-zoh-doh-rahnt* deodorant
diabetyk *dyah-beh-tyhk* diabetic (*n.*)
diagnoza *dyah-gnoh-zah* diagnosis
dla niepalących *dlah n'yeh-pah-lohn-tsyhh* non-smoking
dla palących *dlah pah-lohn-tsyhh* smoking
dla pieszych *dlah pyeh-shyhh* pedestrian (modif)
dlaczego *dlah-cheh-goh* why
dławić się *dwah-veech' sh'yeh* choke
dług *dwuhg* debt
długi *dwuh-gee* long
długopis *dwuh-goh-pees* pen (ballpoint pen)
do (aż ~) *doh (ahzh ~)* until (to a given point)
do dyspozycji *doh dyhs-poh-zyh-tsyee* available
do góry *doh guh-ryh* up
dobry *doh-bryh* good, kind, right (correct)

dobrze _dohb-zheh_ OK

dochód _doh-huht_ income

dodatkowo _doh-daht-koh-voh_ extra (_adv._)

dodatkowy _doh-daht-koh-vyh_ extra, excess (_adj._)

dodawać _doh-dah-vahch'_ add

dogodny _doh-goh-dnyh_ convenient

dok _dohk_ dock

dokładny _doh-kwah-dnyh_ accurate, exact

dokument _doh-kuh-mehnt_ document

dolar _doh-lahr_ dollar

dom _dohm_ home, house

dom towarowy _dohm toh-vah-roh-vyh_ department store

dopiero co _doh-pyeh-roh tsoh_ just (expressing time)

dopóki nie _doh-puh-kee n'yeh_ until (before fulfillment of condition)

doroczny _doh-rohch-nyh_ annual

dorosły _doh-roh-swyh_ adult (_n._)

doskonale _doh-skoh-nah-leh_ perfect (_adv._)

doskonały _doh-skoh-nah-wyh_ perfect (_adj._)

dostać _dohs-tahch'_ get (obtain)

dostarczać _dohs-tahr-chahch'_ deliver

dostawa _doh-stah-vah_ delivery

dostęp _dohs-tehmp_ access (_n._)

dostępny _doh-stehm-pnyh_ available

dosyć _doh-syhch'_ enough (_pron._)

dość _dohsh'ch'_ enough (_pron._)

doświadczenie _dohsh'-fyaht-cheh-n'yeh_ experience (_n._)

dotyk _doh-tyhk_ touch (one of the senses) (_n._)

dotykać _doh-tyh-kahch'_ touch (_v._)

doustny _doh-uhst-nyh_ oral (medicine)

dowód tożsamości _doh-wuht tohsh-sah-mohsh'-ch'ee_ ID card

dowód tożsamości _doh-wuht tohsh-sah-mohsh'-ch'ee_ identification

dozwolony _doh-zvoh-loh-nyh_ allowed

dół _duhw_ bottom (_n._)

dramat _drah-maht_ drama

drażnić _drahzh-n'eech'_ irritate

drewno _drehv-noh_ wood

drewno opałowe _drehv-noh oh-pah-woh-veh_ firewood

drink _dreenk_ drink (alcoholic) (_n._)

droga _droh-gah_ road

drogi _droh-gee_ expensive

drożdże _drohzh-djeh_ yeast

drób _druhp_ poultry

drugi _druh_-gee second (not first)
drukarka druh-_kahr_-kah printer
drzewo _djeh_-voh wood
drzwi djvee door
dużo _duh_-zhoh many, much (_adv._)
duży _duh_-zhyh big, large
DVD dee vee dee DVD
dwa razy dvah _rah_-zyh twice (_adv._)
dwadzieścia dvah-_dj'yehsh'_-ch'yah twenty
dwanaście dvah-_nahsh'_-ch'yeh twelve
dworzec _dvoh_-zhehts station
dworzec autobusowy _dvoh_-zhehts ahw-toh-buh-_soh_-vyh
  bus terminal
dworzec kolejowy _dvoh_-zhehts koh-leh-_yoh_-vyh train
  station
dyktować dyh-_ktoh_-vahch' dictate
dyplomata dyh-ploh-_mah_-tah diplomat
dyskutować (o) dyhs-kuh-_toh_-vahch' (oh) argue
dywan _dyh_-vahn carpet
dywanik dyh-_vah_-n'eek rug
dzbanek _dzbah_-nehk jug
dziadek _dj'yah_-dehk grandfather
działać _dj'yah_-wahch' act (_v._)
działacz _dj'yah_-wahch' activist
działalność gospodarcza dj'yah-_wahl_-nohsh'ch'
  gohs-poh-_dahr_-chah business (commerce)
dziecko _dj'yeh_-tskoh child, kid, baby
dziedzina dj'yeh-_dj'ee_-nah field (academic)
dzielić (się) _dj'yeh_-leech' (sh'yeh) share
dzielnica dj'yehl-_n'ee_-tsah district (neighborhood)
dziennikarz (_masc._)/**dziennikarka** (_fem._) dj'yehn-_n'ee_-
  kahsh/dj'yehn-n'ee-_kahr_-kah journalist
dzień dj'yehn' day, daytime
dzień dobry dj'yehn' _dohb_-ryh hello
dzień powszedni dj'yehn' pohf-_shehd_-n'ee weekday
dzień wolny dj'yehn' _vohl_-nyh holiday (day off)
dziesięć _dj'yeh_-sh'yehn'ch' ten
dziesięciolecie dj'yeh-sh'yehn-ch'yoh-_leh_-ch'yeh decade
dziewczyna dj'yehf-_chyh_-nah girl, girlfriend
dziewczynka dj'yehf-_chyhn_-kah girl
dziewięć _dj'yeh_-vyehn'ch' nine
dziewięćdziesiąt dj'yeh-vyehn'ch'-_dj'yeh_-sh'yohnt ninety
dziewiętnaście dj'yeh-vyehnt-_nahsh'_-ch'yeh nineteen
dziękuję _dj'yehn_-kuh-yeh thank you
dziki _dj'ee_-kee wild

dzisiaj _dj'ee-sh'yahy_ today
dziś wieczorem _dj'eesh' vyeh-choh-rehm_ tonight
dziura _dj'yuh-rah_ hole
dzwon _dzvohn_ bell
dzwonek _dzvoh-nehk_ bell
dzwonić _dzvoh-n'eech'_ call (on telephone)
dźwięk _dj'vyehnk_ sound
dżem _djehm_ jam
dżinsy _djeen-syh_ jeans
dżungla _djuhn-glah_ jungle

E

edukacja _eh-duh-kah-tsyah_ education
egzemplarz _ehg-zehm-plahsh_ copy (book, etc) (_n._)
ekran _eh-krahn_ screen
eksponować _ehks-poh-noh-vahch'_ exhibit (_v._)
eksport _ehks-pohrt_ export (_n._)
eksportować _ehks-pohr-toh-vahch'_ export (_v._)
ekspres _ehks-prehs_ express train
ekspresowy _ehks-preh-soh-vyh_ express (_adj._)
ekstra _ehks-trah_ extra (_adj._)
elektryczność _eh-lehk-tryhch-nohsh'ch'_ electricity
elektryczny _eh-lehk-tryh-chnyh_ electric
e-mail _ee-mehyl_ e-mail
energia _eh-nehr-gyah_ energy
epileptyczny _eh-pee-lehp-tyhch-nyh_ epileptic
etniczny _eht-n'eech-nyh_ ethnic
etykietka, metka _eh-tyh-kyeht-kah, meht-kah_ tag
Europa _eh-uh-roh-pah_ Europe
Europejczyk (_masc._)/**Europejka** (_fem._) _eh-uh-roh-pehy-chyhk/eh-uh-roh-pehy-kah_ European (_n._)
europejski _eh-uh-roh-pehy-skee_ European (_adj._)
ewakuować _eh-vah-kuh-oh-vahch'_ evacuate

F

fajerwerki _fah-yehr-vehr-kee_ fireworks
fajka _fahy-kah_ pipe (smoking)
faks _fahks_ fax (_n._)
faktyczny _fahk-tyh-chnyh_ actual
fałszywy _fahw-shyh-vyh_ false (_adj._)
farba _fahr-bah_ dye (_n._)

farbować *fahr-boh-vahch'* dye (*v.*)
fasola *fah-soh-lah* bean
fast food *fahst fuht* fast food
festiwal *feh-stee-vahl* festival (music)
figa *fee-gah* fig
filiżanka *fee-lee-zhahn-kah* cup
film *feelm* film, movie
fioletowy *fyoh-leh-toh-vyh* purple
firma *feer-mah* business (company)
flaga *flah-gah* flag
flesz *flehsh* flash (camera)
folia aluminiowa *foh-lyah ah-luh-mee-n'yoh-vah*
   aluminum foil
fontanna *fohn-tahn-nah* fountain
formalny *fohr-mahl-nyh* official (*adj.*)
fortepian *fohr-teh-pyahn* piano
fotografowanie z fleszem *foh-toh-grah-foh-vah-n'yeh*
   sfleh-shehm flash photography
fresk *frehsk* mural
fryzjer męski *fryh-zyehr mehn-skee* barber
funt *fuhnt* pound (*n.*)

G

gardło *gahr-dwoh* throat
garnek *gahr-nehk* pot, pan
garnitur *gahr-nee-tuhr* suit (man's)
gazeta *gah-zeh-tah* newspaper
gdzie *gdj'yeh* where
gdziekolwiek *gdj'yeh-kohl-vyehk* anywhere
gładki *gwaht-kee* smooth
głęboki *gwehm-boh-kee* deep
głodny *gwohd-nyh* hungry
głos *gwohs* voice
głosować *gwoh-soh-vahch'* vote (*v.*)
głośny *gwohsh'-nyh* loud
głowa *gwoh-vah* head
główny *gwuhv-nyh* main, chief (*adj.*)
głuchy *gwuh-hyh* deaf
gnić *gn'eech'* rot (*v.*)
godzina *goh-dj'ee-nah* hour, o'clock
godzina policyjna *goh-dj'ee-nah poh-lee-tsyhy-nah*
   curfew
golić (się) *goh-leech' (sh'yeh)* shave

gołąb *goh-wohmp* pigeon
gorący *goh-rohn-tsyh* hot
gorączka *goh-rohnch-kah* fever
gorzki *gohsh-kee* bitter
gospoda *gohs-poh-dah* inn
gospodarka *gohs-poh-dahr-kah* economy
gospodarstwo rolne *goh-spoh-dahr-stfoh rohl-neh* farm
gościnność *gohsh'-ch'een-nohsh'ch'* hospitality
gość *gohsh'ch'* guest, visitor
gotować *goh-toh-vahch'* cook (*v.*)
gotowy *goh-toh-vyh* ready
gotówka *goh-tuhf-kah* cash (*n.*)
góra *guh-rah* top; mountain, mount (*n.*)
gra *grah* game
grać *grahch'* play (*v.*)
gram *grahm* gram
gramatyka *grah-mah-tyh-kah* grammar
granatowy *grah-nah-toh-vyh* navy (color) (*adj.*)
granica grah-n'ee-tsah border
grawerunek *grah-veh-ruh-nehk* engraving
groszek *groh-shehk* pea
groźba *grohzh'-bah* threat
gruby *gruh-byh* fat (about a person) (*adj.*)
grudzień *gruh-dj'yehn'* December
grupa *gruh-pah* group, class
grupa krwi *gruh-pah krfee* blood type
grypa *gryh-pah* flu, influenza
gryźć *gryhsh'ch'* bite (*v.*)
grzebień *gzheh-byehn'* comb
grzeczność *gzhehch-nohsh'ch'* courtesy
grzmot *gzhmoht* thunder
grzyb *gzhyhp* mushroom
guma *guh-mah* rubber
guzik *guh-zh'eek* button
gwałt *gvahwt* rape (*n.*)
gwizdać *gveez-dahch'* whistle (*v.*)

H

hałas *hah-wahs* noise
hamulec *hah-muh-lehts* brake (*n.*)
handel *hahn-dehl* trade (commerce) (*n.*)
handlować *hahn-dloh-vahch'* trade (*v.*)
hasło *hah-swoh* password

hej *hehy* hey (*interjection*)
herbata *hehr-bah-tah* tea
heteroseksualny *heh-teh-roh-sehk-suh-ahl-nyh* heterosexual (*adj.*)
hol *hohl* hall; lobby; lounge (hotel)
homoseksualista *hoh-moh-sehk-suh-ah-lee-stah* homosexual (*n.*)
homoseksualny *hoh-moh-sehk-suh-ahl-nyh* homosexual (*adj.*)
hotel *hoh-tehl* hotel

I

i *ee* and
identyfikować *ee-dehn-tyh-fee-koh-vahch'* identify
idiom *ee-dyohm* idiom
igła *ee-gwah* needle
ignorować *eeg-noh-roh-vahch'* ignore
ilość *ee-lohsh'ch'* amount, number, quantity
imię *ee-myeh* name
imigracja *ee-mee-grah-tsyah* immigration
immigrant (*masc.*)/**imigrantka** (*fem.*) *ee-mee-grahnt/ ee-mee-grahnt-kah* immigrant
import *eem-pohrt* import (*n.*)
importować *eem-pohr-toh-vahch'* import (*v.*)
indywidualny *een-dyh-vee-duh-ahl-nyh* individual (*adj.*)
infekcja *een-fehk-tsyah* infection
informacja *een-fohr-mah-tsyah* information; information desk
informacja telefoniczna *een-fohr-mah-tsyah teh-leh-foh-n'eech-nah* directory assistance
infrastruktura *een-frah-struh-ktuh-rah* infrastructure
inny *een-nyh* other; different (*adj.*)
insekt *een-sehkt* insect
instrukcja obsługi *een-struhk-tsyah ohp-swuh-gee* manual (*n.*)
instrument muzyczny *een-struh-mehnt muh-zyh-chnyh* musical instrument
instytucja *eens-tyh-tuh-tsyah* institution
insulina *een-suh-lee-nah* insulin
internet *een-tehr-neht* Internet
intruz *een-truhz* intruder
intymny *een-tyhm-nyh* intimate
inżynier *een-zhyh-n'yehr* engineer

irytować *ee-ryh-toh-vahch'* irritate
iść *eesh'ch'* go (by foot), walk (*v.*)
iść za *eesh'ch' zah* follow

J

ja *yah* I
jabłko *yahp-koh* apple
jadalnia *yah-dahl-n'yah* dining room
jagnię *yahg-n'yeh* lamb (animal)
jagoda *yah-goh-dah* berry
jajko *yahy-koh* egg
jak *yahk* how
jakiś *yah-keesh'* any
jakość *yah-kohsh'ch'* quality
jaskinia *yah-skee-n'yah* cave
jasny *yahs-nyh* light (of color)
jaszczurka *yahsh-chuhr-kah* lizard
jechać *yeh-hahch'* go (by bus, train, etc.)
jeden *yeh-dehn* one
jedenaście *yeh-deh-nahsh'-ch'yeh* eleven
jednoosobowy *yehd-noh-oh-soh-boh-vyh* single (not double)
jednorazowego użytku *yehd-noh-rah-zoh-veh-goh uh-zhyht-kuh* disposable
jednorazowy *yehd-noh-rah-zoh-vyh* disposable
jednostka *yehd-nohst-kah* individual (*n.*)
jedzenie *yeh-dzeh-n'yeh* food
jesień *yeh-sh'yehn'* autumn, fall (*n.*)
jeszcze raz *yehsh-cheh rahz* again
jeść *yehsh'ch'* eat
jeść obiad *yehsh'ch' oh-byaht* dine
jeśli *yehsh'-lee* if
jezioro *yeh-zh'yoh-roh* lake
jeździć (na) *yehzh'-dj'eech' (nah)* ride (*v.*)
jeździć na łyżwach *yehzh'-dj'eech' nah wyhzh-vahh* skate (*v.*)
jeździć na nartach *yehzh'-dj'eech' nah nahr-tahh* ski (*v.*)
język *yehn-zyhk* language
język angielski *yehn-zyhk ahn-gyehl-skee* English language
języki obce *yehn-zyh-kee ohp-tseh* foreign languages
jogurt *yoh-guhrt* yogurt
jutro *yuh-troh* tomorrow

K

kabel _kah-behl_ wire, cable
kable rozruchowe _kah-bleh rohz-ruh-hoh-veh_ jumper
cables
kakao _kah-kah-oh_ cocoa
kalectwo _kah-lehts-tfoh_ disability
kalendarz _kah-lehn-dahsh_ calendar
kamień _kah-myehn'_ stone
kanał _kah-nahw_ channel
kanapka _kah-nahp-kah_ sandwich
kantor wymiany walut _kahn-tohr vyh-myah-nyh_
vah-luht currency exchange
kapelusz _kah-peh-luhsh_ hat
kaplica _kah-plee-tsah_ chapel
kara _kah-rah_ penalty
karać _kah-rahch'_ punish
karczoch _kahr-chohh_ artichoke
karetka pogotowia _kah-reht-kah poh-goh-toh-vyah_
ambulance
karta _kahr-tah_ card
karta kredytowa _kahr-tah kreh-dyh-toh-vah_ credit card
karta pokładowa _kahr-tah poh-kwah-doh-vah_ boarding
pass
karta telefoniczna _kahr-tah teh-leh-foh-n'eech-nah_
phone card
karta wędkarska _kahr-tah vehnd-kahr-skah_ fishing
license
kaszleć _kahsh-lehch'_ cough (_v._)
katastrofa _kah-tah-stroh-fah_ disaster
katedra _kah-teh-drah_ cathedral
kaucja _kahw-tsyah_ deposit (partial payment)
kawa _kah-vah_ coffee
kawaler (_n. masc._) _kah-vah-lehr_ single (_n._)
kawał _kah-vahw_ trick (_n._)
kawałek _kah-vah-wehk_ piece
kawiarnia _kah-vyahr-n'yah_ café
każdy _kahzh-dyh_ every; anybody, anyone
kąpać się _kohm-pahch' sh'yeh_ bathe
kąpiel _kohm-pyehl_ bath
kąt _kohnt_ corner
kciuk _kch'yuhk_ thumb
kelner (_masc._)/**kelnerka** (_fem._) _kehl-nehr/kehl-nehr-kah_
server (waiter)

kiedy _kyeh-dyh_ when
kiedyś _kyeh-dyhsh'_ once (at one time, formerly)
kiedykolwiek _kyeh-dyh-kohl-vyehk_ ever
kieliszek _kyeh-lee-shehk_ glass (alcoholic drinks)
kiełbasa _kyehw-bah-sah_ sausage
kierunek _kyeh-ruh-nehk_ direction
kieszeń _kyeh-shehn'_ pocket
kij baseballowy _keey behy-zboh-loh-vyh bat_ (equipment used in baseball)
kilka _keel-kah_ some
kilogram _kee-loh-grahm_ kilogram
kilometr _kee-loh-mehtr_ kilometer
kino _kee-noh_ cinema, movie theater
klasa _klah-sah_ class (group)
klaskać _klah-skahch'_ clap
klasyczny _klah-syh-chnyh_ classic
klatka _klaht-kah_ cage
klej _klehy_ glue
klient (_masc._)/**klientka** (_fem._) _klee-yehnt/klee-yehnt-kah_ client, customer
klimat _klee-maht_ climate
klimatyzacja _klee-mah-tyh-zah-tsyah_ air conditioning
klinika _klee-n'ee-kah_ clinic
klub _kluhp_ club
klucz _kluhch_ key
kłamać _kwah-mahch'_ lie (_v._)
kłamstwo _kwahm-stfoh_ lie (_n._)
kłócić się _kwuh-ch'eech' sh'yeh_ argue
kobiecy _koh-byeh-tsyh_ female (_adj._)
kobieta _koh-byeh-tah_ woman, female (_n._)
koc _kohts_ blanket
kochać _koh-hahch'_ love (_v._)
kod pocztowy _kohd pohch-toh-vyh_ postal code
kokos _koh-kohs_ coconut
kolacja _koh-lah-tsyah_ dinner
kolano _koh-lah-noh_ knee
kolej _koh-lehy_ railroad
kolejka _koh-lehy-kah_ queue (_n._)
kółko _kuhw-koh_ circle
kolor _koh-lohr_ color
koło _koh-woh_ wheel; circle
komar _koh-mahr_ mosquito
komedia _koh-meh-dyah_ comedy
komisja _koh-mee-syah_ commission (body)
kompromis _kohm-proh-mees_ compromise

komputer *kohm-puh-tehr* computer
komunikacja *koh-muh-n'ee-kah-tsyah* communication
koncert *kohn-tsehrt* concert
kondom *kohn-dohm* condom
konduktor *kohn-duhk-tohr* conductor
konferencja *kohn-feh-rehn-tsyah* conference
koniec *koh-n'yehts* end (*n.*)
konkretny *kohn-kreh-tnyh* concrete (specific) (*adj.*)
konstytucja *kohns-tyh-tuh-tsyah* constitution
konsulat *kohn-suh-laht* consulate
konsultować się *kohn-suhl-toh-vahch' sh'yeh* consult
konto *kohn-toh* account (banking)
konto bankowe *kohn-toh bahn-koh-veh* bank account
kontrakt *kohn-trahkt* contract
kontrola bagażu *kohn-troh-lah bah-gah-zhuh* baggage
  check
kontrolować *kohn-troh-loh-vahch'* inspect
koń *kohn'* horse
kopać *koh-pahch'* kick
koperta *koh-pehr-tah* envelope
kopia *koh-pyah* copy (*n.*)
kopiować *koh-pyoh-vahch'* copy (*v.*)
korumpować *koh-ruhm-poh-vahch'* corrupt (*v.*)
kosmetyki *kohs-meh-tyh-kee* cosmetics
kostium *kohs-tyuhm* suit (woman's)
kostium kąpielowy *kohs-tyuhm kohm-pyeh-loh-vyh*
  bathing suit
kostka *kohst-kah* ankle
kosz *kohsh* basket
koszerny *koh-shehr-nyh* kosher
koszt *kohsht* cost (*n.*)
kosztować *kohsh-toh-vahch'* cost (*v.*)
kosztować *kohsh-toh-vahch'* taste (*v.*)
koszula *koh-shuh-lah* shirt (man's)
koszyk *koh-shyhk* basket
koszyk na zakupy *koh-shyhk nah zah-kuh-pyh* shopping
  basket
koszykówka *koh-shyh-kuhf-kah* basketball
kościół *kohsh'-ch'yuhw* church
kość *kohsh'ch'* bone
kot *koht* cat
koza *koh-zah* goat
kozak *koh-zahk* boot
kradzież sklepowa *krah-dj'yehsh skleh-poh-vah*
  shoplifting

kraj *krahy* country
krajowy *krah-yoh-vyh* domestic
kran *krahn* faucet
kraść *krahsh'ch'* steal
krawat *krah-vaht* tie (*n.*)
kredyt *kreh-dyht* credit; loan (bank) (*n.*)
krem *krehm* cream (culinary or cosmetic sense)
krem do golenia *krehm doh goh-leh-n'yah* shaving cream
krem z filtrem przeciwsłonecznym *krehm sfeel-trehm psheh-ch'eef-swoh-nehch-nyhm* sunblock
krew *krehf* blood
krewny (*masc.*)/**krewna** (*fem.*) *kreh-vnyh/kreh-vnah* relative (*n.*)
kręgosłup *krehn-goh-swuhp* spine
kroić *kroh-yeech'* cut (*v.*)
krok *krohk* step (*n.*)
krótki *kruht-kee* short (of length)
krwawić *krvah-veech'* bleed
krwisty *krfee-styh* rare (meat)
krytyczna sytuacja *kryh-tyh-chnah syh-tuh-ah-tsyah* emergency
krzesło *ksheh-swoh* chair
krzyczeć *kshyh-chehch'* shout (*v.*)
krzyk *kshyhk* shout (*n.*)
krzywda *kshyhv-dah* harm (*n.*)
krzywdzić *kshyhv-dj'eech'* harm (*v.*)
ksiądz *ksh'yohndz* priest
książka *ksh'yohn-shkah* book
księgarnia *ksh'yehn-gahr-n'yah* bookstore
księgowy *ksh'yehn-goh-vyh* accountant
księżyc *ksh'yehn-zhyhts* moon
kto *ktoh* who (*interrogative*)
ktokolwiek *ktoh-kohl-vyehk* anybody, anyone
ktoś *ktohsh'* someone, anybody, anyone
który *ktuh-ryh* who (*relative*)
któryś *ktuh-ryhsh'* any
kucharz *kuh-hahsh* chef, cook (*n.*)
kuchenka *kuh-hehn-kah* stove
kuchenka mikrofalowa *kuh-hehn-kah mee-kroh-fah-loh-vah* microwave
kuchnia *kuhh-n'yah* kitchen
kukurydza *kuh-kuh-ryh-dzah* corn
kula *kuh-lah* bullet
kule *kuh-leh* crutches
kultura *kuhl-tuh-rah* culture

kupić <u>kuh</u>-peech' get (buy)
kupiec <u>kuh</u>-pyehts merchant
kupować kuh-<u>poh</u>-vahch' buy, purchase (v.)
kurczak <u>kuhr</u>-chahk chicken
kurs wymiany (walut) kuhrs vyh-<u>myah</u>-nyh (<u>vah</u>-luht) exchange rate
kurtka <u>kuhrt</u>-kah jacket (coat)
kwadrans <u>kfah</u>-drahns quarter (time)
kwadrat <u>kfah</u>-draht square (shape)
kwalifikować (się) kfah-lee-fee-<u>koh</u>-vahch' (sh'yeh) qualify
kwarantanna kfah-rahn-<u>tahn</u>-nah quarantine (n.)
kwaśny <u>kfah</u>-sh'nyh sour
kwestia <u>kfehs</u>-tyah issue
kwestionować kfeh-styoh-<u>noh</u>-vahch' dispute (v.)
kwiat kfyaht flower
kwiecień <u>kfyeh</u>-ch'yehn' April

L

lać lahch' pour
lampa <u>lahm</u>-pah lamp
lampa błyskowa <u>lahm</u>-pah bwyh-<u>skoh</u>-vah flash (camera)
laptop <u>lahp</u>-tohp laptop
las lahs forest
latać <u>lah</u>-tahch' fly (v.)
latarka lah-<u>tahr</u>-kah flashlight
lato <u>lah</u>-toh summer
lądować lohn-<u>doh</u>-vahch' land (v.)
lecieć <u>leh</u>-ch'yehch' go (by plane)
leczyć <u>leh</u>-chyhch' treat (give medical care to), cure (v.)
legalny leh-<u>gahl</u>-nyh legal
lek lehk drug, medication
lekarstwo leh-<u>kahr</u>-stfoh cure; drug, medication, medicine, remedy (n.)
lekarz <u>leh</u>-kahzh doctor, physician
lekki <u>lehk</u>-kee light (of weight)
lewy <u>leh</u>-vyh left
liczba <u>leech</u>-bah number (figure)
licznik <u>leech</u>-n'eek meter (apparatus)
liga <u>lee</u>-gah league
limonka lee-<u>mohn</u>-kah lime
lina <u>lee</u>-nah rope
linie lotnicze <u>lee</u>-n'yeh loht-<u>n'ee</u>-cheh airline

lipiec _lee-pyehts_ July
list _leest_ letter
lista _lees-tah_ list
listopad _lee-stoh-paht_ November
litr _leetr_ liter
lodówka _loh-duhf-kah_ refrigerator
lokalizacja _loh-kah-lee-zah-tsyah_ location
lokalny _loh-kahl-nyh_ local
lokator (_masc._)/**lokatorka** (_fem._) _loh-kah-tohr/loh-kah-tohr-kah_ tenant
lot _loht_ flight
lotnisko _loht-n'ee-skoh_ airport
lód _luht_ ice
lubić _luh-beech'_ like (to be fond of)
ludność _luhd-nohsh'ch'_ population
ludowy _luh-doh-vyh_ folk
ludzie _luh-dj'yeh_ people (persons)
ludzki _luhdz-kee_ human (_adj._)
lunch _lahnch_ lunch
lustro _luhs-troh_ mirror
luty _luh-tyh_ February
luźny _luhzh'-nyh_ loose

Ł

ładować _wah-doh-vahch'_ load (_v._)
łagodny _wah-goh-dnyh_ mild (_adj._)
łamać _wah-mahch'_ break (_v._)
łańcuszek _wahn'-tsuh-shehk_ chain (jewelry)
łapać _wah-pahch'_ catch (_v._)
łapać w pułapkę/sidła _wah-pahch' fpuh-wahp-keh/ sh'ee-dwah_ trap (_v._)
łapówka _wah-puhf-kah_ bribe (_n._)
łazienka _wah-zh'yehn-kah_ bathroom
łódź _wuhdj'_ boat
łóżko _wuhzh-koh_ bed
łyżka _wyhsh-kah_ spoon
łyżwa _wyhzh-vah_ skate (_n._)

M

makaron *mah-kah-rohn* noodles, pasta
maksimum *mah-ksee-muhm* maximum (*n.*)
maksymalny *mah-ksyh-mahl-nyh* maximum (*adj.*)
mało *mah-woh* little (*adv.*)
małpa *mahw-pah* monkey
mały *mah-wyh* small, little
małże *mahw-zheh* mussels
małżeństwo *mahw-zhehn'-stfoh* marriage
mapa *mah-pah* map
mapa drogowa *mah-pah droh-goh-vah* road map
marchew *mahr-hehf* carrot
martwić (się) *mahrt-feech' (sh'yeh)* worry (*v.*)
martwy *mahr-tfyh* dead
marynarka *mah-ryh-nahr-kah* jacket (man's)
marynarka wojenna *mah-ryh-nahr-kah voh-yehn-nah*
  navy (*n.*)
masaż *mah-sahzh* massage
masło *mah-swoh* butter
maszyna *mah-shyh-nah* machine
maszynka do golenia *mah-shyhn-kah doh goh-leh-n'yah*
  razor
matematyka *mah-teh-mah-tyh-kah* math
materac *mah-teh-rahts* mattress
materiał *mah-teh-ryahw* fabric
matka *maht-kah* mother
mądrość *mohn-drohsh'ch'* wisdom
mąka *mohn-kah* flour
mąż *mohnzh* husband
mdłości *mdwoh-sh'ch'ee* nausea
meble *meh-bleh* furniture
mechanik *meh-hah-n'eek* mechanic
mecz *mehch* game (sports)
meczet *meh-cheht* mosque
melon *meh-lohn* melon
menedżer *meh-neh-djehr* leader (manager)
menu *meh-n'ee* menu
metal *meh-tahl* metal
metr *mehtr* meter (measurement)
metro *meh-troh* subway
metryka *meh-tryh-kah* birth certificate
mężczyzna *mehn-shchyh-znah* man
mgła *mgwah* fog
miasto *myah-stoh* city

miasto _myah_-stoh town
mieć zaparcie _myehch'zah-pahr_-ch'yeh (to be) constipated
mieć zawroty głowy _myehch'zah-vroh_-tyh _gwoh_-vyh (to feel) dizzy
miednica _myehd-n'ee_-tsah basin
miejsce _myehy_-stseh place, seat; location
miejsce przeznaczenia _myehy_-stseh pzheh-znah-_cheh_-n'yah destination
miejscowy _myehy-stsoh_-vyh local
mierzyć _myeh_-zhyhch' measure (v.)
miesiąc _myeh_-sh'yohnts month
miesiąc miodowy _myeh_-sh'yohnts myoh-_doh_-vyh honeymoon
miesiączka _myeh-sh'yohn_-chkah menstruation
mieszać _myeh_-shahch' mix (v.)
mieszkać _myehsh_-kahch' live (to reside)
mieszkanie _myeh-shkah_-n'yeh apartment
mieszkaniec _myehsh-kah_-n'yehts occupant
międzynarodowy _myehn-dzyh-nah-roh-doh_-vyh international
miękki _myehn_-kee soft
mięsień _myehn_-sh'yehn' muscle
mięso _myehn_-soh meat
mięta _myehn_-tah mint (plant)
migdał _meeg_-dahw almond
migrena mee-_greh_-nah migraine
mila _mee_-lah mile
million _meel_-yohn million
miłość _mee_-wohsh'ch' love (n.)
miły _mee_-wyh nice
minimum mee-_n'ee_-muhm minimum
minuta mee-_nuh_-tah minute (time)
miód myuht honey
mleko _mleh_-koh milk
młody _mwoh_-dyh young
mniej mn'yehy less
mniejszy mn'_yehy_-shyh minor (adj.)
modlić się _mohd_-leech'sh'yeh pray
moment _moh_-mehnt moment
moneta moh-_neh_-tah coin
morderstwo mohr-_dehr_-stfoh murder (n.)
mordować mohr-_doh_-vahch' murder (v.)
morela moh-_reh_-lah apricot
morze _moh_-zheh sea
moskitiera mohs-kee-_tyeh_-rah mosquito net

most *mohst* bridge
motel *moh-tehl* motel
motocykl *moh-toh-tsyhkl* motorcycle
możliwe (że) *moh-zhlee-veh (zheh)* possibly (*adv.*)
móc *muhts* can (*modal verb*)
mój *muhy* mine
mówić *muh-veech'* speak
mrożony *mroh-zhoh-nyh* frozen
mucha *muh-hah* fly (*n.*)
mundur *muhn-duhr* uniform
muzeum *muh-zeh-uhm* museum
muzułmanin (*masc.*)/**muzułmanka** (*fem.*) *muh-zuhw-mah-n'een/muh-zuhw-mahn-kah* Muslim (*n.*)
muzułmański *muh-zuhw-mahn'-skee* Muslim (*adj.*)
muzyk *muh-zyhk* musician
muzyka *muh-zyh-kah* music
my *myh* we
myć się *myhch' sh'yeh* wash (to clean oneself)
mydło *myh-dwoh* soap
mysz *myhsh* mouse
myśl *myhsh'l* thought (*n.*)
myśleć *myhsh'-lehch'* think
myśliwy *myh-sh'lee-vyh* hunter

N

na *nah* on; down
na noc *nah nohts* overnight (*adv.*)
na świeżym powietrzu *nah sh'fyeh-zhyhm poh-vyeh-tzhuh* outdoor (*adj.*)
na zewnątrz *nah zehv-nohntsh* outside
na zewnątrz *nah zehv-nohntzh* out (outside)
nabiał *nah-byahw* dairy
nabożeństwo *nah-boh-zhehn'-stfoh* service (religious)
naczynie *nah-chyh-n'yeh* dish (vessel)
nad *nahd* above, over (*prep.*)
nadgarstek *nahd-gahr-stehk* wrist
nadmiar *nahd-myahr* excess (*n.*)
nadmierny *nahd-myehr-nyh* excess (*adj.*)
nadwyżka *nahd-vyhzh-kah* excess (*n.*)
nadzwyczajny *nahd-zvyh-chahy-nyh* extra (*adj.*)
nagi *nah-gee* naked
nagły wypadek *nah-gwyh vyh-pah-dehk* emergency
nagroda *nah-groh-dah* prize

nagrywać *nah-gryh-vahch'* record (*v.*, on a disc, tape)
najwięcej *nahy-vyehn-tsehy* most (*adv.*)
nalewać *nah-leh-vahch'* pour
namiot *nah-myoht* tent
napadać *nah-pah-dahch'* assault (*v.*)
napadać(na) *nah-pah-dahch'(nah)* attack (*v.*)
napaść *nah-pahsh'ch'* assault (*n.*)
napełniać *nah-pehw-n'yahch'* fill
napiwek *nah-pee-vehk* tip (gratuity)
napój *nah-puhy* beverage, drink (*n.*)
naprawa *nah-prah-vah* repair (*n.*)
naprawiać *nah-prah-vyahch'* repair (*v.*)
naprawić *nah-prah-veech'* fix
naprzeciwko *nah-psheh-ch'eef-koh* opposite
narkotyk *nahr-koh-tyhk* drug (narcotic)
naród *nah-ruht* nation, people
narta *nahr-tah* ski (*n.*)
naruszenie własności *nah-ruh-sheh-n'yeh vwahs-nohsh'-ch'ee* trespassing
narząd *nah-zhohnt* organ (*biol.*)
narzekać *nah-zheh-kahch'* complain
narzędzie *nah-zhehn-dj'yeh* tool
nasienie *nah-sh'yeh-n'yeh* seed
następny *nahs-tehm-pnyh* next
nasz *nahsh* our
naszyjnik *nah-shyhy-n'eek* necklace
natarcie *nah-tahr-ch'yeh* attack (*n.*)
natychmiastowy *nah-tyhh-myahs-toh-vyh* instant (immediate) (*adj.*)
nauczyciel (*masc.*)/**nauczycielka** (*fem.*) *nah-uh-chyh-ch'yehl/nah-uh-chyh-ch'yehl-kah* teacher
nauczyciel (prywatny) *nah-uh-chyh-ch'yehl (pryh-vaht-nyh)* tutor (*n.*)
nauka *nah-uh-kah* science
nawigacja *nah-vee-gah-tsyah* navigation
nazwisko *nahz-vees-koh* surname
nerka *nehr-kah* kidney
nerw *nehrf* nerve
neutralny *neh-uh-trahl-nyh* neutral (*adj.*)
nic *n'eets* nothing
nie *n'yeh* no
nie zgadzać się *n'yeh zgah-dzahch' sh'yeh* disagree
niebezpieczeństwo *n'yeh-behs-pyeh-chehn'-stfoh* danger
niebezpieczeństwo *n'yeh-behz-pyeh-chehn'-stfoh* hazard
niebieski *n'yeh-byeh-skee* blue

niebo _n'yeh_-boh sky
niedaleko n'yeh-dah-_leh_-koh near (prep)
niedługo n'yeh-_dwuh_-goh soon (_adv._)
niedostateczny n'yeh-dohs-tah-_tehch_-nyh insufficient
niedrogi n'yeh-_droh_-gee inexpensive
niegrzeczny n'yeh-_gzheh_-chnyh rude, impolite
nielegalny n'yeh-leh-_gahl_-nyh illegal
niemowlę n'yeh-_moh_-vleh infant, baby
nieoficjalny n'yeh-oh-fee-_tsyahl_-nyh casual (of clothes)
niepełnosprawny n'yeh-pehw-noh-_sprahv_-nyh disabled,
   handicapped
nieporozumienie n'yeh-poh-roh-zuh-_myeh_-n'yeh
   misunderstanding
nieprzytomny n'yeh-pshyh-_tohm_-nyh unconscious
nierówny n'yeh-_ruhv_-nyh rough
niespodzianka n'yeh-spoh-_dj'yahn_-kah surprise (_n._)
nieszczęście n'yeh-_shchehn'_-sh'ch'yeh disaster
nieszczęśliwy n'yeh-shchehn-_sh'lee_-vyh unhappy
nietoperz n'yeh-_toh_-pehzh bat (animal)
nieuprzejmy n'yeh-uh-_pshehy_-myh impolite
niewidomy n'yeh-vee-_doh_-myh blind
niewinny n'yeh-_veen_-nyh innocent
niewygodny n'yeh-vyh-_gohd_-nyh uncomfortable
niezawodny n'yeh-zah-_vohd_-nyh reliable (person, equipment, memory, etc.)
nieznajomy n'yeh-znah-_yoh_-myh stranger
nieznany n'yeh-_znah_-nyh unfamiliar
niezwykły n'yeh-_zvyh_-kwyh unusual
nigdy _n'ee_-gdyh never (_adv._)
nigdzie _n'eeg_-dj'yeh anywhere (_in negative sentences_),
   nowhere (_adv._)
nikt n'eekt anybody, anyone (_in negative sentences_)
niski _n'ees_-kee low; short (_of a person_)
no cóż noh tsuhsh well (expressing hesitation)
   (_interjection_)
no proszę noh _proh_-sheh well (expressing surprise)
   (_interjection_)
noc nohts night
noga _noh_-gah leg
norma _nohr_-mah standard (_n._)
normalny nohr-_mahl_-nyh normal
nos nohs nose
nosić _noh_-sh'eech' carry; wear (of garments)
notatka noh-_taht_-kah note (_n._)
nowy _noh_-vyh new (_adj._)

Nowy Rok _noh-vyh rohk_ New Year's Day

nożyczki _noh-zhyhch-kee_ scissors

nóż _nuhsh_ knife

nuklearny _nuh-kleh-ahr-nyh_ nuclear (_adj._)

numer kierunkowy _nuh-mehr kyeh-ruhn-koh-vyh_ dialing code, country code

numer lotu _nuh-mehr loh-tuh_ flight number

numer miejsca _nuh-mehr myehy-stsah_ seat number

numer telefonu _nuh-mehr teh-leh-foh-nuh_ phone number

nurkować _nuhr-koh-vahch'_ dive

O

o _oh_ about

obca waluta _ohp-tsah vah-luh-tah_ foreign currency

obcy _ohp-tsyh_ strange, foreign (_adj._); stranger (_n._)

obejmować _oh-behy-moh-vahch'_ hug (_v._)

obiad _oh-byaht_ lunch

obiecywać _oh-byeh-tsyh-vahch'_ promise (_v._)

obiektyw _oh-byehk-tyhf_ lens (camera)

objaw _ohb-yahf_ symptom

objazd _ohb-yahst_ detour

obniżka _ohb-neezh-kah_ sale (seasonal, clearance)

obok _oh-bohk_ next to

obolały _oh-boh-lah-wyh_ sore (_adj._)

obowiązkowy _oh-boh-vyohn-skoh-vyh_ mandatory

obozowisko _oh-boh-zoh-vees-koh_ campground

obrabować _oh-brah-boh-vahch'_ rob

obraza _oh-brah-zah_ insult (_n._)

obrazek _oh-brah-zehk_ picture

obrażać _oh-brah-zhahch'_ offend, insult (_v._)

obserwować _ohp-sehr-voh-vahch'_ watch (_v._)

obsługa _ohb-swuh-gah_ service (in a restaurant)

obsługa pokoi _ohp-swuh-gah poh-koh-yee_ room service

obsługiwać _ohb-swuh-gee-vahch'_ serve

obszar _ohp-shahr_ area

obywatel (_masc._)/**obywatelka** (_fem._) _oh-byh-vah-tehl/ oh-byh-vah-tehl-kah_ citizen

ocean _oh-tseh-ahn_ ocean

ocena _oh-tseh-nah_ estimate (_n._)

oceniać _oh-tseh-n'yahch'_ estimate (_v._)

ochotnik _oh-hoht-n'eek_ volunteer (_n._)

ochrona _oh-hroh-nah_ security

odchodzić *ohd-hoh-dj'eech'* leave (depart on foot)
oddychać *ohd-dyh-hahch'* breathe
oddzielny *oht-dj'yehl-nyh* separate (*adj.*)
odjazd *ohd-yahst* departure (of train, bus, etc.)
odjeżdżać *ohd-yehzh-djahch'* leave (depart by vehicle)
odkładać *oht-kwah-dahch'* postpone
odkryty *oht-kryh-tyh* outdoor (*adj.*)
odkurzać *ohd-kuh-zhahch'* dust (*v.*)
odlatywać *ohd-lah-tyh-vahch'* leave (depart by plane)
odlot *ohd-loht* departure (of airplane)
odpoczywać *oht-poh-chyh-vahch'* rest (*v.*)
odpowiadać *oht-poh-vyah-dahch'* reply (*v.*)
odpowiedź *oht-poh-vyehdj'* reply (*n.*)
odprawa celna *oht-prah-vah tsehl-nah* customs
odraczać *ohd-rah-chahch'* postpone
odwiedzać *ohd-vyeh-dzahch'* visit (*v.*)
odwoływać *ohd-voh-wyh-vahch'* cancel
odwoływać się *ohd-voh-wyh-vahch' sh'yeh* appeal (*v.*
   legal, in court)
odwrócić *oht-vruh-ch'eech'* reverse (invert) (*v.*)
odzyskiwać *ohd-zyhs-kee-vahch'* retrieve
officer *oh-fee-tsehr* officer (military)
oficjalny *oh-fee-tsyahl-nyh* formal
oficjalny *oh-fee-tsyahl-nyh* official (*adj.*)
ogień *oh-gyehn'* fire
oglądać *oh-glohn-dahch'* watch (*v.*)
ogłaszać *oh-gwah-shahch'* declare
ogłoszenie *oh-gwoh-sheh-n'yeh* announcement (*n.*)
ogólny *oh-guhl-nyh* general
ograniczać *oh-grah-n'ee-chahch'* limit (*v.*)
ograniczenie prędkości *oh-grah-n'ee-cheh-n'yeh prehnt-
   kohsh'-ch'ee* speed limit
ograniczony *oh-grah-n'ee-choh-nyh* restricted
ogrodzenie *oh-groh-dzeh-n'yeh* fence
ogród *oh-gruht* garden (*n.*)
ogrzewać *oh-gzheh-vahch'* heat (raise temperature) (*v.*)
ojciec *ohy-ch'yehts* father
ojczysty *ohy-chyh-styh* native (*adj.*)
okno *ohk-noh* window
oko *oh-koh* eye
okolica *oh-koh-lee-tsah* neighborhood
około *oh-koh-woh* about
okraść *oh-krahsh'ch'* rob
okres *oh-krehs* period (menstrual), menstruation;
   period (time)

okrąg _oh-krohnk_ circle
okręg _oh-krehng_ district (administrative)
okulary _oh-kuh-lah-ryh_ eyeglasses
olej _oh-lehy_ oil (cooking)
olej napędowy _oh-lehy nah-pehn-doh-vyh_ diesel
oliwka _oh-leef-kah_ olive (_n._)
ołówek _oh-wuh-vehk_ pencil
ołtarz _ohw-tahzh_ altar
on _ohn_ he
ona _oh-nah_ she
oni (_masc._)/**one** (_fem._) _oh-n'ee/oh-neh_ they
ono _oh-noh_ it
oparzenie słoneczne _oh-pah-zheh-n'yeh swoh-nehch-neh_
   sunburn
opcja _ohp-tsyah_ option
opera _oh-peh-rah_ opera
operacja _oh-peh-rah-tsyah_ surgery
operator _oh-peh-rah-tohr_ operator
opieka przedszkolna _oh-pyeh-kah psheht-shkohl-nah_
   childcare
opiekunka do dziecka _oh-pyeh-kuhn-kah doh dj'yeh-_
   tskah babysitter
opłata _oh-pwah-tah_ fee, charge (_n._)
opłata lotniskowa _oh-pwah-tah loht-n'ee-skoh-vah_
   airport tax
opłata pocztowa _oh-pwah-tah pohch-toh-vah_ postage
opłata za przejazd _oh-pwah-tah zah psheh-yahst_ fare
opłata za przejazd (autostradą) _oh-pwah-tah zah_
   psheh-yahst (ahw-toh-strah-dohm) toll
opłata za wstęp _oh-pwah-tah zah fstehmp_ cover charge
opona _oh-poh-nah_ tire (_n._)
opóźniać _oh-puhzh'-n'yahch'_ delay (_v._)
opóźnienie _oh-puhzh'-n'yeh-n'yeh_ delay (_n._)
opóźniony _oh-puhzh'-n'yoh-nyh_ late (delayed)
oprócz _oh-pruhch_ except
opuchlizna _oh-puh-hleez-nah_ swelling
oraz _oh-rahz_ and
organ _ohr-gahn_ organ
organiczny _ohr-gah-n'eech-nyh_ organic
orkiestra _ohr-kyeh-strah_ orchestra
oryginalny _oh-ryh-gee-nahl-nyh_ original
orzechy _oh-zheh-hyh_ nuts
orzeszki ziemne _oh-zhehsh-kee zh'yehm-neh_ peanuts
osiem _oh-sh'yehm_ eight
osiemdziesiąt _oh-sh'yehm-dj'yeh-sh'yohnt_ eighty

osiemnaście *oh-sh'yehm-nahsh'-ch'yeh* eighteen
oskarżać *ohs-kahr-zhahch'* accuse
osłaniać *oh-swah-n'yahch'* cover (*v.*)
osoba *oh-soh-bah* person, individual
osoba cywilna *oh-soh-bah tsyh-veel-nah* civilian (*n.*)
osoba heteroseksualna *oh-soh-bah heh-teh-roh-sehk-suh-ahl-nah* heterosexual (*n.*)
osobisty *oh-soh-bees-tyh* personal
ostateczny termin *ohs-tah-teh-chnyh tehr-meen* deadline
ostatni *ohs-taht-n'ee* last (most recent) (*adj.*)
ostry *ohs-tryh* sharp; spicy
ostrzegać *ohs-tsheh-gahch'* warn
ostrzeżenie *ohs-tsheh-zheh-n'yeh* warning
oszczędzać *ohsh-chehn-dzahch'* save (put away)
oszustwo *oh-shuhs-tfoh* fraud
oś (koła) *ohsh' (koh-wah)* axle
ośmiornica *ohsh'-myohr-n'ee-tsah* octopus
oświata *ohsh'-fyah-tah* education
oświetlenie *ohsh'-fyeht-leh-n'yeh* lighting
otoczenie *oh-toh-cheh-n'yeh* scenery
otrzymywać *oh-tshyh-myh-vahch'* receive
otwarty *oht-fahr-tyh* open (*adj.*)
otwierać *oht-fyeh-rahch'* open (*v.*)
otworzyć *oht-foh-zhyhch'* unlock
owad *oh-vaht* insect
owca *ohf-tsah* sheep
owoc *oh-vohts* fruit
owoce morza *oh-voh-tseh moh-zhah* seafood
oznajmiać *ohz-nahy-myahch'* declare

P

pachnieć *pahh-n'yehch'* smell (*v.* – emit smell)
pacjent (*masc.*)/**pacjentka** (*fem.*) *pahts-yehnt/pahts-yehnt-kah* patient (*n.*)
paczka *pahch-kah* parcel
pada śnieg *pah-dah sh'n'yehg* snow (it's ~ing)
padać *pah-dahch'* rain (*v.*)
pająk *pah-yohnk* spider
pakować *pah-koh-vahch'* pack (*v.*)
palec (u ręki) *pah-lehts (uh rehn-kee)* finger
palić *pah-leech'* smoke (*v.*)
paliwo *pah-lee-voh* fuel
pamiętać *pah-myehn-tahch'* remember

pan *pahn* Mr. (title), sir; you (*sing. masc.*)

pani *pah-n'ee* Mrs. (title), Ms. (title); lady; you (*sing. fem.*)

panna *pahn-nah* single (*n. fem.*); miss, girl

państwo *pahn'-stfoh* nation, state (*n.*); you (*plural form*)

państwo demokratyczne *pahn'-stfoh deh-moh-krah-tyhch-neh* democracy (country)

papier *pah-pyehr* paper

papier toaletowy *pah-pyehr toh-ah-leh-toh-vyh* toilet paper

papieros *pah-pyeh-rohs* cigarette

papryka *pah-pryh-kah* pepper (vegetable)

para *pah-rah* pair

paragon *pah-rah-gohn* receipt, sales receipt

parasol *pah-rah-sohl* umbrella

parę *pah-reh* some

park *pahrk* park (*n.*)

parking *pahr-keeng* parking

parkować *pahr-koh-vahch'* park (*v.*)

parlament *pahr-lah-mehnt* parliament

partner (*masc.*)/**partnerka** (*fem.*) *pahrt-nehr/pahrt-nehr-kah* partner

pas bezpieczeństwa *pahs behs-pyeh-chehn'-stfah* seatbelt

pas ruchu *pahs ruh-huh* lane (for vehicles)

pasażer (*masc.*)/**pasażerka** (*fem.*) *pah-sah-zhehr/pah-sah-zhehr-kah* passenger

pasować *pah-soh-vahch'* fit (*v.*)

pasta do zębów *pahs-tah doh zehm-buhf* toothpaste

paszport *pahsh-pohrt* passport

patrzeć *pah-tshehch'* look (*v.*)

październik *pahzh'-dj'yehr-n'eek* October

pchać *phahch'* push

pchli targ *phlee tahrg* flea market

pchła *phwah* flea

pedał *peh-dahw* pedal (*n.*)

pedał gazu *peh-dahw gah-zuh* accelerator (gas pedal)

pedałować *peh-dah-woh-vahch'* pedal (*v.*)

pełnomocnik *pehw-noh-mohts-n'eek* attorney

pełny *pehw-nyh* full

pensja *pehn-syah* salary

peron *peh-rohn* platform

personel *pehr-soh-nehl* staff

pęcherzyk *pehn-heh-zhyhk* blister

piasek _pyah-sehk_ sand
piątek _pyohn-tehk_ Friday
pić _peech'_ drink (v.)
pieczarka _pyeh-chahr-kah_ mushroom
pieczęć _pyeh-chehnch'_ stamp (official)
pieczony _pyeh-choh-nyh_ roasted
piekarnia _pyeh-kahr-n'yah_ bakery
piekarnik _pyeh-kahr-n'eek_ oven
pielęgniarka _pyeh-lehn-gn'yahr-kah_ nurse
pieluszka _pyeh-luhsh-kah_ diaper
pieniądze _pyeh-n'yohn-dzeh_ money
pień _pyehn'_ trunk (tree)
pieprz _pyehpsh_ pepper (spice)
pierścionek _pyehr-sh'ch'yoh-nehk_ ring
pierwsza klasa _pyehr-fshah klah-sah_ first-class (n.)
pierwszy _pyehr-vshyh_ first
pies _pyehs_ dog
pieszy _pyeh-shyh_ pedestrian (n.)
pięć _pyehn'ch'_ five
pięćdziesiąt _pyehnch'-dj'yeh-sh'yohnt_ fifty
piękny _pyehn-knyh_ beautiful
pięść _pyehnsh'ch'_ fist
piętnaście _pyehnt-nahsh'-ch'yeh_ fifteen
piętro _pyehn-troh_ floor
pijany _pee-yah-nyh_ drunk
piknik _peek-n'eek_ picnic
piła _pee-wah_ saw
piłka _peew-kah_ ball
piłka nożna _peew-kah nohzh-nah_ soccer
piorun _pyoh-ruhn_ thunder
piosenka _pyoh-sehn-kah_ song
pióro _pyuh-roh_ pen
piramida _pee-rah-mee-dah_ pyramid
pisać _pee-sahch'_ write
piwnica _peev-n'ee-tsah_ basement
piwo _pee-voh_ beer
piżama _pee-zhah-mah_ pajamas
plac _plahts_ square (landmark)
plac targowy _plahts tahr-goh-vyh_ marketplace
placek _plah-tsehk_ pie
plan _plahn_ plan, schedule (n.); project (n.)
plan podróży _plahn poh-druh-zhyh_ itinerary
planować _plah-noh-vahch'_ plan (v.)
plastikowy _plah-stee-koh-vyh_ plastic
plaża _plah-zhah_ beach

plaża nudystów _plah_-zhah nuh-_dyhs_-tuhf nudist beach

plecak _pleh_-tsahk backpack, knapsack

plecy _pleh_-tsyh back

plemię _pleh_-myeh tribe

płacić _pwah_-ch'eech' pay

płakać _pwah_-kahch' cry

płaski _pwah_-skee flat

płaszcz pwahshch coat

płatki śniadaniowe _pwah_-tkee sh'n'yah-dah-_n'yoh_-veh cereal

płatny _pwah_-tnyh paid

płeć pwehch' sex (gender)

płomień _pwoh_-myehn' flame

płot pwoht fence

płyn pwyhn fluid, liquid (_n._)

płyn przeciw zamarzaniu pwyhn _psheh_-ch'eef zah-mahr-_zah_-n'yuh antifreeze

płynny _pwyhn_-nyh fluent

płyta _pwyh_-tah record (audio)

płyta kompaktowa (CD) _pwyh_-tah kohm-pah-_ktoh_-vah CD

pływać _pwyh_-vahch' swim (_v._)

po poh after

po drugiej stronie poh _druh_-gyehy _stroh_-n'yeh across

pobliski poh-_blee_-skee nearby (_adj._)

pobyt _poh_-byht stay (_n._)

pocałunek poh-tsah-_wuh_-nehk kiss (_n._)

pociąg _poh_-ch'yohng train

pociąg ekspresowy _poh_-ch'yohng ehks-preh-_soh_-vyh express train

pocić się _poh_-ch'eech' sh'yeh sweat (_v._)

początek poh-_chohn_-tehk beginning

poczekalnia poh-cheh-_kahl_-n'yah lounge (airport)

poczta _pohch_-tah mail (_n._); post office

poczta elektroniczna _pohch_-tah eh-lehk-troh-_n'eech_-nah e-mail

pocztówka pohch-_tuhf_-kah postcard

pod poht under, below

pod ziemią poht zh'_yeh_-myohm underground (_adv._)

podatek poh-_dah_-tehk tax

podatek obrotowy poh-_dah_-tehk oh-broh-_toh_-vyh sales tax

podatek od sprzedaży poh-_dah_-tehk oht spsheh-_dah_-zhyh sales tax

poddawać (się) pohd-_dah_-vahch' (sh'yeh) surrender (_v._)

podejrzany (*masc.*)/**podejrzana** (*fem.*) *poh-dehy-zhah-nyh/poh-dehy-zhah-nah* suspect (*n.*)

podnosić *pohd-noh-sh'eech'* lift (*v.*)

podobać się *poh-doh-bahch' sh'yeh* like (to be attracted to)

podpaska *poht-pahs-kah* sanitary napkin

podpis *poht-pees* signature

podróż *poh-druhzh* travel, trip (*n.*)

podróż tam i z powrotem *pohd-ruhzh tahm ee z poh-vroh-tehm* round-trip

podróżować *poh-druh-zhoh-vahch'* travel (*v.*)

podstawa *poht-stah-vah* base

podstęp *poht-stehmp* trick (*n.*)

poduszka *poh-duhsh-kah* pillow

podwójny *pohd-vuhy-nyh* double

podziemny *poht-zh'yehm-nyh* underground (*adj.*)

pogoda *poh-goh-dah* weather

pogrzeb *poh-gzhehp* funeral

pojawiać się *poh-yah-vyahch' sh'yeh* appear

pojazd *poh-yahst* vehicle

pokazywać *poh-kah-zyh-vahch'* show (*v.*)

pokład *poh-kwaht* deck (boat)

pokojówka *poh-koh-yuhf-kah* maid

pokój *poh-kuhy* peace; room

pokrywa *poh-kryh-vah* lid, cover (*n.*)

pole *poh-leh* field (farm)

pole namiotowe *poh-leh nah-myoh-toh-veh* campground

polecić *poh-leh-ch'eech'* recommend

policja *poh-lee-tsyah* police

polityka *poh-lee-tyh-kah* politics

polować *poh-loh-vahch'* hunt

południe *poh-wuhd-n'yeh* midday, noon; south

połykać *poh-wyh-kahch'* swallow (*v.*)

pomagać *poh-mah-gahch'* assist, help, aid (*v.*)

pomarańcza *poh-mah-rahn'-chah* orange (*n.*)

pomarańczowy *poh-mah-rahn'-choh-vyh* orange (color)

pomidor *poh-mee-dohr* tomato

pomiędzy *poh-myehn-dzyh* among

pomnik *pohm-n'eek* monument, statue

pomoc *poh-mohts* help, aid (*n.*)

pomocy! *poh-moh-tsyh* help!

pompa *pohm-pah* pump (*n.*)

pompować *pohm-poh-vahch'* pump (*v.*)

pomysł *poh-myhsw* idea

ponad *poh-naht* over (above) (*prep.*)

poncz *pohnch* punch (beverage)

poniedziałek *poh-n'yeh-dj'yah-wehk* Monday

poniżej *poh-n'ee-zhehy* below

popiół *poh-pyuhw* ash

popołudnie *poh-poh-wuhd-n'yeh* afternoon

poprawny *poh-prah-vnyh* correct (*adj.*)

pora dzienna *poh-rah dj'yehn-nah* daytime

pora roku *poh-rah roh-kuh* season

poręcz *poh-rehnch* rail (handrail)

porównywać *poh-ruhv-nyh-vahch'* compare

port *pohrt* harbor

portfel *pohrt-fehl* wallet

porywać *poh-ryh-vahch'* kidnap

posiadać *poh-sh'yah-dahch'* own (*v.*)

posiłek *poh-sh'ee-wehk* meal

posłaniec *poh-swah-n'yehts* messenger

posterunek policji *poh-steh-ruh-nehk poh-lee-tsyee* police station

pościel *pohsh'-ch'yehl* bedding

pot *poht* sweat (*n.*)

potrafić *poh-trah-feech'* can (*modal verb*)

potrawa *poh-trah-vah* dish (food)

potrzebować *poh-tsheh-boh-vahch'* need (*v.*)

potwierdzać *poh-tfyehr-dzahch'* confirm

poważny *poh-vahzh-nyh* serious

powiedzieć *poh-vyeh-dj'yehch'* say, tell

powietrze *poh-vyeh-tsheh* air

powitanie *poh-vee-tah-n'yeh* greeting

powód *poh-vuht* reason (*n.*)

powódź *poh-vuhdj'* flood

powtarzać *pohf-tah-zhahch'* repeat

poza *poh-zah* except

poza domem *poh-zah doh-mehm* out (absent, not at home)

poziom *poh-zh'yohm* level, rate (speed)

poznać *pohz-nahch'* meet (make acquaintance of)

pozwalać *poh-zvah-lahch'* allow, permit (*v.*)

pozwolenie *poh-zvoh-leh-n'yeh* permission

pożar *poh-zhahr* fire

pożyczka *poh-zhyhch-kah* loan (borrowed money) (*n.*)

pół *puhw* half

północ *puhw-nohts* midnight; north

północny wschód *puhw-nohts-nyh fs-huht* northeast

północny zachód *puhw-nohts-nyh zah-huht* northwest

później *puhzh'-n'yehy* later

późny _puhzh'-nyh_ late (not early)
praca _prah-tsah_ job
pracodawca _prah-tsoh-dahf-tsah_ employer
pracować _prah-tsoh-vahch'_ work (v.)
pracownik _prah-tsohv-n'eek_ employee
prać _prahch'_ wash (to do laundry)
pralka _prahl-kah_ washing machine
pralnia chemiczna _prahl-n'yah heh-meech-nah_ dry
   cleaner
pralnia samoobsługowa _prahl-n'yah sah-moh-ohb-swuh-_
   goh-vah laundromat
pranie _prah-n'yeh_ laundry
prasować _prah-soh-vahch'_ iron (v.)
prawa człowieka _prah-vah chwoh-vyeh-kah_ human
   rights
prawda _prahv-dah_ truth
prawdopodobnie _prahv-doh-poh-dohb-n'yeh_ probably
prawdziwy _prahv-djee-vyh_ true
prawnik (_masc._)/**prawniczka** (_fem._) _prahv-n'eek/prahv-_
   n'eech-kah lawyer
prawo _prah-voh_ law
prawo jazdy _prah-voh yahz-dyh_ driver's license
prawy _prah-vyh_ right (_adj._, direction)
prąd _prohnd_ power, electricity
preferować _preh-feh-roh-vahch'_ prefer
premia _preh-myah_ bonus
prezerwatywa _preh-zehr-vah-tyh-vah_ condom
prezent _preh-zehnt_ gift
prezes _preh-zehs_ president (company)
prezydent _preh-zyh-dehnt_ president (of State)
prędkościomierz _prehnt-kohsh'-ch'yoh-myehzh_
   speedometer
prędkość _prehnt-kohsh'ch'_ speed
problem _prohb-lehm_ problem, trouble
procent _proh-tsehnt_ percent
proces _proh-tsehs_ trial
produkt _proh-duhkt_ product
profesjonalny _proh-feh-syoh-nahl-nyh_ professional (_adj._)
profesor _proh-feh-sohr_ professor
profil _proh-feel_ profile (side view of face)
program _proh-grahm_ program
projekt _proh-yehkt_ project (n.)
prom _prohm_ ferry
prosić _proh-sh'eech'_ ask (request)
prosperować _proh-speh-roh-vahch'_ flourish

prostokąt *prohs-toh-kohnt* rectangle
prosty *proh-styh* plain; straight
proszę *proh-sheh* please
proszę pana *proh-sheh pah-nah* sir
prośba *prohsh'-bah* request
protest *proh-tehst* protest (*n.*)
protestant (*masc.*)/**protestantka** (*fem.*) *proh-tehs-tahnt/*
proh-tehs-tahnt-kah Protestant
protestować *proh-tehs-toh-vahch'* protest (*v.*)
prowadzić *proh-vah-dj'eech'* drive
prowincja *proh-veen-tsyah* province
prowizja *proh-vee-zyah* commission (reward)
próba *pruh-bah* test (trail, attempt)
próbka *pruhb-kah* sample (*n.*)
próbować *pruh-boh-vahch'* try (*v.*)
prysznic *pryhsh-n'eets* shower
prywatność *pryh-vaht-nohsh'ch'* privacy
prywatny *pryh-vaht-nyh* private (*adj.*)
przebaczać *psheh-bah-chahch'* forgive
przebicie *psheh-bee-ch'yeh* puncture (*n.*)
przebita opona *psheh-bee-tah oh-poh-nah* flat tire
przebudzony *psheh-buh-dzoh-nyh* awake
przeciw *psheh-ch'eev* against
przed *pshehd* before (prep)
przedawkować *psheh-dahf-koh-vahch'* overdose (*v.*)
przedawkowanie *psheh-dahf-koh-vah-n'yeh* overdose (*n.*)
przedmieście *psheht-myehsh'-ch'yeh* suburb
przedmiot *pshehd-myoht* item
przedsiębiorstwo *psheht-sh'yehm-byohr-stfoh* business
(company)
przedstawiać się *psheht-stah-vyahch' sh'yeh* introduce
oneself
przejście *pshehy-sh'ch'yeh* aisle
przekąska *psheh-kohn-skah* snack (*n.*)
przeklinać *psheh-klee-nahch'* swear (curse)
przeliterować *psheh-lee-teh-roh-vahch'* spell
przemoc *psheh-mohts* violence
przenośny *psheh-nohsh'-nyh* portable (*adj.*)
przepraszać *psheh-prah-shahch'* apologize
przepraszam *psheh-prah-shahm* sorry
przerażający *psheh-rah-zhah-yohn-tsyh* scary
przerwa w podróży *pshehr-vah fpoh-druh-zhyh* layover
przerywać *psheh-ryh-vahch'* stop (*v.* - cease)
przesiadać się *psheh-sh'yah-dahch' sh'yeh* transfer (*v.*)
przestępstwo *psheh-stehmp-stfoh* crime

przestraszony *psheh-strah-shoh-nyh* afraid
przesyłka *psheh-syhw-kah* package
przeszkadzać *psheh-shkah-dzahch'* disturb
prześcieradło *pshehsh'-ch'yeh-rahd-woh* sheets
prześwietlić *pshehsh'-fyeht-leech'* x-ray (*v.*)
przetwarzać *pzheh-tfah-zhahch'* recycle
przewodnik *psheh-vohd-n'eek* guide (*n.*); guidebook
przewozić *psheh-voh-zh'eech'* transport (*v.*)
przewód *psheh-wuht* cable, cord
przez *pshehz* through; over (across the top of), across
(*prep.*)
przeziębienie *psheh-zh'yehm-byeh-n'yeh* cold (*n.*)
przeżycie *pzheh-zhyh-ch'yeh* experience (*n.*)
przód *pshuht* front
przybywać *pshyh-byh-vahch'* arrive, come
przychodnia *pshyh-hohd-n'yah* clinic
przychodzić *pshyh-hoh-dj'eech'* come
przydział *pshyh-dj'yahw* ration
przyjaciel (*masc.*)/**przyjaciółka** (*fem.*) *pshyh-yah-ch'yehl/pshyh-yah-ch'yuhw-kah* friend
przyjemny *pshyh-yehm-nyh* pleasant
przyjęcie *pshyh-yehn-ch'yeh* admission (to school);
party (social)
przyjeżdżać *pshyh-yehzh-djahch'* come
przyjmować *pshyhy-moh-vahch'* admit (to school)
przykład *pshyh-kwahd* example
przykrywać *pshyh-kryh-vahch'* cover (*v.*)
przyłączyć (się) *pshyh-wohn-chyhch' (sh'yeh)* join
przymierzalnia *pshyh-myeh-zhahl-n'yah* fitting room,
changing room
przynosić *pshyh-noh-sh'eech'* bring (*v.*)
przypadek *pshyh-pah-dehk* event
przypominać *pshyh-poh-mee-nahch'* remind
przyroda *pshyh-roh-dah* nature
przyprowadzać *pshyh-proh-vah-dzahch'* bring (*v.*)
przysięgać *pshyh-sh'yehn-gahch'* swear (take an oath)
przystanek *pshyh-stah-nehk* stop (*n.*)
przyszłość *pshyh-shwohsh'ch'* future
przywódca *pshyh-wuht-tsah* leader (political)
przywozić *pshyh-voh-zh'eech'* bring (*v.*)
psycholog *psyh-hoh-lohg* psychologist
pszczoła *pshchoh-wah* bee
pszenica *psheh-n'ee-tsah* wheat
publiczne środki transportu *puh-bleech-neh sh'rohd-kee trahns-pohr-tuh* public transportation

publiczność *puh-bleech-nohsh'ch'* public (*n.*)
publiczny *puh-bleech-nyh* public (*adj.*)
pudełko *puh-dehw-koh* case, box (container)
pukać *puh-kahch'* knock
punkt kontrolny *puhnkt kohn-trohl-nyh* checkpoint
pusty *puh-styh* empty
pustynia *puh-styh-n'yah* desert (*n.*)
pyszny *pyhsh-nyh* delicious
pytać *pyh-tahch'* ask (inquire)
pytanie *pyh-tah-n'yeh* question (*n.*)

R

rabat *rah-baht* discount
raca *rah-tsah* flare
rachunek *rah-huh-nehk* bill, check; sales receipt
rachunek bankowy *rah-huh-nehk bahn-koh-vyh* bank
  account
radio *rah-dyoh* radio
radzić się *rah-dj'eech' sh'yeh* consult
ramię *rah-myeh* arm; shoulder
rano *rah-noh* morning
ratować *rah-toh-vahch'* rescue, save
raz *rahz* once (one time)
razem *rah-zehm* together
realizować (czek) *reh-ah-lee-zoh-vahch' (chehk)* cash (*v.*)
recepcja *reh-tsehp-tsyah* front desk
recepta *reh-tsehp-tah* prescription
region *reh-gyohn* region
regularny *reh-guh-lahr-nyh* regular
referencje *reh-feh-rehn-tsyeh* reference
rejestracja *reh-yeh-strah-tsyah* registration
rejon *reh-yohn* district (administrative)
rekin *reh-keen* shark
reklama *reh-klah-mah* advertisement
rekord *reh-kohrt* record (sports)
religia *reh-lee-gyah* religion
reporter *reh-pohr-tehr* reporter
republika *reh-puh-blee-kah* republic
restauracja *rehs-tahw-rah-tsyah* restaurant
reszta *rehsh-tah* change (money)
rewolucja *reh-voh-luh-tsyah* revolution
rezerwacja *reh-zehr-vah-tsyah* reservation
rezerwować *reh-zehr-voh-vahch'* reserve

reżim _reh-zheem_ regime
ręcznik _rehnch-n'eek_ towel
ręcznik kąpielowy _rehn-chn'eek kohm-pyeh-loh-vyh_ bath towel
ręka _rehn-kah_ hand; arm
robak _roh-bahk_ worm
robić _roh-beech'_ do
robić na drutach _roh-beech' nah druh-tahh_ knit
rock _rohk_ rock (music)
rocznica _roh-chn'ee-tsah_ anniversary
roczny _rohch-nyh_ annual
rodzaj _roh-dzahy_ kind, type (_n._)
rodzic _roh-dj'eets_ parent
rodzina _roh-dj'ee-nah_ family
rok _rohk_ year
rolnictwo _rohl-n'eets-tfoh_ agriculture
romans _roh-mahns_ romance
romantyczny _roh-mahn-tyhchnyh_ romantic
rondelek _rohn-deh-lehk_ pan
ropa naftowa _roh-pah nahf-toh-vah_ oil (petroleum)
roślina _roh-sh'lee-nah_ plant (_n._)
rower _roh-vehr_ bicycle
rozbijać _rohz-bee-yahch'_ break (_v._)
rozbijać obóz _rohz-bee-yahch' oh-buhz_ camp (_v._)
rozdarcie _rohz-dahr-ch'yeh_ rip (_n._)
rozdział _rohz-dj'yahw_ chapter
rozdzielić _rohz-dj'yeh-leech'_ separate (to set apart)
rozdzierać _rohz-dj'yeh-rahch'_ rip (_v._)
rozkład _rohz-kwaht_ schedule (_n._)
rozkwitać _rohz-kfee-tahch'_ flourish
rozmawiać _rohz-mah-vyahch'_ talk
rozmiar _rohz-myahr_ size
rozpinać _rohz-pee-nahch'_ undo
rozpoznawać _rohz-pohz-nah-vahch'_ recognize, identify
rozprawa _rohz-prah-vah_ trial
rozrywka _rohz-ryhv-kah_ entertainment
rozsądny _rohz-sohn-dnyh_ reasonable
rozumieć _roh-zuh-myehch'_ understand
róg _ruhg_ corner
również _ruhv-nyehsh_ also
równy _ruhv-nyh_ equal, even, smooth
różny _ruhzh-nyh_ different (_adj._)
ruch uliczny _ruhh uh-leech-nyh_ traffic
ruchome schody _ruh-hoh-meh s hoh-dyh_ escalator
rugby _rahg-bee_ rugby

ruiny *ruh-yee-nyh* ruins
rura *ruh-rah* pipe (conduit)
rura kanalizacyjna *ruh-rah kah-nah-lee-zah-tsyhy-nah* drain
ruszać (się) *ruh-shahch' (sh'yeh)* move (*v.*)
ryba *ryh-bah* fish (*n.*)
rybak *ryh-bahk* fisherman
rynek *ryh-nehk* marketplace
ryzyko *ryh-zyh-koh* risk (*n.*)
ryzykować *ryh-zyh-koh-vahch'* risk (*v.*)
ryż *ryhzh* rice
rzadki *zhaht-kee* rare (unusual)
rząd *zhohnt* government
rządzić *zhohn-dj'eech'* rule (*v.*)
rzecz *zhehch* thing
rzeczywisty *zheh-chyh-vee-styh* actual
rzeka *zheh-kah* river
rzeźba *zhehzh'-bah* sculpture
rzeźnik *zhehzh'-n'eek* butcher
rzucać *zhuh-tsahch'* throw (*v.*)

S

sad *saht* orchard
sala konferencyjna *sah-lah kohn-feh-rehn-tsyhy-nah* conference room
salon fryzjerski *sah-lohn fryh-zyehr-skee* salon (hair)
salon kosmetyczny *sah-lohn kohs-meh-tyhch-nyh* salon (beauty)
sałata *sah-wah-tah* lettuce
sałatka *sah-waht-kah* salad
sam (*masc.*)/**sama** (*fem.*) *sahm/sah-mah* alone
samochód *sah-moh-huht* automobile
samochód *sah-moh-huht* car
samolot *sah-moh-loht* airplane, plane
samoobsługa *sah-moh-ohb-swuh-gah* self-service
sandały *sahn-dah-wyh* sandals
sankcja *sahnk-tsyah* sanction (*n.*)
sankcjonować *sahnk-tsyoh-noh-vahch'* sanction (*v.*)
sanktuarium *sahn-ktuh-ah-ryuhm* sanctuary (holy place)
satelita *sah-teh-lee-tah* satellite
sąd *sohnd* court

sąsiad (*masc.*)/**sąsiadka** (*fem.*) <u>sohn</u>-sh'yaht/sohn-<u>sh'yaht</u>-kah neighbor
scena <u>stseh</u>-nah scene
sceneria stseh-<u>neh</u>-ryah scenery
schody <u>s-hoh</u>-dyh stairs
schowek na bagaż <u>s-hoh</u>-vehk nah <u>bah</u>-gahzh locker
schronienie s-hroh-<u>n'yeh</u>-n'yeh refuge, shelter (*n.*)
schronisko (młodzieżowe) s-hroh-<u>n'ees</u>-koh (mwoh-dj'yeh-<u>zhoh</u>-veh) hostel
sejf sehyf safe (*n.*)
sekcja <u>sehk</u>-tsyah section
sekretarz (*masc.*)/**sekretarka** (*fem.*) seh-<u>kreh</u>-tahsh/seh-kreh-<u>tahr</u>-kah secretary
seks sehks sex
sekunda seh-<u>kuhn</u>-dah second (time unit)
seminarium seh-mee-<u>nah</u>-ryuhm seminar
senat <u>seh</u>-naht senate
senator seh-<u>nah</u>-tohr senator
senior <u>seh</u>-n'yohr senior (*n.*)
senny <u>sehn</u>-nyh drowsy
ser (żółty) sehr (<u>zhuhw</u>-tyh) cheese
serce <u>sehr</u>-tseh heart
serwer <u>sehr</u>-vehr server (computer)
serwetka sehr-<u>veht</u>-kah napkin
sezonowy seh-zoh-<u>noh</u>-vyh seasonal
sędzia <u>sehn'</u>-dj'yah judge, referee (*n.*)
siadać <u>sh'yah</u>-dahch' sit
siedem <u>sh'yeh</u>-dehm seven
siedemdziesiąt sh'yeh-dehm-dj'yeh-sh'yohnt seventy
siedemnaście sh'yeh-dehm-nahsh'-ch'yeh seventeen
sierpień <u>sh'yehr</u>-pyehn' August
silnik <u>sh'eel</u>-n'eek engine, motor
siłownia sh'ee-<u>wohv</u>-n'yah gym
siodło <u>sh'yoh</u>-dwoh saddle
siostra <u>sh'yoh</u>-strah sister
siostrzenica sh'yohs-tsheh-<u>n'ee</u>-tsah niece (sister's daughter)
siostrzeniec sh'yohs-<u>tsheh</u>-n'yehts nephew (sister's son)
skakać <u>skah</u>-kahch' jump
skaleczenie skah-leh-<u>cheh</u>-n'yeh cut (*n.*)
skała <u>skah</u>-wah rock (stone)
skaner <u>skah</u>-nehr scanner
skarpetka skahr-<u>peht</u>-kah sock
sklep sklehp shop, store (*n.*)
sklep spożywczy sklehp spoh-<u>zhyf</u>-chyh grocery store

sklep z używaną odzieżą *sklehp zuh-zyh-vah-nohm oh-dj'yeh-zhohm* secondhand store
sklepik całodobowy *skleh-peek tsah-woh-doh-boh-vyh* convenience store
sklepikarz *skleh-pee-kahsh* shopkeeper
skomplikowany *skohm-plee-koh-vah-nyh* complicated
skorumpowany *skoh-ruhm-poh-vah-nyh* corrupt (*adj.*)
skorupiak *skoh-ruh-pyahk* shellfish
skóra *skuh-rah* leather
skóra *skuh-rah* skin
skręcić *skrehn-ch'eech'* turn
skrzydło *skshyh-dwoh* wing
skrzynka pocztowa *skshyhn-kah pohch-toh-vah* postbox
skrzyżowanie *skshyh-zhoh-vah-n'yeh* intersection
skrzyżowanie BE *skshyh-zhoh-vah-n'yeh* junction (intersection)
słodki *swoht-kee* sweet (taste)
słodycze *swoh-dyh-cheh* candy
słoik *swoh-yeek* jar
słońce *swohn'-tseh* sun
słownik *swohv-n'eek* dictionary
słowo *swoh-voh* word
słuchać *swuh-hahch'* listen
słucham? *swuh-hahm* pardon?
służący (*masc.*)/**służąca** (*fem.*) *swuh-zhohn-tsyh/swuh-zhohn-tsah* servant
słyszeć *swyh-shehch'* hear
smak *smahk* flavor
smak *smahk* taste (*n.*)
smażyć *smah-zhyhch'* fry (*v.*)
smutny *smuht-nyh* sad
sobota *soh-boh-tah* Saturday
soczewka *soh-chehf-kah* lens (optical)
soja *soh-yah* soy
sok *sohk* juice
sos *sohs* sauce
sól *suhl* salt
spacer *spah-tsehr* walk (*n.*)
spacerować *spah-tseh-roh-vahch'* walk (*v.*)
spać *spahch'* sleep
specjalny *speh-tsyahl-nyh* special
spędzać *spehn-dzahch'* spend (time)
spis *spees* directory
spłacać *spwah-tsahch'* repay
spodnie *spohd-n'yeh* pants

sport *spohrt* sport
sporty *spohr-tyh* sports (*n*.pl.)
spotkać, spotkać się (z kimś) *spoht-kahch' sh'yeh
(skeemsh')* meet (come together, encounter)
spotkanie *spoht-kah-n'yeh* meeting
spód *spuht* bottom (*n*.)
spódnica *spuhd-n'ee-tsah* skirt
spragniony *sprahg-n'yoh-nyh* thirsty
sprawa *sprah-vah* case (legal proceedings)
sprawa *sprah-vah* issue
sprawdzać *sprahv-dzahch'* check, inspect (*v*.)
sprawdzić *sprahv-dj'eech'* see (inspect)
sprawiedliwość *sprah-vyeh-dlee-vohsh'ch'* justice
sprzedany *spsheh-dah-nyh* sold
sprzedawać *spsheh-dah-vahch'* sell
sprzedaż *spsheh-dahzh* sale (selling)
sprzęgło *spzhehn-gwoh* clutch pedal
sprzęt *spshehnt* equipment
spuszczać wodę *spuhsh-chahch' voh-deh* flush
srebrny *sreh-brnyh* silver (*adj*.)
srebro *sreh-broh* silver (*n*.)
stacja *stah-tsyah* station
stacja metra *stah-tsyah meh-trah* metro station
stać *stahch'* stand (*v*.)
stać w kolejce *stahch' fkoh-lehy-tseh* queue (*v*.)
stąd (oddalony ~) *stohnt (ohd-dah-loh-nyh ~)* away
stadion *stah-dyohn* stadium
stały *stah-wyh* permanent (*adj*.)
standard *stahn-dahrt* standard (*n*.)
stanu wolnego *stah-nuh vohl-neh-goh* single (unmarried)
Stany Zjednoczone *stah-nyh zyehd-noh-choh-neh*
   United States
starszy *stahr-shyh* senior (*adj*.)
stary *stah-ryh* old
statek *stah-tehk* ship (*n*.)
statek *stah-tehk* boat
stawać się *stah-vahch' sh'yeh* become (*v*.)
stek *stehk* steak
sterylny *steh-ryhl-nyh* sterile
sto *stoh* hundred
stomatolog *stoh-mah-toh-lohg* dentist
stopa *stoh-pah* foot
stosunek *stoh-suh-nehk* ratio
stół *stuhw* table
stracić *strah-ch'eech'* lose (a person)

strażnik _strahzh-n'eek_ guard (_n._)

strona _stroh-nah_ page; side

strzec się _stshehts sh'yeh_ beware

strzelać _stsheh-lahch'_ shoot

strzykawka _stshyh-kahf-kah_ syringe

student _stuh-dehnt_ student (college, university)

studiować _stuh-dyoh-vahch'_ study (_v._)

stulecie _stuh-leh-ch'yeh_ century

styczeń _styh-chehn'_ January

substancja chemiczna _suhp-stahn-tsyah heh-meech-nah_ chemical (_n._)

suchy _suh-hyh_ dry (_adj._)

sukienka _suh-kyehn-kah_ dress (_n._)

suknia _suhk-n'yah_ dress (_n._)

supermarket _suh-pehr-mahr-keht_ supermarket

surowy _suh-roh-vyh_ raw

suszarka _suh-shahr-kah_ dryer

suszyć; suszyć się _suh-shyhch'; suh-shyhch' sh'yeh_ dry (_v._)

swędzieć _sfehn-dj'yehch'_ itch

sygnalizować _syhg-nah-lee-zoh-vahch'_ signal (_v._)

sygnał _syhg-nahw_ signal (_n._)

Sylwester _syhl-vehs-tehr_ New Year's Eve

sylwetka _syhl-veht-kah_ profile (biographical sketch)

symbol _syhm-bohl_ symbol

syn _syhn_ son

synagoga _syh-nah-goh-gah_ synagogue

sypialnia _syh-pyahl-n'yah_ bedroom

syrena _syh-reh-nah_ siren

system _syhs-tehm_ system

szacować _shah-tsoh-vahch'_ estimate (_v._)

szacunek _shah-tsuh-nehk_ respect (_n._); estimate (_n._)

szafka _shahf-kah_ cabinet

szalik _shah-leek_ scarf

szampan _shahm-pahn_ champagne

szampon _shahm-pohn_ shampoo

szanować _shah-noh-vahch'_ respect (_v._)

szatnia _shaht-n'yah_ changing room

szczepić _shcheh-peech'_ vaccinate

szczęśliwy _shchehn-sh'lee-vyh_ happy; lucky

szczoteczka do zębów _shchoh-tehch-kah doh zehm-buhf_ toothbrush

szczur _shchuhr_ rat

szczyt _shchyht_ peak

szef kuchni _shehf kuh-chn'ee_ chef

szesnaście _shehs-nahsh'-ch'yeh_ sixteen

sześć *shehsh'ch'* six
sześćdziesiąt *shehsh'ch'-dj'yeh-sh'yohnt* sixty
szew *shehf* stitch (medical)
szklanka *shklahn-kah* glass (non-alcoholic drinks)
szkodnik *shkohd-n'eek* pest
szkodzić *shkoh-dj'eech'* harm (v.)
szkolnictwo *shkohl-n'eets-tfoh* education
szkoła *shkoh-wah* school
szlak *shlahk* trail
szmatka, ścierka *shmaht-kah, sh'ch'yehr-kah* cloth
sznur *shnuhr* cord
szorstki *shohr-stkee* rough
szpital *shpee-tahl* hospital
sztuczne ognie *shtuh-chneh ohg-n'yeh* fireworks
sztuka *shtuh-kah* art; play (theater), show (n.)
sztuka ludowa *shtuh-kah luh-doh-vah* folk art
szuflada *shuh-flah-dah* drawer
szukać *shuh-kahch'* seek
szybki *shyhp-kee* quick, rapid
szyć *shyhch'* sew
szyja *shyh-yah* neck
szyna *shyh-nah* rail (transportation)

Ś

ściana *sh'ch'yah-nah* wall
ściana skalna *sh'ch'yah-nah skahl-nah* cliff
ścieżka *sh'ch'yeh-shkah* footpath
ścieżka *sh'ch'yehsh-kah* path
ślub *sh'luhp* wedding
śmiać się *sh'myahch' sh'yeh* laugh (v.)
śmieci *sh'myeh-ch'ee* trash, litter (n.)
śmiecić *sh'myeh-ch'eech'* litter (v.)
śmietana *sh'myeh-tah-nah* cream (*culinary*)
śniadanie *sh'n'yah-dah-n'yeh* breakfast
śnieg *sh'n'yehg* snow (n.)
śpiący *sh'pyohn-tsyh* drowsy
śpieszyć się *sh'pyeh-shyhch' sh'yeh* hurry
śpiewać *sh'pyeh-vahch'* sing
śpiwór *sh'pee-vuhr* sleeping bag
średni *sh'reh-dn'ee* middle, medium (*adj.*)
środa *sh'roh-dah* Wednesday
środek *sh'roh-dehk* middle (n.)

środek antykoncepcyjny *sh'roh-dehk ahn-tyh-kohn-tsehp-tsyhy-nyh* contraceptive (*n.*)
środek odkażający *sh'roh-dehk oht-kah-zhah-yohn-tsyh* antiseptic
środek odstraszający owady *sh'roh-dehk oht-strah-shah-yohn-tsyh oh-vah-dyh* insect repellant
środek przeciwbólowy *sh'roh-dehk psheh-ch'eev-buh-loh-vyh* painkiller
środek uspokajający *sh'roh-dehk uhs-poh-kah-yah-yohn-tsyh* sedative
środek znieczulający *sh'roh-dehk zn'yeh-chuh-lah-yohn-tsyh* anesthetic
środkowy *sh'rohd-koh-vyh* middle (*adj.*)
śruba *sh'ruh-bah* screw
śrubokręt *sh'ruh-boh-krehnt* screwdriver
świadectwo pracy *sh'fyah-dehts-tfoh prah-tsyh* reference
świat *sh'fyaht* world
światło *sh'fyah-twoh* light (*n.*)
świątynia *sh'fyohn-tyh-n'yah* temple
świecki *sh'fyeh-tskee* secular
świetnie *sh'fyeht-n'yeh* great (*adv.*)
świetny *sh'fyeht-nyh* great (*adj.*)
świeży *sh'fyeh-zhyh* fresh
święto *sh'fyehn-toh* festival, holiday (religious)
święty *sh'fyehn-tyh* holy, sacred
świnia *sh'fee-n'yah* pig
świt *sh'feet* dawn

T

tabletka *tah-bleht-kah* pill
tabletki nasenne *tah-bleht-kee nah-sehn-neh* sleeping pills
taca *tah-tsah* tray
tajemnica *tah-yehm-n'ee-tsah* mystery, secret
tak *tahk* yes
taki sam *tah-kee sahm* same
taksówka *tahk-suhf-kah* cab, taxi
talerz *tah-lehsh* plate
tam *tahm* there
tampon *tahm-pohn* tampon
tamto *tahm-toh* that
tani *tah-n'ee* cheap
tańczyć *tahn'-chyhch'* dance (*v.*)

taras _tah-rahs_ deck (terrace)
taśma _tahsh'-mah_ tape (_n._)
teatr _teh-ahtr_ theater
telefon _teh-leh-fohn_ phone, telephone
telefon komórkowy _teh-leh-fohn koh-muhr-koh-vyh_ mobile phone
telefon publiczny _teh-leh-fohn puh-bleech-nyh_ public telephone
telewizja _teh-leh-vee-zyah_ television
telewizja kablowa _teh-leh-vee-zyah kah-bloh-vah_ cable TV
temperatura _tehm-peh-rah-tuh-rah_ temperature
tempo _tehm-poh_ rate (level)
ten (_masc._)/**ta** (_fem._)/**to** (_neut._) _tehn/tah/toh_ this
teraz _teh-rahs_ now
teren _teh-rehn_ area
termin _tehr-meen_ date (_n._)
terrorysta _tehr-roh-ryhs-tah_ terrorist
terytorium _teh-ryh-toh-ryuhm_ territory
test _tehst_ test (exam)
teściowa _tehsh'-ch'yoh-vah_ mother-in-law
tętno _tehnt-noh_ pulse
tkanina _tkah-n'ee-nah_ fabric
tlen _tlehn_ oxygen
tłuc _twuhts_ break (_v._)
tłum _twuhm_ crowd
tłumacz _twuh-mahch_ translator
tłumacz ustny _twuh-mahch uhst-nyh_ interpreter
tłumaczenie ustne _twuh-mah-cheh-n'yeh uhst-neh_ interpretation
tłumaczyć _twuh-mah-chyhch'_ translate
tłumaczyć ustnie _twuh-mah-chyhch' uhst-n'yeh_ interpret
tłuszcz _twuhshch_ fat (_n._)
to _toh_ it; that
toaleta (WC) _toh-ah-leh-tah_ lavatory, toilet, bathroom
toaleta publiczna _toh-ah-leh-tah puh-bleech-nah_ public toilet
tonąć _toh-nohnch'_ drown
topić się _toh-peech' sh'yeh_ melt; drown (_v._)
torba _tohr-bah_ bag
torebka _toh-rehp-kah_ purse
tort _tohrt_ cake
tortura _tohr-tuh-rah_ torture (_n._)
torturować _tohr-tuh-roh-vahch'_ torture (_v._)

towary *toh-_vah_-ryh* goods
towarzystwo (*accompanying people*) *toh-vah-_zhyh_-stfoh* company
towarzysz (*masc.*)/**towarzyszka** (*fem.*) *toh-_vah_-zhyhsh/toh-vah-_zhyhsh_-kah* companion
tradycja *trah-_dyh_-tsyah* tradition
tradycyjny *trah-dyh-_tsyhy_-nyh* traditional
traktować *trahk-_toh_-vahch'* treat (behave towards)
transplantacja *trahns-plahn-_tah_-tsyah* transplant (*n.*)
transport *_trahns_-pohrt* transportation
transportować *trahns-pohr-_toh_-vahch'* transport (*v.*)
trasa *_trah_-sah* route
trawa *_trah_-vah* grass
trochę *_troh_-heh* some
trójkąt *_truhy_-kohnt* triangle
trucizna *truh-_ch'eez_-nah* poison
trudny *_truhd_-nyh* difficult (*adj.*)
trwały *_trvah_-wyh* permanent (*adj.*)
trzęsienie ziemi *tshehn-_sh'yeh_-n'yeh _zh'yeh_-mee* earthquake
trzy *tshyh* three
trzydzieści *tshyh-_dj'yehsh'_-ch'ee* thirty
tunel *_tuh_-nehl* tunnel
turysta (*masc.*)/**turystka** (*fem.*) *tuh-_ryhs_-tah/tuh-_ryhst_-kah* tourist, visitor
tusz *tuhsh* ink
tutaj *_tuh_-tahy* here
tuzin *_tuh_-zh'een* dozen
twardy *_tfahr_-dyh* hard (texture)
twarz *tfahzh* face
ty *tyh* you (*sing.*)
tydzień *_tyh_-dj'yehn'* week
tylko *_tyhl_-koh* only
tylny *_tyhl_-nyh* rear (*adj.*)
tymczasowy *tyhm-chah-_soh_-vyh* temporary
tysiąc *_tyh_-sh'yohnts* thousand

U

ubezpieczenie *uh-behz-pyeh-_cheh_-n'yeh* insurance
ubezpieczenie zdrowotne *uh-behz-pyeh-_cheh_-n'yeh zdroh-_voht_-neh* health insurance
ubierać *uh-_byeh_-rahch'* wear (of garments)

ubierać się *uh-byeh-rahch' sh'yeh* dress (*v.*)
ubranie *uh-brah-n'yeh* clothing
ucho *uh-hoh* ear
uchodźca *uh-hohdj'-tsah* refugee
uczciwy *uhch-ch'ee-vyh* honest
uczeń *uh-chehn'* student (primary ~, secondary ~)
uczulenie *uh-chuh-leh-n'yeh* allergy
uczyć się *uh-chyhch' sh'yeh* learn, study
uderzać pięścią *uh-deh-zhahch' pyehn'sh'-ch'yohm* punch
  (to hit)
udo *uh-doh* thigh
udogodnienia *uh-doh-goh-dn'yeh-n'yah* amenities
udzielać lekcji (prywatnych) *uh-dj'yeh-lahch' lehk-tsyee*
  (pryh-vaht-nyhh) tutor (*v.*)
ufać *uh-fahch'* trust (*v.*)
ugoda *uh-goh-dah* settlement (agreement)
ugryzienie owada *uh-gryh-zh'yeh-n'yeh oh-vah-dah*
  insect bite
układanka *uh-kwah-dahn-kah* puzzle (jigsaw)
ukradziony *uh-krah-dj'yoh-nyh* stolen
ukrywać *uh-kryh-vahch'* conceal
ulica *uh-lee-tsah* street
uliczka *uh-leech-kah* alley, avenue, lane
umeblowany *uh-meh-bloh-vah-nyh* furnished
umieć *uh-myehch'* can (*modal verb*)
umierać *uh-myeh-rahch'* die
umowa *uh-moh-vah* contract
umówione spotkanie *uh-muh-vyoh-neh spoht-kah-n'yeh*
  appointment
umysłowy *uh-myh-swoh-wyh* mental (*adj.*)
umywalka *uh-myh-vahl-kah* sink, basin (in bathroom)
unia *uh-n'yah* union
unikać *uh-n'ee-kahch'* avoid
uniform *uh-n'ee-fohrm* uniform
uniwersytet *uh-n'ee-vehr-syh-teht* university
upadać *uh-pah-dahch'* fall (*v.*)
upał *uh-pahw* heat (hot temperature) (*n.*)
upośledzenie *uh-poh-sh'leh-dzeh-n'yeh* disability
uprzejmość *uh-pshehy-mohsh'ch'* courtesy
uprzejmy *uh-pshehy-myh* polite
uraz *uh-rahz* injury
urlop *uhr-lohp* vacation (from a job)
urodziny *uh-roh-dj'ee-nyh* birthday
urządzenie *uh-zhohn-dzeh-n'yeh* machine
urzędnik *uh-zhehnd-n'eek* official (*n.*)

usta _uhs-tah_ mouth
ustny _uhst-nyh_ oral
usuwać _uhu-suh-vahch'_ remove
uszkodzenie _uhsh-koh-dzeh-n'yeh_ damage (_n._)
uśmiechać się _uhsh'-myeh-hahch' sh'yeh_ smile
uważać _uh-vah-zhahch'_ beware
używać _uh-zhyh-vahch'_ use (_v._)

W

w ciąży _fch'yohn-zhyh_ pregnant
w dół _vduhw_ down
w jedną stronę _vyehd-nohm stroh-neh_ one-way
w końcu _fkohn'-tsuh_ eventually
w pierwszej klasie _fpyehr-fshehy klah-sh'yeh_ first-class
  (_adj._)
w porządku _fpoh-zhohn-tkuh_ OK
w przyszłym roku _fpshyh-shwyhm roh-kuh_ next year
w środku _fsh'roh-tkuh_ inside
w zeszłym roku _v zehsh-wyhm roh-kuh_ last year
wagon sypialny _vah-gohn syh-pyahl-nyh_ sleeping car
wakacje _vah-kah-tsyeh_ vacation (from school)
walizka _vah-leez-kah_ suitcase
waluta _vah-luh-tah_ currency
wanilia _vah-n'ee-lyah_ vanilla (_n._)
wanna _vahn-nah_ bathtub
warga _vahr-gah_ lip
warsztat _vahrsh-taht_ shop (workshop) (_n._)
warsztat naprawczy _vahrsh-taht nah-prahv-chyh_ repair
  shop
warzywo _vah-zhyh-voh_ vegetable
ważyć _vah-zhyhch'_ weigh
wąchać _vohn-hahch'_ smell (_v._ – sniff)
wąski _vohn-skee_ narrow
wąsy _vohn-syh_ moustache
wątroba _vohn-troh-bah_ liver
wąż _vohnzh_ snake
wchodzić _fhoh-dj'eech'_ enter
wczesny _fcheh-snyh_ early (_adj._)
wcześnie _fcheh-sh'n'yeh_ early (_adv._)
wczoraj _fchoh-rahy_ yesterday
we śnie _veh sh'n'yeh_ asleep
weekend _wee-kehnt_ weekend

wegetarianin (*masc.*)/**wegetarianka** (*fem.*) *veh-geh-tah-ryah-n'een/veh-geh-tah-ryahn-kah* vegetarian (*n.*)

wegetariański *veh-geh-tah-ryahn'-skee* vegetarian (*adj.*)

wejście *vehysh'-ch'yeh* entrance, entry

wejść *vehysh'ch'* enter

welon *veh-lohn* veil (*n.*)

wełna *vehw-nah* wool

wesele *veh-seh-leh* wedding

wewnątrz (budynku) *vehv-nohntzh (buh-dyhn-kuh)* indoor

wędka *vehnd-kah* fishing rod

wędkarstwo *vehnd-kahr-stfoh* fishing

wędkarz *vehnt-kahzh* fisherman

wędrować pieszo *vehn-droh-vahch' pyeh-shoh* hike

węzeł *vehn-zehw* knot

wiadomość (*sing.*)/**wiadomości** (*plural*) *vyah-doh-mohsh'ch'/vyah-doh-mohsh'-ch'ee* news, message

wiarygodny *vyah-ryh-gohd-nyh* reliable (witness, account, information, etc.)

wiatr *vyahtr* wind

widelec *vee-deh-lehts* fork

widok *vee-dohk* view (*n.*)

widzieć *vee-dj'yehch'* see (witness)

wieczór *vyeh-chuhr* evening

wiedzieć *vyeh-dj'yehch'* know

wiek *vyehk* age, century

wieko *vyeh-koh* lid, cover (*n.*)

wieprzowina *vyehp-shoh-vee-nah* pork

wiersz *vyehrsh* poem

wierzyć *vyeh-zhyhch'* believe

wieś *vyehsh'* village

więcej *vyehn-tsehy* more (*adv.*)

więzienie *vyehn-zh'yeh-n'yeh* jail, prison

więzień *vyehn-zh'yehn'* prisoner

winda *veen-dah* elevator

winny *veen-nyh* guilty

wino *vee-noh* wine

winogrono *vee-noh-groh-noh* grape

wiosna *vyoh-snah* spring

wirus *vee-ruhs* virus

wirus HIV *vee-ruhs heef* HIV

witaj (*sing.*)/**witajcie** (*plural*) *vee-tahy/vee-tahy-ch'yeh* welcome

wiza *vee-zah* visa

wiza wjazdowa *vee-zah vyahz-doh-vah* entry visa

wizyta *vee-zyh-tah* appointment, visit (*n.*)

wjazd *vyahst* ramp; entry

władza *vwah-dzah* authority (power)

władza ustawodawcza *vwah-dzah uh-stah-voh-dahf-chah* legislature

własność *vwahs-nohsh'ch'* property

własność prywatna *vwahs-nohsh'ch' pryh-vaht-nah* private property

własny pokój *vwahs-nyh poh-kuhy* private room

właściciel *vwahsh'-ch'ee-ch'yehl* owner (*n.*)

właściwy *vwahsh'-ch'ee-vyh* proper, right (correct)

właśnie ta (*fem.*) *vwahsh'-n'yeh tah* very (*adj.*)

właśnie ten (*masc.*) *vwahsh'-n'yeh tehn* very (*adj.*)

włosy *vwoh-syh* hair

wnosić oskarżenie *vnoh-sh'eech' ohs-kahr-zheh-n'yeh* prosecute

woda *voh-dah* water

wojna *vohy-nah* war

wojsko *vohy-skoh* army

wojskowy *vohy-skoh-vyh* military

wokół *voh-kuhw* around

woleć *voh-lehch'* prefer

wolny *vohl-nyh* free (available); slow

wolny od cła *vohl-nyh oht tswah* duty-free

wolny pokój *vohl-nyh poh-kuhy* vacancy

wołowina *voh-woh-vee-nah* beef

wózek *vuh-zehk* cart; trolley

wózek inwalidzki *vuh-zehk een-vah-leedz-kee* wheelchair

wpłata *fpwah-tah* deposit (bank)

wpływ *fpwyhf* influence

wpuszczać *fpuhsh-chahch'* admit (to a museum, etc)

wrażliwy *vrah-zhlee-vyh* sensitive

wrogi *vroh-gee* hostile

wrócić *vruh-ch'eech'* return (*v.*)

wróg *vruhg* enemy

wróżka *vruhsh-kah* fortune teller

wrzesień *vzheh-sh'yehn'* September

wrzeszczeć *vzhehsh-chehch'* yell (*v.*)

wschód *fs-huht* east

wskazać *fskah-zahch'* point (*v.*)

wskazówki *fskah-zuhf-kee* directions

wskrzesić (*fig.*: custom, language) *fsksheh-sh'eech'* revive (*v.*)

wspinać się *fspee-nahch' sh'yeh* climb

współpracownik *fspuhw-prah-tsohv-n'eek* associate (*n.*)
wstążka *fstohn-zhkah* ribbon
wstęp *fstehmp* admission (to a museum, etc)
wstrząs mózgu *fstshohns muhz-guh* concussion
wstrzykiwać *fstshyh-kee-vahch'* inject
wszy *fshyh* lice
wszyscy *fshyhs-tsyh* all (everybody) (*pron.*)
wszystko *fshyhs-tkoh* all (everything) (*pron.*)
wściekły *fsh'ch'yeh-kwyh* mad (*adj.*)
wtargnięcie *ftahrg-n'yehn'-ch'yeh* trespassing
wtedy *fteh-dyh* then (time) (*adv.*)
wtorek *ftoh-rehk* Tuesday
wujek *vuh-yehk* uncle
wy *vyh* you (*plural*)
wybierać *vyh-byeh-rahch'* pick (select)
wybierać *vyh-byeh-rahch'* select (*v.*)
wybierać numer *vyh-byeh-rahch' nuh-mehr* dial
wybory *vyh-boh-ryh* election
wybór *vyh-buhr* selection, option
wybrzeże *vyh-bzheh-zheh* coast
wycieczka *vyh-ch'yehch-kah* trip (*n.*)
wycierać *vyh-ch'yeh-rahch'* wipe (*v.*)
wycofanie (się) *vyh-tsoh-fah-n'yeh (sh'yeh)* withdrawal
wycofywać (się) *vyh-tsoh-fyh-vahch' (sh'yeh)* withdraw
wydarzenie *vyh-dah-zheh-n'yeh* event
wydatek *vyh-dah-tehk* expense
wydawać *vyh-dah-vahch'* spend (money)
wydawać się *vyh-dah-vahch' sh'yeh* seem
wygodny *vyh-goh-dnyh* comfortable, convenient
wygody *vyh-goh-dyh* amenities
wygrywać *vyh-gryh-vahch'* win
wyjaśniać *vyh-yahsh'-n'yahch'* explain
wyjście *vyhysh'-ch'yeh* exit (*n.*)
wykaz *vyh-kahz* directory
wykluczać *vyh-kluh-chahch'* exclude
wyleczyć *vyh-leh-chyhch'* cure (*v.*)
wyłączony *vyh-wohn-choh-nyh* off (*adv./adj.*)
wymagać *vyh-mah-gahch'* require
wymawiać *vyh-mah-vyahch'* pronounce
wymeldowywać się *vyh-mehl-doh-vahch' sh'yeh*
  check out
wymieniać *vyh-myeh-n'yahch'* exchange (*v.*)
wymiotować *vyh-myoh-toh-vahch'* vomit (*v.*)
wynagrodzenie *vyh-nah-groh-dzeh-n'yeh* compensation
wynająć *vyh-nah-yohn'ch'* rent (*v.*)

wynik _vyh-n'eek_ score
wypadek _vyh-pah-dehk_ accident
wyposażenie _vyh-poh-sah-zheh-n'yeh_ equipment
wyposażony _vyh-poh-sah-zhoh-nyh_ furnished
wyprzedany _vyh-psheh-dah-nyh_ sold out
wyprzedaż _vyh-psheh-dahzh_ sale (seasonal, clearance)
wysłać (pocztą) _vyh-swahch' (pohch-tohm)_ mail (v.)
wysoki _vyh-soh-kee_ tall
wysokość _vyh-soh-kohsh'ch'_ altitude
wyspa _vyhs-pah_ island
wystarczająco _vyh-stahr-chah-yohn-tsoh_ enough (adv.)
wystawiać _vyh-stah-vyahch'_ exhibit (v.)
wysychać _vyh-syh-hahch'_ dry (v.)
wysyłać _vyh-syh-wahch'_ send
wzgórze _vzguh-zheh_ hill
wzrok _vzrohk_ sight
wzwyż _vzvyhzh_ up
wzywać _vzyh-vahch'_ summon (v.)

Z

z dnia na dzień _zdn'yah nah dj'yehn'_ overnight (adj.)
z powodu _spoh-voh-duh_ because of
z wyjątkiem _zvyh-yohnt-kyehm_ except
za _zah_ behind
zabawa _zah-bah-vah_ fun
zabieg _zah-byehg_ surgery
zabijać _zah-bee-yahch'_ kill
zabraniać _zah-brah-n'yahch'_ prohibit
zachowywać się _zah-hoh-vyh-vahch' sh'yeh_ act (v.)
zachód _zah-huht_ west
zaczynać (się) _zah-chyh-nahch' (sh'yeh)_ start (v.)
zadośćuczynienie _zah-dohsh'ch'-uh-chyh-n'yeh-n'yeh_ remedy (legal)
zaginiony _zah-gee-n'yoh-nyh_ lost (of a person)
zagraniczny _zah-grah-n'eech-nyh_ foreign
zajazd _zah-yahst_ inn
zajezdnia _zah-yehzd-n'yah_ depot
zajęcia _zah-yehn-ch'yah_ class (course)
zajęty _zah-yehn-tyh_ busy
zakaźny _zah-kahzh'-nyh_ contagious
zakażać _zah-kah-zhahch'_ infect
zakażony _zah-kah-zhoh-nyh_ infected
zakład _zahk-waht_ institution

zakładnik *zah-kwahd-n'eek* hostage
zakonnica *zah-kohn-n'ee-tsah* nun
zakopywać *zah-koh-pyh-vahch'* bury
zakręt *zah-krehnt* corner
zakup *zah-kuhp* purchase (*n.*)
zakwaterowanie *zah-kfah-teh-roh-vah-n'yeh*
  accommodations
zaliczka *zah-leech-kah* deposit (against damage)
zamarznięty *zah-mahr-zn'yehn-tyh* frozen
zamawiać *zah-mah-vyahch'* order
zamek *zah-mehk* lock (*n.*)
zamek błyskawiczny *zah-mehk bwyhs-kah-veech-nyh*
  zipper
zameldować się *zah-mehl-doh-vahch' sh'yeh* check in
zamężna *zah-mehn-zhnah* married (of a woman)
zamieszki *zah-myehsh-kee* riot
zamknięty *zahm-kn'yehn-tyh* closed
zamówienie *zah-muh-vyeh-n'yeh* order (*n.*)
zamrażać *zah-mrah-zhahch'* freeze
zamykać *zah-myh-kahch'* shut, close (*v.*)
zamykać na klucz *zah-myh-kahch' nah kluhch* lock (*v.*)
zanieczyszczenie *zah-n'yeh-chyhsh-cheh-n'yeh* pollution
zanim *zah-n'eem* until (before fulfillment of condition)
zaopatrzenie *zah-oh-pah-tsheh-n'yeh* supplies
zapach *zah-pahh* odor
zapalenie wyrostka robaczkowego *zah-pah-leh-n'yeh*
  vyh-rohst-kah roh-bahch-koh-veh-goh appendicitis
zapalić *zah-pah-leech'* start (of a car)
zapasowy *zah-pah-soh-vyh* spare (*adj.*)
zapasy *zah-pah-syh* supplies
zapisywać *zah-pee-syh-vahch'* note (*v.*)
zapłata *zah-pwah-tah* payment
zapłon *zahp-wohn* ignition
zapominać *zah-poh-mee-nahch'* forget
zaprosić *zah-proh-sh'eech'* invite
zaprzeczać *zah-psheh-chahch'* deny
zapytanie *zah-pyh-tah-n'yeh* inquiry
zaraźliwy *zah-rah-zh'lee-vyh* contagious
zasada *zah-sah-dah* rule (*n.*)
zaskakiwać *zahs-kah-kee-vahch'* surprise (*v.*)
zastępować *zah-stehm-poh-vahch'* replace, substitute (*v.*)
zastrzyk *zahs-tshyhk* shot (medicine)
zatrucie pokarmowe *zah-truh-ch'yeh poh-kahr-moh-veh*
  food poisoning

zatrzasnąć sobie drzwi *zah-tshahs-nohnch' soh-byeh djvee* lock oneself out

zatrzymać *zah-tshyh-mahch'* keep (*v.*)

zatrzymać, zatrzymać się *zah-tshyh-mahch', zah-tshyh-mahch' sh'yeh* halt, stop (*v.* bring/come to a halt)

zatrzymać się *zah-tshyh-mahch' sh'yeh* stay (in a hotel)

zatyczka *zah-tyhch-kah* plug

zaufanie *zah-uh-fah-n'yeh* trust (*n.*)

zawał *zah-vahw* heart attack

zawiadomienie *zah-vyah-doh-myeh-n'yeh* announcement (*n.*)

zawinąć *zah-vee-nohn'ch'* wrap (*v.*)

zawodowy *zah-voh-doh-vyh* professional (*adj.*)

zawód *zah-vuht* occupation

zawsze *zah-fsheh* always (*adv.*)

ząb *zohmp* tooth

zbierać *zbyeh-rahch'* collect, pick (pluck, gather)

zbiornik *zbyohr-n'eek* reservoir

zbrodnia *zbroh-dn'yah* crime

zdanie *zdah-n'yeh* sentence

zdjęcie *zdyehn'-ch'yeh* photograph

zdjęcie rentgenowskie *zdyehn'-ch'yeh rehnt-geh-nohfs-kyeh* x-ray (*n.*)

zdolny *zdohl-nyh* able (*adj.*)

zdrowie *zdroh-vyeh* health

zegar *zeh-gahr* clock

zegarek *zeh-gah-rehk* watch (*n.*)

zepsuty *zehp-suh-tyh* broken; corrupt (*adj.*); rotten

zero *zeh-roh* zero

zestaw *zehs-tahf* kit

zeszły *zehsh-wyh* last (previous) (*adj.*)

zewnętrzny *zehv-nehn-tshnyh* outdoor (*adj.*)

zezwolenie *zehz-voh-leh-n'yeh* license, permit (*n.*)

zgadzać się *zgah-dzahch' sh'yeh* agree

zgłaszać *zgwah-shahch'* declare

zgłosić *zgwoh-sh'eech'* report (*v.*)

zgniły *zgn'ee-wyh* rotten

zgubić *zguh-beech'* lose (an item)

zgubiony *zguh-byoh-nyh* lost (of an item)

zgwałcić *zgvahw-ch'eech'* rape (*v.*)

ziarno *zh'yahr-noh* seed

zielony *zh'yeh-loh-nyh* green

ziemia *zh'yeh-myah* earth, dirt, soil, ground (*n.*)

ziemniak *zh'yehm-n'yahk* potato

zima *zh'ee-mah* winter

zimny _zh'ee-mnyh_ cold (_adj._)
zioło _zh'yoh-woh_ herb
zlew _zlehf_ sink (in kitchen)
złodziej _zwoh-dj'yehy_ thief
złoto _zwoh-toh_ gold (_n._)
złoty _zwoh-tyh_ gold (_adj._)
zły _zwyh_ angry; bad; wrong
zmarły _zmahr-wyh_ dead
zmiana _zmyah-nah_ change (alteration)
zmieniać _zmyeh-n'yahch'_ change (_v._)
znaczek _znah-chehk_ stamp (postal)
znajdować _znahy-doh-vahch'_ find
znak _znahk_ sign
zniszczenie _zn'eesh-cheh-n'yeh_ damage (_n._)
zniżka _zn'eezh-kah_ discount
znowu _znoh-vuh_ again
zobaczyć _zoh-bah-chyhch'_ see (notice)
zoo _zoh_ zoo
zostać _zoh-stahch'_ stay (_v._)
zostawać _zoh-stah-vahch'_ become (_v._)
zostawiać _zohs-tah-vyahch'_ leave (cause to remain)
zranienie _zrah-n'yeh-n'yeh_ injury
zrobić _zroh-beech'_ make (_v._)
zrywać _zryh-vahch'_ pick (pluck, gather)
zupa _zuh-pah_ soup
związek _zvyohn-zehk_ relationship, union
zwiedzanie _zvyeh-dzah-n'yeh_ sightseeing
zwierzę _zvyeh-zheh_ animal
zwierzę (domowe) _zvyeh-zheh (doh-moh-veh)_ pet
zwlekać _zvleh-kahch'_ delay (_v._)
zwłoka _zvwoh-kah_ delay (_n._)
zwracać _zvrah-tsahch'_ repay
zwrot _zvroht_ phrase
zwrot pieniędzy _zvroht pyeh-n'yehn-dzyh_ refund
zwrócić _zvruh-ch'eech'_ return (give back) (_v._)
zwyczajny _zvyh-chahy-nyh_ ordinary
zwykły _zvyh-kwyh_ usual, ordinary
zysk _zyhsk_ profit (_n._)

Ź

źle _zh'leh_ wrong (_adv._)
źródło _zh'ruh-dwoh_ source

Ż

żaden _zhah-dehn_ any (in negative sentences)
żakiet _zhah-kyeht_ jacket (woman's)
żądanie _zhohn-dah-n'yeh_ demand (_n._)
żebrak _zheh-brahk_ beggar
żebro _zheh-broh_ rib
żeglować _zheh-gloh-vahch'_ sail (_v._)
żelazko _zheh-lahs-koh_ iron (_n._)
żeński _zhehn'-skee_ female (_adj._)
żołądek _zhoh-wohn-dehk_ stomach (organ)
żołnierz _zhohw-n'yehzh_ soldier
żona _zhoh-nah_ wife
żonaty _zhoh-nah-tyh_ married (of a man)
żółty _zhuhw-tyh_ yellow
żuć _zhuhch'_ chew
życie _zhyh-ch'yeh_ life
życie nocne _zhyh-ch'yeh nohts-neh_ nightlife
życiorys _zhyh-ch'yoh-ryhs_ resume (_n._)
życzliwy _zhyhch-lee-vyh_ kind (_adj._)
żyć _zhyhch'_ live (to be alive)
Żyd (_masc._)/**Żydówka** (_fem._) _zhyht/zhyh-duhf-kah_ Jew
żyła _zhyh-wah_ vein
żywy _zhyh-vyh_ alive

English-Polish
Dictionary

A

able (*adj.*) zdolny *zdohl-nyh*
able (*v.* **be ~ to**) być w stanie *bych' fstah-n'yeh*
about o; około *oh; oh-koh-woh*
above nad *nahd*
academy academia *ah-kah-deh-myah*
accelerator (gas pedal) pedał gazu *peh-dahw gah-zuh*
accent akcent *ahk-tsehnt*
accept akceptować *ahk-tsehp-toh-vahch'*
access (*n.*) dostęp *dohs-tehmp*
accident wypadek *vyh-pah-dehk*
accommodation zakwaterowanie *zah-kfah-teh-roh-vah-n'yeh*
account (banking) konto *kohn-toh*
accountant księgowy *ksh'yehn-goh-vyh*
accurate dokładny *doh-kwah-dnyh*
accuse oskarżać *ohs-kahr-zhahch'*
acre (0.4 hectares) akr (0,4 hektara) *ahkr*
across przez; po drugiej stronie *pshehz; poh druh-gyehy stroh-n'yeh*
act (*v.*) zachowywać się; działać *zah-hoh-vyh-vahch' sh'yeh; dj'yah-wahch'*
activist aktywista *ahk-tyh-vee-stah*; działacz *dj'yah-wahch'*
activity czynność *chyhn-nohsh'ch'*
actor aktor *ahk-tohr*
actual rzeczywisty; faktyczny *zheh-chyh-vee-styh; fahk-tyh-chnyh*
add dodawać *doh-dah-vahch'*
address (*n.*) adres *ah-drehs*
administration administracja *ahd-mee-n'ee-strah-tsyah*
admission (to school) przyjęcie *pshyh-yehn-ch'yeh*
admission (to a museum, etc) wstęp *fstehmp*
admit (to school) przyjmować *pshyhy-moh-vahch'*; **(to a museum, etc)** wpuszczać *fpuhsh-chahch'*
adult (*n.*) dorosły *doh-roh-swyh*
advertisement reklama *reh-klah-mah*
afraid przestraszony *psheh-strah-shoh-nyh*
after po *poh*
afternoon popołudnie *poh-poh-wuhd-n'yeh*
again znowu; jeszcze raz *znoh-vuh; yehsh-cheh rahz*
against przeciw *psheh-ch'eev*
age wiek *vyehk*

agency (*n.*) agencja *ah-gehn-tsyah*
agent agent *ah-gehnt*
agree zgadzać się *zgah-dzahch' sh'yeh*
agriculture rolnictwo *rohl-n'eets-tfoh*
aid (*n.*) pomoc *poh-mohts*
aid (*v.*) pomagać *poh-mah-gahch'*
AIDS AIDS *ehyts*
air powietrze *poh-vyeh-tsheh*
air conditioning klimatyzacja *klee-mah-tyh-zah-tsyah*
airline linie lotnicze *lee-n'yeh loht-n'ee-cheh*
airplane samolot *sah-moh-loht*
airport lotnisko *loht-n'ee-skoh*
airport tax opłata lotniskowa *oh-pwah-tah loht-n'ee-
   skoh-vah*
aisle przejście *pshehy-sh'ch'yeh*
alarm (warning signal) alarm *ah-lahrm;* (~ **clock**)
   budzik *buh-dj'eek*
alcohol alkohol *ahl-koh-hohl*
alive żywy *zhyh-vyh*
all (*pron.*) wszyscy (everybody); wszystko (everything) *fshyhs-tsyh; fshyhs-tkoh*
allergy uczulenie; alergia *uh-chuh-leh-n'yeh;
   ah-lehr-gyah*
alley uliczka *uh-leech-kah*
allow pozwalać *poh-zvah-lahch'*
allowed dozwolony *doh-zvoh-loh-nyh*
almond migdał *meeg-dahw*
alone sam (*masc.*)/sama (*fem.*) *sahm/sah-mah*
also również *ruhv-nyehsh*
altar ołtarz *ohw-tahzh*
altitude wysokość *vyh-soh-kohsh'ch'*
aluminum foil folia aluminiowa *foh-lyah ah-luh-mee-
   n'yoh-vah*
always (*adv.*) zawsze *zah-fsheh*
ambassador ambasador *ahm-bah-sah-dohr*
ambulance karetka pogotowia *kah-reht-kah poh-goh-
   toh-vyah*
amenities udogodnienia, wygody *uh-doh-goh-dn'yeh-
   n'yah; vyh-goh-dyh*
among pomiędzy *poh-myehn-dzyh*
amount (*n.*) ilość *ee-lohsh'ch'*
and i; oraz *ee; oh-rahz*
anemic anemiczny *ah-neh-mee-chnyh*
anesthetic środek znieczulający *sh'roh-dehk zn'yeh-
   chuh-lah-yohn-tsyh*

angry zły *zwyh*
animal zwierzę <u>zvyeh</u>-*zheh*
ankle kostka <u>kohst</u>-*kah*
anniversary rocznica *roh-<u>chn'ee</u>-tsah*
announcement(*n.*) ogłoszenie; zawiadomienie *oh-gwoh-<u>sheh</u>-n'yeh; zah-vyah-doh-<u>myeh</u>-n'yeh*
annual roczny; doroczny <u>rohch</u>-*nyh; doh-<u>rohch</u>-nyh*
antibiotics antybiotyki *ahn-tyh-byoh-<u>tyh</u>-kee*
antifreeze płyn przeciw zamarzaniu *pwyhn <u>psheh</u>-ch'eef zah-mahr-<u>zah</u>-n'yuh*
antique antyk <u>ahn</u>-*tyhk*
antiseptic środek odkażający *sh'<u>roh</u>-dehk oht-kah-zhah-<u>yohn</u>-tsyh*
any jakiś; któryś <u>yah</u>-*keesh';* <u>ktuh</u>-*ryhsh';* **(in negative sentences)** żaden <u>zhah</u>-*dehn*
anybody ktoś; ktokolwiek; każdy *ktohsh'; ktoh-<u>kohl</u>-vyehk;* <u>kahzh</u>-*dyh;* **(in negative sentences)** nikt *n'eekt*
anyone ktoś; ktokolwiek; każdy *ktohsh'; ktoh-<u>kohl</u>-vyehk;* <u>kahzh</u>-*dyh;* **(in negative sentences)** nikt *n'eekt*
anywhere gdziekolwiek *gdj'yeh-<u>kohl</u>-vyehk;* **(in negative sentences)** nigdzie <u>n'eeg</u>-*dj'yeh*
apartment mieszkanie *myeh-<u>shkah</u>-n'yeh*
apologize przepraszać *psheh-<u>prah</u>-shahch'*
appeal (*v.*) błagać <u>bwah</u>-*gahch';* (*v.* **legal, in court**) apelować, odwoływać się *ah-peh-<u>loh</u>-vahch', ohd-voh-<u>wyh</u>-vahch' sh'yeh*
appear pojawiać się *poh-<u>yah</u>-vyahch' sh'yeh*
appendicitis zapalenie wyrostka robaczkowego *zah-pah-<u>leh</u>-n'yeh vyh-<u>rohst</u>-kah roh-bahch-koh-<u>veh</u>-goh*
appetite apetyt *ah-<u>peh</u>-tyht*
apple jabłko <u>yahp</u>-*koh*
appointment umówione spotkanie, wizyta *uh-muh-<u>vyoh</u>-neh spoht-<u>kah</u>-n'yeh; vee-<u>zyh</u>-tah*
apricot morela *moh-<u>reh</u>-lah*
April kwiecień <u>kfyeh</u>-*ch'yehn'*
architecture architektura *ahr-hee-tehk-<u>tuh</u>-rah*
area obszar, teren <u>ohp</u>-*shahr;* <u>teh</u>-*rehn*
argue dyskutować (o); kłócić się *dyhs-kuh-<u>toh</u>-vahch' (oh);* <u>kwuh</u>-*ch'eech' sh'yeh*
arm ramię; ręka <u>rah</u>-*myeh;* <u>rehn</u>-*kah*
army armia; wojsko <u>ahr</u>-*myah;* <u>vohy</u>-*skoh*
around wokół <u>voh</u>-*kuhw*
arrest (*v.*) aresztować *ah-reh-<u>shtoh</u>-vahch'*
arrive przybywać *pshyh-<u>byh</u>-vahch'*
art sztuka <u>shtuh</u>-*kah*

arthritis artretyzm *ahr-treh-tyhzm*
artichoke karczoch *kahr-chohh*
ash popiół *poh-pyuhw*
ask (inquire) pytać *pyh-tahch';* **(request)** prosić *proh-sh'eech'*
asleep we śnie *veh sh'n'yeh*
aspirin aspiryna *ah-spee-ryh-nah*
assault (*n.*) atak; napaść *ah-tahk; nah-pahsh'ch'*
assault (*v.*) atakować; napadać *ah-tah-koh-vahch'; nah-pah-dahch'*
assist (help) pomagać *poh-mah-gahch';* **(cooperate with)** asystować *ah-syh-stoh-vahch'*
associate (*n.*) współpracownik *fspuhw-prah-tsohv-n'eek*
asthma astma *ahst-mah*
ATM bankomat *bahn-koh-maht*
attack (*n.*) atak; natarcie *ah-tahk; nah-tahr-ch'yeh*
attack (*v.*) atakować; napadać(na) *ah-tah-koh-vahch'; nah-pah-dahch' (nah)*
attorney pełnomocnik; adwokat *pehw-noh-mohts-n'eek; ahd-voh-kaht*
August sierpień *sh'yehr-pyehn'*
author autor *ahw-tohr*
authority władza (power); autorytet (influence) *vwah-dzah; ahw-toh-ryh-teht*
automatic automatyczny *ahw-toh-mah-tyhch-nyh*
automatic transmission automatyczna skrzynia biegów *ahw-toh-mah-tyhch-nah skshyh-n'yah byeh-guhf*
automobile samochód *sah-moh-huht*
autumn jesień *yeh-sh'yehn'*
available dostępny; do dyspozycji *doh-stehm-pnyh; doh dyhs-poh-zyh-tsyee*
avenue aleja; uliczka *ah-leh-yah; uh-leech-kah*
avoid unikać *uh-n'ee-kahch'*
awake przebudzony *psheh-buh-dzoh-nyh*
away (oddalony) stąd; daleko od *(ohd-dah-loh-nyh) stohnt; dah-leh-koh ohd*
axle oś (koła) *ohsh' (koh-*ziecko, niemowlę *dj'yeh-tskoh; n'yeh-moh-vleh*

B

baby wipes chusteczki do pielęgnacji niemowląt *huh-stehch-kee doh pyeh-lehn-gnah-tsyee n'yeh-mohv-lohnt*
babysitter opiekunka do dziecka *oh-pyeh-kuhn-kah doh dj'yeh-tskah*
back plecy *pleh-tsyh*
backpack plecak *pleh-tsahk*
bad zły *zwyh*
bag torba *tohr-bah*
baggage bagaż *bah-gahzh*
baggage check kontrola bagażu *kohn-troh-lah bah-gah-zhuh*
bakery piekarnia *pyeh-kahr-n'yah*
balcony balkon *bahl-kohn*
ball piłka *peew-kah*
banana banan *bah-nahn*
bandage bandaż *bahn-dahzh*
bank bank *bahnk*
bank account konto bankowe; rachunek bankowy *kohn-toh bahn-koh-veh; rah-huh-nehk bahn-koh-vyh*
bar bar *bahr*
barber fryzjer męski *fryh-zyehr mehn-skee*
barrel beczka *beh-chkah*
barrier bariera *bah-ryeh-rah*
base podstawa; baza *poht-stah-vah; bah-zah*
basement piwnica *peev-n'ee-tsah*
basin miednica; umywalka *myehd-n'ee-tsah; uh-myh-vahl-kah*
basket kosz; koszyk *kohsh; koh-shyhk*
basketball koszykówka *koh-shyh-kuhf-kah*
bat nietoperz (animal); kij baseballowy (equipment used in baseball) *n'yeh-toh-pehzh; keey behy-zboh-loh-vyh*
bath kąpiel *kohm-pyehl*
bath towel ręcznik kąpielowy *rehn-chn'eek kohm-pyeh-loh-vyh*
bathe kąpać się *kohm-pahch' sh'yeh*
bathing suit kostium kąpielowy *kohs-tyuhm kohm-pyeh-loh-vyh*
bathroom łazienka *wah-zh'yehn-kah;* **(public toilet)** toaleta *toh-ah-leh-tah, WC vuh tseh*
bathtub wanna *vahn-nah*
battery akumulator *ah-kuh-muh-lah-tohr*

battle (*n.*) bitwa _beet_-fah
beach plaża _plah_-zhah
bean fasola fah-_soh_-lah
beautiful piękny _pyehn_-knyh
because of z powodu spoh-_voh_-duh
become (*v.*) stawać się; zostawać _stah_-vahch' sh'yeh; zoh-_stah_-vahch'
bed łóżko _wuhzh_-koh
bedding pościel _pohsh'_-ch'yehl
bedroom sypialnia syh-_pyahl_-n'yah
bee pszczoła _pshchoh_-wah
beef wołowina voh-woh-_vee_-nah
beer piwo _pee_-voh
before (*prep.*) przed pshehd
beggar żebrak _zheh_-brahk
beginning początek poh-_chohn_-tehk
behind za zah
believe wierzyć _vyeh_-zhyhch'
bell dzwon; dzwonek dzvohn; _dzvoh_-nehk
below poniżej; pod poh-_n'ee_-zhehy; pohd
berry jagoda yah-_goh_-dah
beverage napój _nah_-puhy
beware strzec się, uważać stshehts sh'yeh; uh-_vah_-zhahch'
bible biblia _beeb_-lyah
bicycle rower _roh_-vehr
big duży _duh_-zhyh
bill rachunek rah-_huh_-nehk
birth certificate akt urodzenia, metryka ahkt uh-roh-_dzeh_-n'yah, meh-_tryh_-kah
birthday urodziny uh-roh-_dj'ee_-nyh
bite (*v.*) gryźć gryhsh'ch'
bitter gorzki _gohsh_-kee
black czarny _chahr_-nyh
blanket koc kohts
bleed krwawić _krvah_-veech'
bless błogosławić bwoh-goh-_swah_-veech'
blind niewidomy n'yeh-vee-_doh_-myh
blister pęcherzyk; bąbel pehn-_heh_-zhyhk; _bohm_-behl
blood krew krehf
blood type grupa krwi _gruh_-pah krfee
blue niebieski n'yeh-_byeh_-skee
boarding pass karta pokładowa _kahr_-tah poh-kwah-_doh_-vah
boat statek; łódź _stah_-tehk; wuhdj'
body ciało _ch'yah_-woh

bomb bomba _bohm-bah_
bone kość _kohsh'ch'_
bonus premia _preh-myah_
book książka _ksh'yohn-shkah_
bookstore księgarnia _ksh'yehn-gahr-n'yah_
boot but, kozak _buht, koh-zahk_
border granica _grah-n'ee-tsah_
bottle butelka _buh-tehl-kah_
bottom (_n._) dół; spód _duhw; spuht_
box pudełko (container) _puh-dehw-koh_
boy chłopiec _hwoh-pyehts_
boyfriend chłopak _hwoh-pahk_
brake (_n._) hamulec _hah-muh-lehts_
bread chleb _hlehp_
break (_v._) tłuc, łamać, rozbijać _twuhts, wah-mahch', rohz-bee-yahch'_
breakfast śniadanie _sh'n'yah-dah-n'yeh_
breathe oddychać _ohd-dyh-hahch'_
bribe (_n._) łapówka _wah-puhf-kah_
brick cegła _tseh-gwah_
bridge most _mohst_
bring przynosić; przywozić; przyprowadzać _pshyh-noh-sh'eech'; pshyh-voh-zh'eech'; pshyh-proh-vah-dzahch'_
broken zepsuty _zehp-suh-tyh_
brother brat _braht_
brown brązowy _brohn-zoh-vyh_
building budynek _buh-dyh-nehk_
bull byk _byhk_
bullet kula _kuh-lah_
bureaucracy biurokracja _byuh-roh-krah-tsyah_
bury zakopywać _zah-koh-pyh-vahch'_
bus autobus _ahw-toh-buhs_
bus terminal dworzec autobusowy _dvoh-zhehts ahw-toh-buh-soh-vyh_
business (commerce) biznes, działalność gospodarcza _beez-nehs, dj'yah-wahl-nohsh'ch' gohs-poh-dahr-chah;_ **(company)** firma, przedsiębiorstwo _feer-mah, psheht-sh'yehm-byohr-stfoh_
busy zajęty _zah-yehn-tyh_
but (_conj._) ale _ah-leh_
butcher rzeźnik _zhehzh'-n'eek_
butter masło _mah-swoh_
button guzik _guh-zh'eek_
buy kupować _kuh-poh_-vaksówka _tahk-suhf-kah_

C

cabinet szafka _shahf-kah_
cable kabel, przewód _kah-behl, psheh-wuht_
cable TV telewizja kablowa _teh-leh-vee-zyah kah-bloh-vah_
café kawiarnia _kah-vyahr-n'yah_
cage klatka _klaht-kah_
cake ciasto, tort _ch'yah-stoh, tohrt_
calendar kalendarz _kah-lehn-dahsh_
call (on telephone) dzwonić _dzvoh-n'eech'_
camera aparat fotograficzny _ah-pah-raht foh-toh-grah-fee-chnyh_
camp (_v._) rozbijać obóz _rohz-bee-yahch' oh-buhz_
campground obozowisko, pole namiotowe _oh-boh-zoh-vees-koh, poh-leh nah-myoh-toh-veh_
can (_modal verb_) móc; umieć, potrafić _muhts; uh-mye-hch', poh-trah-feech'_
cancel odwoływać, anulować _ohd-voh-wyh-vahch', ah-nuh-loh-vahch'_
candy cukierek, słodycze _tsuh-kyeh-rehk, swoh-dyh-cheh_
car samochód; auto _sah-moh-huht; ahw-toh_
card karta _kahr-tah_
carpet dywan _dyh-vahn_
carrot marchew _mahr-hehf_
carry nosić _noh-sh'eech'_
carry-on bagaż podręczny _bah-gahzh poh-drehn-chnyh_
cart wózek _vuh-zehk_
case (container) pudełko _puh-dehw-koh;_ **(legal proceedings)** sprawa _sprah-vah_
cash (_v._) realizować (czek) _reh-ah-lee-zoh-vahch' (chehk)_
cash (_n._) gotówka _goh-tuhf-kah_
casual (of clothes) nieoficjalny _n'yeh-oh-fee-tsyahl-nyh_
cat kot _koht_
catch (_v._) chwytac, łapać _hfyh-tahch', wah-pahch'_
cathedral katedra _kah-teh-drah_
cattle bydło _byh-dwoh_
cave jaskinia _yah-skee-n'yah_
CD płyta kompaktowa, CD _pwyh-tah kohm-pah-ktoh-vah, see dee_
cement cement _tseh-mehnt_
cemetery cmentarz _tsmehn-tahzh_
cent cent _tsehnt_
center centrum _tsehn-truhm_

century wiek, stulecie *vyehk, stuh-leh-ch'yeh*
cereal płatki śniadaniowe *pwah-tkee sh'n'yah-dah-n'yoh-veh*
chain (jewelry) łańcuszek *wahn'-tsuh-shehk*
chair krzesło *ksheh-swoh*
champagne szampan *shahm-pahn*
change (*v.*) zmieniać *zmyeh-n'yahch'*
change (*n.*) **(alteration)** zmiana *zmyah-nah;* **(money)**
  reszta *rehsh-tah*
changing room szatnia; przymierzalnia *shaht-n'yah;*
  pshyh-myeh-zhahl-n'yah
channel kanał *kah-nahw*
chapel kaplica *kah-plee-tsah*
chapter rozdział *rohz-dj'yahw*
charge (*n.*) opłata *oh-pwah-tah*
cheap tani *tah-n'ee*
check (*v.*) sprawdzać *sprahv-dzahch'*
check (*n.*) **(bank)** czek *chehk;* **(bill)** rachunek *rah-huh-nehk*
check in zameldować się *zah-mehl-doh-vahch' sh'yeh*
check out wymeldowywać się *vyh-mehl-doh-vahch'*
  sh'yeh
checkpoint punkt kontrolny *puhnkt kohn-trohl-nyh*
cheese ser (żółty) *sehr (zhuhw-tyh)*
chef kucharz; szef kuchni *kuh-hahzh; shehf kuh-chn'ee*
chemical (*n.*) substancja chemiczna *suhp-stahn-tsyah*
  heh-meech-nah
chew żuć *zhuhch'*
chicken kurczak *kuhr-chahk*
chickpeas ciecierzyca *ch'yeh-ch'yeh-zhyh-tsah*
chief (*adj.*) główny *gwuhv-nyh*
child dziecko *dj'yeh-tskoh*
childcare opieka przedszkolna *oh-pyeh-kah psheht-shkohl-nah*
chocolate czekolada *cheh-koh-lah-dah*
choke dławić się *dwah-veech' sh'yeh*
church kościół *kohsh'-ch'yuhw*
cigarette papieros *pah-pyeh-rohs*
cinema kino *kee-noh*
cinnamon cynamon *tsyh-nah-mohn*
circle koło, okrąg, kółko *koh-who, oh-krohnk, kuhw-koh*
citizen obywatel (*masc.*)/obywatelka (*fem.*) *oh-byh-vah-tehl/oh-byh-vah-tehl-kah*
city miasto *myah-stoh*

civilian (*n.*) osoba cywilna; cywil (colloquial) *oh-<u>soh</u>-bah tsyh-<u>veel</u>-nah; <u>tsyh</u>-veel*

clap klaskać *<u>klah</u>-skahch'*

class (course) zajęcia *zah-<u>yehn</u>-ch'yah;* **(group)** klasa, grupa *<u>klah</u>-sah, <u>gruh</u>-pah*

classic klasyczny *klah-<u>syh</u>-chnyh*

clean czysty *<u>chyh</u>-styh*

client klient (*masc.*)/klientka (*fem.*) *<u>klee</u>-yehnt/klee-<u>yehnt</u>-kah*

cliff ściana skalna *sh'<u>ch'yah</u>-nah skahl-nah*

climate klimat *<u>klee</u>-maht*

climb wspinać się *<u>fspee</u>-nahch' sh'yeh*

clinic klinika; przychodnia *klee-<u>n'ee</u>-kah; pshyh-<u>hohd</u>-n'yah*

clock zegar *<u>zeh</u>-gahr*

close (*adv.*) blisko *<u>blee</u>-skoh*

close (*v.*) zamykać *zah-<u>myh</u>-kahch'*

closed zamknięty *zahm-<u>kn'yehn</u>-tyh*

cloth szmatka, ścierka *<u>shmaht</u>-kah, sh'<u>ch'yehr</u>-kah*

clothing ubranie *uh-<u>brah</u>-n'yeh*

club klub *kluhp*

clutch pedal sprzęgło *<u>spzhehn</u>-gwoh*

coast wybrzeże *vyh-<u>bzheh</u>-zheh*

coat płaszcz *pwahshch*

cocoa kakao *kah-<u>kah</u>-oh*

coconut kokos *<u>koh</u>-kohs*

coffee kawa *<u>kah</u>-vah*

coin moneta *moh-<u>neh</u>-tah*

cold (*adj.*) zimny *<u>zh'ee</u>-mnyh*

cold (*n.*) przeziębienie *psheh-zh'yehm-<u>byeh</u>-n'yeh*

collect zbierać *<u>zbyeh</u>-rahch'*

color kolor *<u>koh</u>-lohr*

comb grzebień *<u>gzheh</u>-byehn'*

come przychodzić, przyjeżdżać, przybywać (arrive) *pshyh-<u>hoh</u>-dj'eech', pshyh-<u>yehzh</u>-djahch', pshyh-<u>byh</u>-vahch'*

comedy komedia *koh-<u>meh</u>-dyah*

comfortable wygodny *vyh-<u>goh</u>-dnyh*

commission komisja (body); prowizja (reward) *koh-<u>mee</u>-syah; proh-<u>vee</u>-zyah*

communication komunikacja *koh-muh-n'ee-<u>kah</u>-tsyah*

companion towarzysz (*masc.*)/towarzyszka (*fem.*) *toh-<u>vah</u>-zhyhsh/toh-vah-<u>zhyhsh</u>-kah*

company towarzystwo (accompanying people); firma (business) *toh-vah-<u>zhyh</u>-stfoh; <u>feer</u>-mah*

compare porównywać *poh-ruhv-<u>nyh</u>-vahch'*

compensation wynagrodzenie *vyh-nah-groh-dzeh-n'yeh*
complain narzekać *nah-zheh-kahch'*
complicated skomplikowany *skohm-plee-koh-vah-nyh*
compromise kompromis *kohm-proh-mees*
computer komputer *kohm-puh-tehr*
conceal ukrywać *uh-kryh-vahch'*
concert koncert *kohn-tsehrt*
concrete (*adj.*) konkretny (specific) *kohn-kreh-tnyh*
concrete (*n.*) beton (building material) *beh-tohn*
concussion wstrząs mózgu *fstshohns muhz-guh*
condom kondom, prezerwatywa *kohn-dohm, preh-zehr-vah-tyh-vah*
conductor konduktor *kohn-duhk-tohr*
conference konferencja *kohn-feh-rehn-tsyah*
conference room sala konferencyjna *sah-lah kohn-feh-rehn-tsyhy-nah*
confirm potwierdzać *poh-tfyehr-dzahch'*
(to be) constipated mieć zaparcie *myehch' zah-pahr-ch'yeh*
constitution konstytucja *kohns-tyh-tuh-tsyah*
consulate konsulat *kohn-suh-laht*
consult radzić się, konsultować się *rah-dj'eech' sh'yeh, kohn-suhl-toh-vahch' sh'yeh*
contagious zaraźliwy, zakaźny *zah-rah-zh'lee-vyh, zah-kahzh'-nyh*
contraception antykoncepcja *ahn-tyh-kohn-tsehp-tsyah*
contraceptive (*n.*) środek antykoncepcyjny *sh'roh-dehk ahn-tyh-kohn-tsehp-tsyhy-nyh*
contract umowa, kontrakt *uh-moh-vah, kohn-trahkt*
convenience store sklepik całodobowy *skleh-peek tsah-woh-doh-boh-vyh*
convenient dogodny, wygodny *doh-goh-dnyh, vyh-goh-dnyh*
cook (*n.*) kucharz *kuh-hahsh*
cook (*v.*) gotować *goh-toh-vahch'*
copy (*n.*) kopia, egzemplarz (book, etc) *koh-pyah, ehg-zehm-plahsh*
copy (*v.*) kopiować *koh-pyoh-vahch'*
cord sznur, przewód *shnuhr, psheh-wuht*
corn kukurydza *kuh-kuh-ryh-dzah*
corner róg, kąt, zakręt *ruhg, kohnt, zah-krehnt*
correct (*adj.*) poprawny *poh-prah-vnyh*
corrupt (*adj.*) zepsuty, skorumpowany *zehp-suh-tyh, skoh-ruhm-poh-vah-nyh*

corrupt (v.) deprawować (deprave), korumpować *deh-prah-voh-vahch', koh-ruhm-poh-vahch'*
cosmetics kosmetyki *kohs-meh-tyh-kee*
cost (n.) koszt *kohsht*
cost (v.) kosztować *kohsh-toh-vahch'*
cotton bawełna *bah-vehw-nah*
cough (v.) kaszleć *kahsh-lehch'*
country kraj *krahy*
country code numer kierunkowy kraju *nuh-mehr kyeh-ruhn-koh-vyh krah-yuh*
court sąd *sohnd*
courtesy grzeczność, uprzejmość *gzhehch-nohsh'ch', uh-pshehy-mohsh'ch'*
cover (n.) pokrywa, wieko (lid) *poh-kryh-vah, vyeh-koh*
cover (v.) przykrywać, osłaniać *pshyh-kryh-vahch', oh-swah-n'yahch'*
cover charge opłata za wstęp *oh-pwah-tah zah fstehmp*
cream śmietana (culinary); krem (culinary or cosmetic sense) *sh'myeh-tah-nah; krehm*
credit kredyt *kreh-dyht*
credit card karta kredytowa *kahr-tah kreh-dyh-toh-vah*
crime zbrodnia, przestępstwo *zbroh-dn'yah, psheh-stehmp-stfoh*
crowd tłum *twuhm*
crutches kule *kuh-leh*
cry płakać *pwah-kahch'*
culture kultura *kuhl-tuh-rah*
cup filiżanka *fee-lee-zhahn-kah*
cure (n.) lekarstwo *leh-kahr-stfoh*
cure (v.) leczyć, wyleczyć *leh-chyhch', vyh-leh-chyhch'*
curfew godzina policyjna; cisza nocna (hotel) *goh-dj'ee-nah poh-lee-tsyhy-nah; ch'ee-shah nohts-nah*
currency waluta *vah-luh-tah*
currency exchange kantor wymiany walut *kahn-tohr vyh-myah-nyh vah-luht*
customer klient *klee-yehnt*
customs odprawa celna *oht-prah-vah tsehl-nah*
customs declaration deklaracja celna *deh-klah-rah-tsyah tsehl-nah*
customs duty cło *tswoh*
cut (n.) cięcie, skaleczenie *ch'yehn'-ch'yeh, skah-leh-cheh-n'yeh*
cut (v.) kroić, ciąć *kroh-yeech', ch'yohn'ch'*

D

dairy nabiał _nah_-byahw
damage (_n._) zniszczenie, uszkodzenie zn'eesh-_cheh_-n'yeh, uhsh-koh-_dzeh_-n'yeh
dance (_v._) tańczyć _tahn'_-chyhch'
danger niebezpieczeństwo n'yeh-behs-pyeh-_chehn'_-stfoh
dark ciemny _ch'yehm_-nyh
date (_n._) data, termin _dah_-tah, _tehr_-meen
date of birth data urodzenia _dah_-tah uh-roh-_dzeh_-n'yah
daughter córka _tsuhr_-kah
dawn świt sh'feet
day dzień dj'yehn'
daytime dzień; pora dzienna dj'yehn'; _poh_-rah _dj'yehn_-nah
dead zmarły, martwy _zmahr_-wyh, _mahr_-tfyh
deadline ostateczny termin ohs-tah-_teh_-chnyh _tehr_-meen
deaf głuchy _gwuh_-hyh
debt dług dwuhg
decade dekada, dziesięciolecie deh-_kah_-dah, dj'yeh-sh'yehn-ch'yoh-_leh_-ch'yeh
December grudzień _gruh_-dj'yehn'
decide decydować deh-tsyh-_doh_-vahch'
decision decyzja deh-_tsyh_-zyah
deck (boat) pokład _poh_-kwaht; **(terrace)** taras _tah_-rahs
declare ogłaszać, oznajmiać, zgłaszać oh-_gwah_-shahch', ohz-_nahy_-myahch', _zgwah_-shahch'
deep głęboki gwehm-_boh_-kee
delay (_n._) zwłoka, opóźnienie _zvwoh_-kah, oh-puhzh'-_n'yeh_-n'yeh
delay (_v._) opóźniać, zwlekać oh-_puhzh'_-n'yahch', _zvleh_-kahch'
delicious pyszny _pyhsh_-nyh
deliver dostarczać dohs-_tahr_-chahch'
delivery dostawa doh-_stah_-vah
demand (_n._) żądanie zhohn-_dah_-n'yeh
democracy (country) państwo demokratyczne _pahn'_-stfoh deh-moh-krah-_tyhch_-neh; **(system)** demokracja deh-moh-_krah_-tsyah
dentist stomatolog, dentysta stoh-mah-_toh_-lohg, dehn-_tyhs_-tah
deny zaprzeczać zah-_psheh_-chahch'
deodorant dezodorant deh-zoh-_doh_-rahnt
department store dom towarowy dohm toh-vah-_roh_-vyh

departure (of train, bus, etc.) odjazd *ohd-yahst;* **(of airplane)** odlot *ohd-loht*
deposit (bank) wpłata *fpwah-tah;* **(against damage)** zaliczka *zah-leech-kah;* **(partial payment)** kaucja *kahw-tsyah*
depot zajezdnia *zah-yehzd-n'yah*
desert (*n.*) pustynia *puh-styh-n'yah*
desk biurko *byuhr-koh*
dessert deser *deh-sehr*
destination cel podróży; miejsce przeznaczenia *tsehl poh-druh-zhyh; myehy-stseh pzheh-znah-cheh-n'yah*
detergent detergent *deh-tehr-gehnt*
detour objazd *ohb-yahst*
diabetic (*n.*) cukrzyk, diabetyk *tsuh-kshyhk, dyah-beh-tyhk*
diagnosis diagnoza *dyah-gnoh-zah*
dial wybierać numer *vyh-byeh-rahch' nuh-mehr*
dialing code numer kierunkowy *nuh-mehr kyeh-ruhn-koh-vyh*
diaper pieluszka *pyeh-luhsh-kah*
diarrhea biegunka *byeh-guhn-kah*
dictate dyktować *dyh-ktoh-vahch'*
dictionary słownik *swohv-n'eek*
die umierać *uh-myeh-rahch'*
diesel olej napędowy *oh-lehy nah-pehn-doh-vyh*
different (*adj.*) różny, inny *ruhzh-nyh, een-nyh*
difficult (*adj.*) trudny *truhd-nyh*
dine jeść obiad *yehsh'ch' oh-byaht*
dining room jadalnia *yah-dahl-n'yah*
dinner kolacja *koh-lah-tsyah*
diplomat dyplomata *dyh-ploh-mah-tah*
direction kierunek *kyeh-ruh-nehk*
directions wskazówki *fskah-zuhf-kee*
directory spis, wykaz *spees, vyh-kahz*
directory assistance informacja telefoniczna *een-fohr-mah-tsyah teh-leh-foh-n'eech-nah*
dirt brud (mess); ziemia (soil) *bruhd; zh'yeh-myah*
dirty brudny *bruhd-nyh*
disability kalectwo, upośledzenie *kah-lehts-tfoh, uh-poh-sh'leh-dzeh-n'yeh*
disabled niepełnosprawny *n'yeh-pehw-noh-sprahv-nyh*
disagree nie zgadzać się *n'yeh zgah-dzahch' sh'yeh*

disaster katastrofa, nieszczęście *kah-tah-stroh-fah, n'yeh-shchehn'-sh'ch'yeh*

discount zniżka, rabat _zn'eezh-kah, rah-baht_
disease choroba _hoh-roh-bah_
dish potrawa, danie (food); naczynie (vessel) _poh-trah-vah, dah-n'yeh; nah-chyh-n'yeh_
disposable jednorazowy, jednorazowego użytku _yehd-noh-rah-zoh-vyh, yehd-noh-rah-zoh-veh-goh uh-zhyht-kuh_
dispute (_v._) kwestionować _kfeh-styoh-noh-vahch'_
district (admin) okręg, rejon _oh-krehng, reh-yohn;_
  (neighborhood) dzielnica _dj'yehl-n'ee-tsah_
disturb przeszkadzać _psheh-shkah-dzahch'_
dive nurkować _nuhr-koh-vahch'_
(to feel) dizzy mieć zawroty głowy _myehch' zah-vroh-tyh gwoh-vyh_
do robić _roh-beech'_
dock dok _dohk_
doctor lekarz _leh-kahzh_
document dokument _doh-kuh-mehnt_
dog pies _pyehs_
dollar dolar _doh-lahr_
domestic krajowy _krah-yoh-vyh_
door drzwi _djvee_
double podwójny _pohd-vuhy-nyh_
dough ciasto _ch'yah-stoh_
down na; w dół _nah; vduhw_
downtown (w) centrum miasta _ftsehn-truhm myah-stah_
dozen tuzin _tuh-zh'een_
drain rura kanalizacyjna _ruh-rah kah-nah-lee-zah-tsyhy-nah_
drama dramat _drah-maht_
drawer szuflada _shuh-flah-dah_
dress (_n._) sukienka, suknia _suh-kyehn-kah, suhk-n'yah_
dress (_v._) ubierać się _uh-byeh-rahch' sh'yeh_
drink (_n._) napój (liquid); drink (alcoholic) _nah-puhy; dreenk_
drink (_v._) pić _peech'_
drive prowadzić _proh-vah-dj'eech'_
driver's license prawo jazdy _prah-voh yahz-dyh_
drown topić się, tonąć _toh-peech' sh'yeh, toh-nohnch'_
drowsy senny, śpiący _sehn-nyh, sh'pyohn-tsyh_
drug (medicine) lek, lekarstwo _lehk, leh-kahr-stfoh;_
  (narcotic) narkotyk _nahr-koh-tyhk_
drunk pijany _pee-yah-nyh_
dry (_adj._) suchy _suh-hyh_
dry (_v._) suszyć; suszyć się; wysychać _suh-shyhch'; suh-shyhch' sh'yeh; vyh-syh-hahch'_

dry cleaner pralnia chemiczna _prahl_-n'yah heh-_meech_-nah

dryer suszarka suh-_shahr_-kah

dust (_v._) odkurzać ohd-_kuh_-zhahch'

duty-free wolny od cła _vohl_-nyh oht tswah

DVD DVD dee vee dee

dye (_n._) farba _fahr_-bah

dye (_v._) farbować fahr-_boh_-vahch'

E

ear ucho _uh_-hoh

earache ból ucha buhl _uh_-hah

early (_adj._) wczesny _fcheh_-snyh

early (_adv._) wcześnie _fcheh_-sh'n'yeh

earth ziemia _zh'yeh_-myah

earthquake trzęsienie ziemi tshehn-_sh'yeh_-n'yeh _zh'yeh_-mee

east wschód _fs_-huht

eat jeść yehsh'ch'

economy gospodarka gohs-poh-_dahr_-kah

education szkolnictwo, edukacja, oświata shkohl-_n'eets_-tfoh, eh-duh-_kah_-tsyah, ohsh'-_fyah_-tah

egg jajko _yahy_-koh

eight osiem _oh_-sh'yehm

eighteen osiemnaście oh-sh'yehm-_nahsh'_-ch'yeh

eighty osiemdziesiąt oh-sh'yehm-_dj'yeh_-sh'yohnt

election wybory vyh-_boh_-ryh

electric elektryczny eh-lehk-_tryh_-chnyh

electricity elektryczność, prąd eh-lehk-_tryhch_-nohsh'ch', prohnd

elevator winda _veen_-dah

eleven jedenaście yeh-deh-_nahsh'_-ch'yeh

e-mail poczta elektroniczna, e-mail _pohch_-tah eh-lehk-troh-_n'eech_-nah, _ee_-mehyl

embassy ambasada ahm-bah-_sah_-dah

emergency nagły wypadek; krytyczna sytuacja _nah_-gwyh vyh-_pah_-dehk; kryh-_tyh_-chnah syh-tuh-_ah_-tsyah

employee pracownik prah-_tsohv_-n'eek

employer pracodawca prah-tsoh-_dahf_-tsah

empty pusty _puh_-styh

end (_n._) koniec _koh_-n'yehts

enemy wróg vruhg

energy energia eh-_nehr_-gyah

engine silnik _sh'eel-n'eek_
engineer inżynier _een-zhyh-n'yehr_
English language język angielski _yehn-zyhk ahn-gyehl-skee_
engraving grawerunek _grah-veh-ruh-nehk_
enough (_adv._) wystarczająco _vyh-stahr-chah-yohn-tsoh_
enough (_pron._) dość, dosyć _dohsh'ch', doh-syhch'_
enter wejść, wchodzić _vehysh'ch', fhoh-dj'eech'_
entertainment rozrywka _rohz-ryhv-kah_
entire cały, całkowity _tsah-wyh, tsahw-koh-vee-tyh_
entrance wejście _vehysh'-ch'yeh_
entry wejście, wjazd _vehysh'-ch'yeh, vyahst_
entry visa wiza wjazdowa _vee-zah vyahz-doh-vah_
envelope koperta _koh-pehr-tah_
epileptic epileptyczny _eh-pee-lehp-tyhch-nyh_
equal równy _ruhv-nyh_
equipment wyposażenie, sprzęt _vyh-poh-sah-zheh-n'yeh, spshehnt_
escalator ruchome schody _ruh-hoh-meh s hoh-dyh_
estimate (_n._) szacunek, ocena _shah-tsuh-nehk, oh-tseh-nah_
estimate (_v._) szacować, oceniać _ah-tsoh-vahch', oh-tseh-n'yahch'_
ethnic etniczny _eht-n'eech-nyh_
Europe Europa _eh-uh-roh-pah_
European (_adj._) europejski _eh-uh-roh-pehy-skee_
European (_n._) Europejczyk (_masc._)/Europejka (_fem._) _eh-uh-roh-pehy-chyhk/eh-uh-roh-pehy-kah_
evacuate ewakuować _eh-vah-kuh-oh-vahch'_
even równy _ruhv-nyh_
evening wieczór _vyeh-chuhr_
event wydarzenie, przypadek _vyh-dah-zheh-n'yeh, pshyh-pah-dehk_
eventually w końcu _fkohn'-tsuh_
ever kiedykolwiek _kyeh-dyh-kohl-vyehk_
every każdy _kahzh-dyh_
exact dokładny _doh-kwahd-nyh_
examine badać (inspect) _bah-dahch'_
example przykład _pshyh-kwahd_
except oprócz, poza, z wyjątkiem _oh-pruhch, poh-zah, zvyh-yohnt-kyehm_
excess (_adj._) nadmierny, dodatkowy _nahd-myehr-nyh, doh-daht-koh-vyh_
excess (_n._) nadwyżka, nadmiar _nahd-vyhzh-kah, nahd-myahr_

exchange (*v.*) wymieniać *vyh-myeh-n'yahch'*
exchange rate kurs wymiany (walut) *kuhrs vyh-myah-nyh (vah-luht)*
exclude wykluczać *vyh-kluh-chahch'*
exhibit (*v.*) wystawiać, eksponować *vyh-stah-vyahch', ehks-poh-noh-vahch'*
exit (*n.*) wyjście *vyhysh'-ch'yeh*
expense wydatek *vyh-dah-tehk*
expensive drogi *droh-gee*
experience (*n.*) doświadczenie, przeżycie *dohsh'-fyaht-cheh-n'yeh, pzheh-zhyh-ch'yeh*
expiration date data ważności *dah-tah vahzh-nohsh'-ch'ee*
explain wyjaśniać *vyh-yahsh'-n'yahch'*
export (*n.*) eksport *ehks-pohrt*
export (*v.*) eksportować *ehks-pohr-toh-vahch'*
express (*adj.*) ekspresowy *ehks-preh-soh-vyh*
express train ekspres, pociąg ekspresowy *ehks-prehs, poh-ch'yohng ehks-preh-soh-vyh*
extra (*adj.*) dodatkowy, nadzwyczajny, ekstra *doh-daht-koh-vyh, nahd-zvyh-chahy-nyh, ehks-trah*
extra (*adv.*) dodatkowo *doh-daht-koh-voh*
eye oko *oh-koh*
eyeglasses okulary *oh-kuh-lah* tkanina, materiał *tkah-n'ee-nah, mah-teh-ryahw*

F

face twarz *tfahzh*
fall (*n.*) **(autumn)** jesień *yeh-sh'yehn'*
fall (*v.*) upadać *uh-pah-dahch'*
false (*adj.*) fałszywy *fahw-shyh-vyh*
family rodzina *roh-dj'ee-nah*
far (*adj.*) daleki *dah-leh-kee*
far (*adv.*) daleko *dah-leh-koh*
fare opłata za przejazd *oh-pwah-tah zah psheh-yahst*
farm gospodarstwo rolne *goh-spoh-dahr-stfoh rohl-neh*
fast food fast food *fahst fuht*
fat (*adj.*) gruby (pertaining to a person) *gruh-byh*
fat (*n.*) tłuszcz *twuhshch*
father ojciec *ohy-ch'yehts*
faucet kran *krahn*
fax (*n.*) faks *fahks*
February luty *luh-tyh*

fee opłata *oh-pwah-tah*
feel czuć; czuć się *chuhch'; chuhch' sh'yeh*
female (*adj.*) żeński, kobiecy *zhehn'-skee, koh-byeh-tsyh*
female (*n.*) kobieta *koh-byeh-tah*
fence płot, ogrodzenie *pwoht, oh-groh-dzeh-n'yeh*
ferry prom *prohm*
festival (**religious**) święto *sh'fyehn-toh;* (**music**) festiwal *feh-stee-vahl*
fever gorączka *goh-rohnch-kah*
field (**farm**) pole *poh-leh;* (**academic**) dziedzina *dj'yeh-dj'ee-nah;* (**sports**) boisko *boh-yee-skoh*
fifteen piętnaście *pyehnt-nahsh'-ch'yeh*
fifty pięćdziesiąt *pyehnch'-dj'yeh-sh'yohnt*
fig figa *fee-gah*
fill napełniać *nah-pehw-n'yahch'*
film film *feelm*
find znajdować *znahy-doh-vahch'*
finger palec (u ręki) *pah-lehts (uh rehn-kee)*
fire pożar; ogień *poh-zhahr; oh-gyehn'*
fire alarm alarm pożarowy *ah-lahrm poh-zhah-roh-vyh*
firewood drewno opałowe *drehv-noh oh-pah-woh-veh*
fireworks sztuczne ognie; fajerwerki *shtuh-chneh ohg-n'yeh; fah-yehr-vehr-kee*
first pierwszy *pyehr-vshyh*
first-aid kit apteczka *ahp-tehch-kah*
first-class (*adj.*) w pierwszej klasie *fpyehr-fshehy klah-sh'yeh*
first-class (*n.*) pierwsza klasa *pyehr-fshah klah-sah*
fish (*n.*) ryba *ryh-bah*
fisherman wędkarz; rybak *vehnt-kahzh; ryh-bahk*
fishing wędkarstwo *vehnd-kahr-stfoh*
fishing license karta wędkarska *kahr-tah vehnd-kahr-skah*
fishing rod wędka *vehnd-kah*
fist pięść *pyehnsh'ch'*
fit (*v.*) pasować *pah-soh-vahch'*
fitting room przymierzalnia *pshyh-myeh-zhahl-n'yah*
five pięć *pyehn'ch'*
fix naprawić *nah-prah-veech'*
flag flaga *flah-gah*
flame płomień *pwoh-myehn'*
flare raca *rah-tsah*
flash flesz; lampa błyskowa (phot) *flehsh; lahm-pah bwyh-skoh-vah*

flash photography fotografowanie z fleszem *foh-toh-grah-foh-vah-n'yeh sfleh-shehm*
flashlight latarka *lah-tahr-kah*
flat płaski *pwah-skee*
flat tire przebita opona *psheh-bee-tah oh-poh-nah*
flavor smak *smahk*
flea pchła *phwah*
flea market pchli targ *phlee tahrg*
flight lot *loht*
flight number numer lotu *nuh-mehr loh-tuh*
flood powódź *poh-vuhdj'*
floor piętro *pyehn-troh*
flour mąka *mohn-kah*
flourish rozkwitać, prosperować *rohz-kfee-tahch', proh-speh-roh-vahch'*
flower kwiat *kfyaht*
flu grypa *gryh-pah*
fluent płynny *pwyhn-nyh*
fluid (*n.*) płyn *pwyhn*
flush spuszczać wodę *spuhsh-chahch' voh-deh*
fly (*n.*) mucha *muh-hah*
fly (*v.*) latać *lah-tahch'*
fog mgła *mgwah*
folk ludowy *luh-doh-vyh*
folk art sztuka ludowa *shtuh-kah luh-doh-vah*
follow iść za *eesh'ch' zah*
food jedzenie *yeh-dzeh-n'yeh*
food poisoning zatrucie pokarmowe *zah-truh-ch'yeh poh-kahr-moh-veh*
foot stopa *stoh-pah*
football (soccer) piłka nożna *peew-kah nohzh-nah*
footpath ścieżka *sh'ch'yeh-shkah*
forehead czoło *choh-woh*
foreign zagraniczny, obcy *zah-grah-n'eech-nyh, ohp-tsyh*
foreign currency obca waluta *ohp-tsah vah-luh-tah*
foreign languages języki obce *yehn-zyh-kee ohp-tseh*
forest las *lahs*
forget zapominać *zah-poh-mee-nahch'*
forgive przebaczać *psheh-bah-chahch'*
fork widelec *vee-deh-lehts*
formal oficjalny *oh-fee-tsyahl-nyh*
fortune teller wróżka *vruhsh-kah*
forty czterdzieści *chtehr-dj'yehsh'-ch'ee*
fountain fontanna *fohn-tahn-nah*
four cztery *chteh-ryh*

fourteen czternaście *chtehr-nahsh'-ch'yeh*
fraud oszustwo *oh-shuhs-tfoh*
free (available) wolny *vohl-nyh;* **(without charge)**
bezpłatny *behz-pwaht-nyh*
freeze zamrażać *zah-mrah-zhahch'*
fresh świeży *sh'fyeh-zhyh*
Friday piątek *pyohn-tehk*
friend przyjaciel (*masc.*)/przyjaciółka (*fem.*) *pshyh-yah-ch'yehl/pshyh-yah-ch'yuhw-kah*
front przód *pshuht*
front desk recepcja *reh-tsehp-tsyah*
frozen zamarznięty; mrożony *zah-mahr-zn'yehn-tyh; mroh-zhoh-nyh*
fruit owoc *oh-vohts*
fry (*v.*) smażyć *smah-zhyhch'*
fuel paliwo *pah-lee-voh*
full pełny *pehw-nyh*
fun zabawa *zah-bah-vah*
funeral pogrzeb *poh-gzhehp*
furnished umeblowany, wyposażony *uh-meh-bloh-vah-nyh, vyh-poh-sah-zhoh-nyh*
furniture meble *meh-bleh*
future przyszłość *pshyh-shwohsh'ch'*

G

game gra *grah;* **(sports)** mecz *mehch*
garden (*n.*) ogród *oh-gruht*
gas tank bak *bahk*
gasoline benzyna *behn-zyh-nah*
gear bieg *byehg*
general ogólny *oh-guhl-nyh*
get (obtain) dostać *dohs-tahch';* **(buy)** kupić *kuh-peech'*
gift prezent *preh-zehnt*
girl dziewczynka; dziewczyna *dj'yehf-chyhn-kah; dj'yehf-chyh-nah*
girlfriend dziewczyna *dj'yehf-chyh-nah*
give dawać *dah-vahch'*
glass (non-alcoholic drinks) szklanka *shklahn-kah;* **(alcoholic drinks)** kieliszek (alcoholic drinks) *kyeh-lee-shehk*
glasses (optical) okulary *oh-kuh-lah-ryh*
glue klej *klehy*

go (by foot) iść *eesh'ch'*; **(by bus, train, etc.)** jechać
   yeh-hahch'; **(by plane)** lecieć *leh-ch'yehch'*
goat koza *koh-zah*
gold (*adj.*) złoty *zwoh-tyh*
gold (*n.*) złoto *zwoh-toh*
good dobry *doh-bryh*
goods towary, artykuły *toh-vah-ryh, ahr-tyh-kuh-wyh*
government rząd *zhohnt*
gram gram *grahm*
grammar gramatyka *grah-mah-tyh-kah*
grandfather dziadek *dj'yah-dehk*
grandmother babcia *bahp-ch'yah*
grape winogrono *vee-noh-groh-noh*
grass trawa *trah-vah*
great (*adj.*) świetny *sh'fyeht-nyh*
great (*adv.*) świetnie *sh'fyeht-n'yeh*
green zielony *zh'yeh-loh-nyh*
greeting powitanie *poh-vee-tah-n'yeh*
grocery store sklep spożywczy *sklehp spoh-zhyf-chyh*
ground (*n.*) ziemia *zh'yeh-myah*
group grupa *gruh-pah*
guard (*n.*) strażnik *strahzh-n'eek*
guest gość *gohsh'ch'*
guide (*n.*) przewodnik *psheh-vohd-n'eek*
guidebook przewodnik *psheh-vohd-n'eek*
guilty winny *veen-nyh*
gun broń *brohn'*
gym siłownia *sh'ee-wohv-n'yah*

H

hair włosy *vwoh-syh*
half pół *puhw*
hall hol *hohl*
halt zatrzymać (się) *zah-tshyh-mahch' (sh'yeh)*
hand ręka *rehn-kah*
handicapped niepełnosprawny *n'yeh-pehw-noh-sprahv-
   nyh*
happy szczęśliwy *shchehn-sh'lee-vyh*
harbor port *pohrt*
hard (texture) twardy *tfahr-dyh*; **(difficult)** ciężki
   ch'yehn-zhkee
harm (*n.*) krzywda *kshyhv-dah*

harm (*v.*) krzywdzić; szkodzić <u>kshyhv</u>-dj'eech'; <u>shkoh</u>-dj'eech'

hat kapelusz kah-<u>peh</u>-luhsh

hazard niebezpieczeństwo n'yeh-behz-pyeh-<u>chehn'</u>-stfoh

he on ohn

head głowa <u>gwoh</u>-vah

health zdrowie <u>zdroh</u>-vyeh

health insurance ubezpieczenie zdrowotne uh-behz-pyeh-<u>cheh</u>-n'yeh zdroh-<u>voht</u>-neh

hear słyszeć <u>swyh</u>-shehch'

heart serce <u>sehr</u>-tseh

heart attack atak serca, zawał <u>ah</u>-tahk <u>sehr</u>-tsah, <u>zah</u>-vahw

heat (*n.*) upał <u>uh</u>-pahw

heat (*v.*) ogrzewać oh-<u>gzheh</u>-vahch'

heavy ciężki <u>ch'yehn</u>-zhkee

hello dzień dobry dj'yehn' <u>dohb</u>-ryh

help (*n.*) pomoc <u>poh</u>-mohts

help! (*interjection*) pomocy! poh-<u>moh</u>-tsyh

herb zioło <u>zh'yoh</u>-woh

here tutaj <u>tuh</u>-tahy

heterosexual (*adj.*) heteroseksualny heh-teh-roh-sehk-suh-<u>ahl</u>-nyh

heterosexual (*n.*) osoba heteroseksualna oh-<u>soh</u>-bah heh-teh-roh-sehk-suh-<u>ahl</u>-nah

hey! (*interjection*) hej hehy

highway autostrada ahw-toh-<u>strah</u>-dah

hike wędrować pieszo vehn-<u>droh</u>-vahch' <u>pyeh</u>-shoh

hill wzgórze <u>vzguh</u>-zheh

HIV wirus HIV <u>vee</u>-ruhs heef

hole dziura <u>dj'yuh</u>-rah

holiday dzień wolny (day off); święto (church) dj'yehn' <u>vohl</u>-nyh; sh'<u>fyehn</u>-toh

holy święty sh'<u>fyehn</u>-tyh

home dom dohm

homeless bezdomny behz-<u>dohm</u>-nyh

homosexual (*adj.*) homoseksualny hoh-moh-sehk-suh-<u>ahl</u>-nyh

homosexual (*n.*) homoseksualista hoh-moh-sehk-suh-ah-<u>lee</u>-stah

honest uczciwy uhch-<u>ch'ee</u>-vyh

honey miód myuht

honeymoon miesiąc miodowy <u>myeh</u>-sh'yohnts myoh-<u>doh</u>-vyh

horse koń kohn'

hospital szpital _shpee-tahl_
hospitality gościnność _gohsh'-ch'een-nohsh'ch'_
hostage zakładnik _zah-kwahd-n'eek_
hostel schronisko (młodzieżowe) _s-hroh-n'ees-koh (mwoh-dj'yeh-zhoh-veh)_
hostile wrogi _vroh-gee_
hot gorący _goh-rohn-tsyh_
hotel hotel _hoh-tehl_
hour godzina _goh-dj'ee-nah_
house dom _dohm_
how jak _yahk_
hug (_v._) obejmować _oh-behy-moh-vahch'_
human (_adj._) ludzki _luhdz-kee_
human (_n._) człowiek _chwoh-vyehk_
human rights prawa człowieka _prah-vah chwoh-vyeh-kah_
hundred sto _stoh_
hungry głodny _gwohd-nyh_
hunt polować _poh-loh-vahch'_
hunter myśliwy _myh-sh'lee-vyh_
hurry śpieszyć się _sh'pyeh-shyhch' sh'yeh_
hurt boleć _boh-lehch'_
husband mąż _moyah_

I

ice lód _luht_
ID card dowód tożsamości _doh-wuht tohsh-sah-mohsh'-ch'ee_
idea pomysł _poh-myhsw_
identification dowód tożsamości _doh-wuht tohsh-sah-mohsh'-ch'ee_
identify identyfikować, rozpoznawać _ee-dehn-tyh-fee-koh-vahch', rohz-pohz-nah-vahch'_
idiom idiom _ee-dyohm_
if jeśli; czy _yehsh'-lee; chyh_
ignition zapłon _zahp-wohn_
ignore ignorować _eeg-noh-roh-vahch'_
illegal nielegalny _n'yeh-leh-gahl-nyh_
illness choroba _hoh-roh-bah_
immigrant immigrant (_masc._)/imigrantka (_fem._) _ee-mee-grahnt/ee-mee-grahnt-kah_
immigration imigracja _ee-mee-grah-tsyah_
impolite niegrzeczny, nieuprzejmy _n'yeh-gzhehch-nyh, n'yeh-uh-pshehy-myh_

import (*n.*) import _eem-pohrt_
import (*v.*) importować _eem-pohr-toh-vahch'_
income dochód _doh-huht_
incorrect błędny _bwehn-dnyh_
individual (*adj.*) indywidualny _een-dyh-vee-duh-ahl-nyh_
individual (*n.*) osoba; jednostka _oh-soh-bah; yehd-nohst-kah_
indoor wewnątrz (budynku) _vehv-nohntzh (buh-dyhn-kuh)_
inexpensive niedrogi _n'yeh-droh-gee_
infant niemowlę _n'yeh-moh-vleh_
infect zakażać _zah-kah-zhahch'_
infected zakażony _zah-kah-zhoh-nyh_
infection infekcja _een-fehk-tsyah_
influence wpływ _fpwyhf_
influenza grypa _gryh-pah_
information informacja _een-fohr-mah-tsyah_
information desk informacja _een-fohr-mah-tsyah_
infrastructure infrastruktura _een-frah-struh-ktuh-rah_
inject wstrzykiwać _fstshyh-kee-vahch'_
injury uraz; zranienie _uh-rahz; zrah-n'yeh-n'yeh_
ink atrament; tusz _ah-trah-mehnt; tuhsh_
inn zajazd; gospoda _zah-yahst; gohs-poh-dah_
innocent niewinny _n'yeh-veen-nyh_
inquiry zapytanie _zah-pyh-tah-n'yeh_
insect owad, insekt _oh-vaht, een-sehkt_
insect bite ugryzienie owada _uh-gryh-zh'yeh-n'yeh oh-vah-dah_
insect repellant środek odstraszający owady _sh'roh-dehk oht-strah-shah-yohn-tsyh oh-vah-dyh_
inside w środku _fsh'roh-tkuh_
inspect badać, sprawdzać, kontrolować _bah-dahch', sprahv-dzahch', kohn-troh-loh-vahch'_
instant (*adj.*) natychmiastowy (immediate) _nah-tyhh-myahs-toh-vyh_
institution instytucja; zakład _eens-tyh-tuh-tsyah; zahk-waht_
insufficient niedostateczny _n'yeh-dohs-tah-tehch-nyh_
insulin insulina _een-suh-lee-nah_
insult (*n.*) obraza _oh-brah-zah_
insult (*v.*) obrażać _oh-brah-zhahch'_
insurance ubezpieczenie _uh-behz-pyeh-cheh-n'yeh_
international międzynarodowy _myehn-dzyh-nah-roh-doh-vyh_
Internet internet _een-tehr-neht_

interpret tłumaczyć ustnie *twuh-mah-chyhch' uhst-n'yeh*
interpretation tłumaczenie ustne *twuh-mah-cheh-n'yeh uhst-neh*
interpreter tłumacz ustny *twuh-mahch uhst-nyh*
intersection skrzyżowanie *skshyh-zhoh-vah-n'yeh*
intimate intymny; bliski *een-tyhm-nyh; blees-kee*
introduce oneself przedstawiać się *psheht-stah-vyahch' sh'yeh*
intruder intruz *een-truhz*
invite zaprosić *zah-proh-sh'eech'*
iron (*n.*) żelazko *zheh-lahs-koh*
iron (*v.*) prasować *prah-soh-vahch'*
irritate irytować, drażnić *ee-ryh-toh-vahch', drahzh-n'eech'*
island wyspa *vyhs-pah*
issue sprawa, kwestia *sprah-vah, kfehs-tyah*
it to, ono *toh, oh-noh*
itch swędzieć *sfehn-dj'yehch'*
item przedmiot *pshehd-myoht*
itinerary plan podróży *plahn poh-druh-zhyh*

J

jacket marynarka (man's); żakiet (woman's); kurtka (coat) *mah-ryh-nahr-kah; zhah-kyeht; kuhrt-kah*
jail więzienie *vyehn-zh'yeh-n'yeh*
jam dżem *djehm*
January styczeń *styh-chehn'*
jar słoik *swoh-yeek*
jeans dżinsy *djeen-syh*
Jew Żyd (*masc.*)/Żydówka (*fem.*) *zhyht/zhyh-duhf-kah*
jewelry biżuteria *bee-zhuh-teh-ryah*
job praca *prah-tsah*
join przyłączyć (się) *pshyh-wohn-chyhch' (sh'yeh)*
journalist dziennikarz (*masc.*)/dziennikarka (*fem.*) *dj'yehn-n'ee-kahsh/dj'yehn-n'ee-kahr-kah*
judge sędzia *sehn-dj'yah*
jug dzbanek *dzbah-nehk*
juice sok *sohk*
July lipiec *lee-pyehts*
jump skakać *skah-kahch'*
jumper cables kable rozruchowe *kah-bleh rohz-ruh-hoh-veh*
junction (intersection) skrzyżowanie BE *skshyh-zhoh-vah-n'yeh*

June czerwiec _chehr_-vyehts
jungle dżungla _djuhn_-glah
just (expressing time) dopiero co doh-_pyeh_-roh tsoh
justice sprawiedliwość sprah-vyeh-_dlee_-vohsh'ch'

K

keep (_v._) zatrzymać zah-_tshyh_-mahch'
kettle czajnik _chahy_-n'eek
key klucz kluhch
kick kopać _koh_-pahch'
kid dziecko _dj'yeh_-tskoh
kidnap porywać poh-_ryh_-vahch'
kidney nerka _nehr_-kah
kill zabijać zah-_bee_-yahch'
kilogram kilogram kee-_loh_-grahm
kilometer kilometr kee-_loh_-mehtr
kind (_adj._) dobry, życzliwy _dohb_-ryh, zhyhch-_lee_-vyh
kind (_n._) rodzaj _roh_-dzahy
kiss (_n._) pocałunek poh-tsah-_wuh_-nehk
kiss (_v._) całować tsah-_woh_-vahch'
kit zestaw _zehs_-tahf
kitchen kuchnia _kuhh_-n'yah
knapsack plecak, chlebak _pleh_-tsahk, _hleh_-bahk
knee kolano koh-_lah_-noh
knife nóż nuhsh
knit robić na drutach _roh_-beech' nah _druh_-tahh
knock pukać _puh_-kahch'
knot węzeł _vehn_-zehw
know wiedzieć _vyeh_-dj'yehch'
kosher koszerny koh-_shehr_-nyh

L

lady pani _pah_-n'ee
lake jezioro yeh-_zh'yoh_-roh
lamb (animal) jagnię, baranek _yahg_-n'yeh, bah-_rah_-nehk;
   (food) baranina bah-rah-_n'ee_-nah
lamp lampa _lahm_-pah
land (_v._) lądować lohn-_doh_-vahch'
lane (narrow street) uliczka uh-_leech_-kah; **(for vehicles)**
   pas ruchu pahs _ruh_-huh
language język _yehn_-zyhk

laptop laptop _lahp-tohp_

large duży _duh-zhyh_

last (_adj._) (**most recent**) ostatni; (**previous**) zeszły
ohs-taht-n'ee; zehsh-wyh

last year w zeszłym roku _v zehsh-wyhm roh-kuh_

late (**not early**) późny _puhzh'-nyh;_ (**delayed**) opóźniony
oh-puhzh'-n'yoh-nyh

later później _puhzh'-n'yehy_

laugh (_v._) śmiać się _sh'myahch' sh'yeh_

laundromat pralnia samoobsługowa _prahl-n'yah
sah-moh-ohb-swuh-goh-vah_

laundry pranie _prah-n'yeh_

lavatory toaleta _toh-ah-leh-tah_

law prawo _prah-voh_

lawyer prawnik (_masc._)/prawniczka (_fem._) _prahv-n'eek/
prahv-n'eech-kah_

layover przerwa w podróży _pshehr-vah fpoh-druh-zhyh_

leader (**political**) przywódca _pshyh-wuht-tsah;_
(**manager**) menedżer _meh-neh-djehr_

league liga _lee-gah_

learn uczyć się _uh-chyhch' sh'yeh_

leather skóra _skuh-rah_

leave (**depart by vehicle**) odjeżdżać _ohd-yehzh-djahch';_
(**depart on foot**) odchodzić _ohd-hoh-dj'eech';_ (**depart
by plane**) odlatywać _ohd-lah-tyh-vahch';_ (**cause to
remain**) zostawiać _zohs-tah-vyahch'_

left lewy _leh-vyh_

leg noga _noh-gah_

legal legalny _leh-gahl-nyh_

legislature władza ustawodawcza _vwah-dzah uh-stah-
voh-dahf-chah_

lemon cytryna _tsyh-tryh-nah_

lens (**optical**) soczewka _soh-chehf-kah;_ (**camera**)
obiektyw _oh-byehk-tyhf_

less mniej _mn'yehy_

letter list _leest_

lettuce sałata _sah-wah-tah_

level poziom _poh-zh'yohm_

library biblioteka _bee-blyoh-teh-kah_

lice wszy _fshyh_

license zezwolenie _zehz-voh-leh-n'yeh_

lid wieko, pokrywka _vyeh-koh, poh-kryhf-kah_

lie (_n._) kłamstwo _kwahm-stfoh_

lie (_v._) kłamać _kwah-mahch'_

life życie _zhyh-ch'yeh_

lift (*n.*) winda (elevator) *veen-dah*
lift (*v.*) podnosić *pohd-noh-sh'eech'*
light (*adj.*) **(of weight)** lekki *lehk-kee;* **(of color)** jasny
 yahs-nyh
light (*n.*) światło *sh'fyah-twoh*
lighting oświetlenie *ohsh'-fyeht-leh-n'yeh*
like (to be fond of) lubić *luh-beech';* **(to be attracted
 to)** podobać się *poh-doh-bahch' sh'yeh*
lime limonka *lee-mohn-kah*
limit (*v.*) ograniczać *oh-grah-n'ee-chahch'*
lip warga *vahr-gah*
liquid (*n.*) płyn *pwyhn*
liquor alkohol *ahl-koh-hohl*
list lista *lees-tah*
listen słuchać *swuh-hahch'*
liter litr *leetr*
litter (*n.*) śmieci *sh'myeh-ch'ee*
litter (*v.*) śmiecić *sh'myeh-ch'eech'*
little (*adj.*) mały *mah-wyh*
little (*adv.*) mało *mah-woh*
live (to be alive) żyć *zhyhch';* **(to reside)** mieszkać
 myehsh-kahch'
liver wątroba *vohn-troh-bah*
lizard jaszczurka *yahsh-chuhr-kah*
load (*v.*) ładować *wah-doh-vahch'*
loaf bochenek (chleba) *boh-heh-nehk (hleh-bah)*
loan (*n.*) **(borrowed money)** pożyczka *poh-zhyhch-
 kah;* **(bank)** kredyt *kreh-dyht*
lobby hol *hohl*
local lokalny, miejscowy *loh-kahl-nyh, myehy-stsoh-vyh*
location miejsce, lokalizacja *myehy-stseh, loh-kah-lee-
 zah-tsyah*
lock (*n.*) zamek *zah-mehk*
lock (*v.*) zamykać na klucz *zah-myh-kahch' nah kluhch*
lock oneself out zatrzasnąć sobie drzwi *zah-tshahs-
 nohnch' soh-byeh djvee*
locker schowek na bagaż *s-hoh-vehk nah bah-gahzh*
long długi *dwuh-gee*
look (*v.*) patrzeć *pah-tshehch'*
loose luźny *luhzh'-nyh*
lose (an item) zgubić *zguh-beech';* **(a person)** stracić
 strah-ch'eech'
lost (of an item) zgubiony *zguh-byoh-nyh;* **(of a person)** zaginiony *zah-gee-n'yoh-nyh*
loud głośny *gwohsh'-nyh*

lounge (hotel) hol, bar *hohl, bahr;* **(airport)**
poczekalnia *poh-cheh-kahl-n'yah*
love (*n.*) miłość *mee-wohsh'ch'*
love (*v.*) kochać *koh-hahch'*
low niski *n'ees-kee*
lucky szczęśliwy *shchehn-sh'lee-vyh*
luggage bagaż *bah-gahzh*
lunch obiad, lunch *oh-byaht, lahnch*

M

machine maszyna; urządzenie *mah-shyh-nah; uh-zhohn-*
dzeh-n'yeh
mad (*adj.*) wściekły *fsh'ch'yeh-kwyh*
maid pokojówka *poh-koh-yuhf-kah*
mail (*n.*) poczta *pohch-tah*
mail (*v.*) wysłać (pocztą) *vyh-swahch' (pohch-tohm)*
main (*adj.*) główny *gwuhv-nyh*
make (*v.*) zrobić *zroh-beech'*
man mężczyzna *mehn-shchyh-znah*
mandatory obowiązkowy *oh-boh-vyohn-skoh-vyh*
manual (*n.*) instrukcja obsługi *een-struhk-tsyah ohp-*
swuh-gee
many dużo *duh-zhoh*
map mapa *mah-pah*
marketplace plac targowy; rynek *plahts tahr-goh-vyh;*
ryh-nehk
marriage małżeństwo *mahw-zhehn'-stfoh*
married (of a man) żonaty *zhoh-nah-tyh;* **(of a**
woman) zamężna *zah-mehn-zhnah*
marry (~ someone) brać ślub z (kimś) *brahch' sh'luhp z*
(keemsh')
massage masaż *mah-sahzh*
math matematyka *mah-teh-mah-tyh-kah*
mattress materac *mah-teh-rahts*
maximum (*adj.*) maksymalny *mah-ksyh-mahl-nyh*
maximum (*n.*) maksimum *mah-ksee-muhm*
mayor burmistrz *buhr-meestsh*
meal posiłek *poh-sh'ee-wehk*
measure (*v.*) mierzyć *myeh-zhyhch'*
meat mięso *myehn-soh*
mechanic mechanik *meh-hah-n'eek*
medication lek, lekarstwo *lehk, leh-kahr-stfoh*
medicine lekarstwo *leh-kahr-stfoh*

medium (*adj.*) średni; M *sh'rehd-n'ee; ehm*
meet (make acquaintance of) poznać *pohz-nahch';*
  (come together, encounter) spotkać, spotkać się (z
  kimś) *spoht-kahch' sh'yeh (skeemsh')*
meeting spotkanie *spoht-kah-n'yeh*
melon melon *meh-lohn*
melt (*v.*) topić się *toh-peech' sh'yeh*
member członek *chwoh-nehk*
menstruation miesiączka, okres *myeh-sh'yohn-chkah,*
  oh-krehs
mental (*adj.*) umysłowy *uh-myh-swoh-wyh*
menu menu *meh-n'ee*
merchant kupiec *kuh-pyehts*
message wiadomość *vyah-doh-mohsh'ch'*
messenger posłaniec *poh-swah-n'yehts*
metal metal *meh-tahl*
meter (apparatus) licznik *leech-n'eek;* **(measurement)**
  metr *mehtr*
metro station stacja metra *stah-tsyah meh-trah*
microwave kuchenka mikrofalowa *kuh-hehn-kah mee-*
  kroh-fah-loh-vah
midday południe *poh-wuhd-n'yeh*
middle (*adj.*) średni, środkowy *sh'reh-dn'ee, sh'rohd-koh-*
  vyh
middle (*n.*) środek *sh'roh-dehk*
midnight północ *puhw-nohts*
migraine migrena *mee-greh-nah*
mild (*adj.*) łagodny *wah-goh-dnyh*
mile mila *mee-lah*
military wojskowy *vohy-skoh-vyh*
milk mleko *mleh-koh*
million milion *meel-yohn*
mine mój *muhy*
minimum minimum *mee-n'ee-muhm*
minor (*adj.*) mniejszy *mn'yehy-shyh*
mint (plant) mięta *myehn-tah;* **(candy)** cukierek miętowy *tsuh-kyeh-rehk myehn-toh-vyh*
minute minuta (time) *mee-nuh-tah*
mirror lustro *luhs-troh*
misunderstanding nieporozumienie *n'yeh-poh-roh-zuh-*
  myeh-n'yeh
mix (*v.*) mieszać *myeh-shahch'*
mobile phone telefon komórkowy *teh-leh-fohn koh-*
  muhr-koh-vyh
moment chwila, moment *hfee-lah, moh-mehnt*

Monday poniedziałek *poh-n'yeh-dj'yah-wehk*
money pieniądze *pyeh-n'yohn-dzeh*
monkey małpa *mahw-pah*
month miesiąc *myeh-sh'yohnts*
monument pomnik *pohm-n'eek*
moon księżyc *ksh'yehn-zhyhts*
more (*adv.*) więcej *vyehn-tsehy*
morning rano *rah-noh*
mosque meczet *meh-cheht*
mosquito komar *koh-mahr*
mosquito net moskitiera *mohs-kee-tyeh-rah*
most (*adv.*) najwięcej *nahy-vyehn-tsehy*
motel motel *moh-tehl*
mother matka *maht-kah*
mother-in-law teściowa *tehsh'-ch'yoh-vah*
motion sickness choroba lokomocyjna *hoh-roh-bah*
  loh-koh-moh-tsyhy-nah
motor silnik (engine) *sh'eel-n'eek*
motorcycle motocykl *moh-toh-tsyhkl*
mount (*n.*) góra *guh-rah*
mountain góra *guh-rah*
mouse mysz *myhsh*
moustache wąsy *vohn-syh*
mouth usta *uhs-tah*
move (*v.*) ruszać (się) *ruh-shahch' (sh'yeh)*
movie film *feelm*
movie theater kino *kee-noh*
Mr. (title) pan *pahn*
Mrs. (title) pani *pah-n'ee*
Ms. (title) pani *pah-n'ee*
much (*adv.*) dużo *duh-zhoh*
mud błoto *bwoh-toh*
mural fresk *frehsk*
murder (*n.*) morderstwo *mohr-dehr-stfoh*
murder (*v.*) mordować *mohr-doh-vahch'*
muscle mięsień *myehn-sh'yehn'*
museum muzeum *muh-zeh-uhm*
mushroom grzyb; pieczarka *gzhyhp; pyeh-chahr-kah*
music muzyka *muh-zyh-kah*
musical instrument instrument muzyczny *een-struh-*
  mehnt muh-zyh-chnyh
musician muzyk *muh-zyhk*
Muslim (*adj.*) muzułmański *muh-zuhw-mahn'-skee*
Muslim (*n.*) muzułmanin (*masc.*)/muzułmanka (*fem.*)
  muh-zuhw-mah-n'een/muh-zuhw-mahn-kah

mussels małże _mahw_-zheh
mystery tajemnica tah-yehm-_n'ee_-tsah

N

naked nagi _nah_-gee
name imię _ee_-myeh
napkin serwetka sehr-_veht_-kah
narrow wąski _vohn_-skee
nation (people) naród _nah_-ruht; **(state)** państwo
  pahn'-stfoh
native (_adj._) ojczysty ohy-_chyh_-styh
nature przyroda pshyh-_roh_-dah
nausea mdłości _mdwoh_-sh'ch'ee
navigation nawigacja nah-vee-_gah_-tsyah
navy (_n._) marynarka wojenna mah-ryh-_nahr_-kah voh-
  yehn-nah
navy (_adj._) granatowy (color) grah-nah-_toh_-vyh
near (_prep._) niedaleko n'yeh-dah-_leh_-koh
nearby (_adj._) pobliski poh-_blee_-skee
neck szyja _shyh_-yah
necklace naszyjnik nah-_shyhy_-n'eek
need (_v._) potrzebować poh-tsheh-_boh_-vahch'
needle igła _ee_-gwah
neighbor sąsiad (_masc._)/sąsiadka (_fem._) _sohn_-sh'yaht/
  sohn-_sh'yaht_-kah
neighborhood okolica oh-koh-_lee_-tsah
nephew (sister's son) siostrzeniec sh'yohs-_tsheh_-n'yehts;
  (brother's son) bratanek brah-_tah_-nehk
nerve nerw nehrf
neutral (_adj._) neutralny neh-uh-_trahl_-nyh
never (_adv._) nigdy _n'ee_-gdyh
new (_adj._) nowy _noh_-vyh
New Year Nowy Rok _noh_-vyh rohk
New Year's Day Nowy Rok _noh_-vyh rohk
New Year's Eve Sylwester syhl-_vehs_-tehr
news wiadomość (_sing._), wiadomości (_pl._) vyah-_doh_-
  mohsh'ch', vyah-doh-_mohsh'_-ch'ee
newspaper gazeta gah-_zeh_-tah
next następny nahs-_tehm_-pnyh
next to obok _oh_-bohk
next year w przyszłym roku _fpshyh_-shwyhm _roh_-kuh
nice miły _mee_-wyh
niece (sister's daughter) siostrzenica sh'yohs-tsheh-

_n'ee_-tsah; **(brother's daughter)** bratanica _brah-tah-_
_n'ee_-tsah

night noc _nohts_

nightlife życie nocne _zhyh_-ch'yeh _nohts_-neh

nine dziewięć _dj'yeh_-vyehn'ch'

nineteen dziewiętnaście dj'yeh-vyehnt-_nahsh'_-ch'yeh

ninety dziewięćdziesiąt dj'yeh-vyehn'ch'-_dj'yeh_-sh'yohnt

no nie _n'yeh_

noise hałas _hah_-wahs

non-smoking dla niepalących dlah n'yeh-pah-_lohn_-tsyhh

noodles makaron mah-_kah_-rohn

noon południe poh-_wuhd_-n'yeh

normal normalny nohr-_mahl_-nyh

north północ _puhw_-nohts

northeast północny wschód puhw-_nohts_-nyh _fs-huht_

northwest północny zachód puhw-_nohts_-nyh _zah_-huht

nose nos _nohs_

note (_n._) notatka noh-_taht_-kah

note (_v._) zapisywać zah-pee-_syh_-vahch'

nothing nic _n'eets_

November listopad lee-_stoh_-paht

now teraz _teh_-rahs

nowhere (_adv._) nigdzie _n'eeg_-dj'yeh

nuclear (_adj._) nuklearny nuh-kleh-_ahr_-nyh

nudist beach plaża nudystów _plah_-zhah nuh-_dyhs_-tuhf

number (figure) liczba _leech_-bah; **(amount, quantity)**
ilość _ee_-lohsh'ch'

nun zakonnica zah-kohn-_n'ee_-tsah

nurse pielęgniarka pyeh-lehn-_gn'yahr_-kah

nuts orzechy oh-_zheh_-hyh

O

occupant mieszkaniec myehsh-_kah_-n'yehts

occupation zawód _zah_-vuht

ocean ocean oh-_tseh_-ahn

o'clock godzina goh-_dj'ee_-nah

October październik pahzh'-_dj'yehr_-n'eek

octopus ośmiornica ohsh'-myohr-_n'ee_-tsah

odor zapach zah-pahh

off (_adv./adj._) wyłączony vyh-wohn-_choh_-nyh

offend obrażać oh-_brah_-zhahch'

office biuro _byuh_-roh

officer (military) officer oh-_fee_-tsehr

official (*adj.*) oficjalny, formalny *oh-fee-tsyahl-nyh, fohr-mahl-nyh*
official (*n.*) urzędnik *uh-zhehnd-n'eek*
often (*adv.*) często *chehn-stoh*
oil (cooking) olej *oh-lehy;* **(petroleum)** ropa naftowa *roh-pah nahf-toh-vah*
OK w porządku; dobrze *fpoh-zhohn-tkuh; dohb-zheh*
old stary *stah-ryh*
olive (*n.*) oliwka *oh-leef-kah*
on na *nah*
once (one time) raz *rahz;* **(at one time, formerly)** kiedyś *kyeh-dyhsh'*
one jeden *yeh-dehn*
one-way w jedną stronę *vyehd-nohm stroh-neh*
onion cebula *tseh-buh-lah*
only tylko *tyhl-koh*
open (*adj.*) otwarty *oht-fahr-tyh*
open (*v.*) otwierać *oht-fyeh-rahch'*
opera opera *oh-peh-rah*
operator operator *oh-peh-rah-tohr*
opposite naprzeciwko *nah-psheh-ch'eef-koh*
option opcja; wybór *ohp-tsyah, vyh-buhr*
or albo *ahl-boh*
oral ustny *uhst-nyh;* **(medicine)** doustny *doh-uhst-nyh*
orange (color) (*adj.*) pomarańczowy *poh-mah-rahn'-choh-vyh*
orange (*n.*) pomarańcza *poh-mah-rahn'-chah*
orchard sad *saht*
orchestra orkiestra *ohr-kyeh-strah*
order (*n.*) zamówienie *zah-muh-vyeh-n'yeh*
order (*v.*) zamawiać *zah-mah-vyahch'*
ordinary zwykły *zvyh-kwyh,* zwyczajny *zvyh-chahy-nyh*
organ organ *ohr-gahn;* **(biol.)** narząd *nah-zhohnt*
organic organiczny *ohr-gah-n'eech-nyh*
original oryginalny *oh-ryh-gee-nahl-nyh*
other inny *een-nyh*
our nasz *nahsh*
out (outside) na zewnątrz *nah zehv-nohntzh;* **(absent, not at home)** poza domem *poh-zah doh-mehm*
outdoor (*adj.*) zewnętrzny, odkryty, na świeżym powietrzu *zehv-nehn-tshnyh, oht-kryh-tyh, nah sh'fyeh-zhyhm poh-vyeh-tzhuh*
outside na zewnątrz *nah zehv-nohntsh*
oven piekarnik *pyeh-kahr-n'eek*

over (*prep.*) **(across the top of)** przez *pshehz*; **(above)** nad, ponad *naht, poh-naht*

overdose (*n.*) przedawkowanie *psheh-dahf-koh-vah-n'yeh*

overdose (*v.*) przedawkować *psheh-dahf-koh-vahch'*

overnight (*adj.*) z dnia na dzień *zdn'yah nah dj'yehn'*

overnight (*adv.*) na noc *nah nohts*

own (*v.*) posiadać *poh-sh'yah-dahch'*

owner (*n.*) właściciel *vwahsh'-ch'ee-ch'yehl*

oxygen tlen *tlehn*

P

pack (*v.*) pakować *pah-koh-vahch'*

package przesyłka *psheh-syhw-kah*

page strona *stroh-nah*

paid płatny *pwah-tnyh*

pain ból *buhl*

painful bolesny *boh-lehs-nyh*

painkiller środek przeciwbólowy *sh'roh-dehk psheh-ch'eev-buh-loh-vyh*

pair para *pah-rah*

pajamas piżama *pee-zhah-mah*

pan garnek, rondelek *gahr-nehk, rohn-deh-lehk*

pants spodnie *spohd-n'yeh*

paper papier *pah-pyehr*

parcel paczka *pahch-kah*

pardon? słucham? *swuh-hahm*

parent rodzic *roh-dj'eets*

park (*n.*) park *pahrk*

park (*v.*) parkować *pahr-koh-vahch'*

parking parking *pahr-keeng*

parliament parlament *pahr-lah-mehnt*

partner partner (*masc.*)/partnerka (*fem.*) *pahrt-nehr/pahrt-nehr-kah*

party przyjęcie (social) *pshyh-yehn'-ch'yeh*

passenger pasażer (*masc.*)/pasażerka (*fem.*) *pah-sah-zhehr/pah-sah-zhehr-kah*

passport paszport *pahsh-pohrt*

password hasło *hah-swoh*

pasta makaron *mah-kah-rohn*

pastry ciastko *ch'yahst-koh*

path ścieżka *sh'ch'yehsh-kah*

patience cierpliwość *ch'yehr-plee-vohsh'ch'*

patient (*n.*) pacjent (*masc.*)/pacjentka (*fem.*) *pahts-yehnt/pahts-yehnt-kah*
pavement chodnik *hohd-n'eek*
pay płacić *pwah-ch'eech'*
payment zapłata *zah-pwah-tah*
pea groszek *groh-shehk*
peace pokój *poh-kuhy*
peach brzoskwinia *bzhohs-kfee-n'yah*
peak szczyt *shchyht*
peanuts orzeszki ziemne *oh-zhehsh-kee zh'yehm-neh*
pedal (*n.*) pedał *peh-dahw*
pedal (*v.*) pedałować *peh-dah-woh-vahch'*
pedestrian (*adj.*) dla pieszych *dlah pyeh-shyhh*
pedestrian (*n.*) pieszy *pyeh-shyh*
pen pióro *pyuh-roh*; (**ballpoint pen**) długopis *dwuh-goh-pees*
penalty kara *kah-rah*
pencil ołówek *oh-wuh-vehk*
people (**persons**) ludzie *luh-dj'yeh;* (**nation**) naród *nah-ruht*
pepper (**spice**) pieprz *pyehpsh;* (**vegetable**) papryka *pah-pryh-kah*
percent procent *proh-tsehnt*
perfect (*adj.*) doskonały *doh-skoh-nah-wyh*
perfect (*adv.*) doskonale *doh-skoh-nah-leh*
period (**time**) okres *oh-krehs;* (**menstrual**) okres *oh-krehs*
permanent (*adj.*) stały, trwały *stah-wyh, trvah-wyh*
permission pozwolenie *poh-zvoh-leh-n'yeh*
permit (*v.*) pozwalać *poh-zvah-lahch'*
permit (*n.*) zezwolenie *zeh-zvoh-leh-n'yeh*
person osoba *oh-soh-bah*
personal osobisty *oh-soh-bees-tyh*
pest szkodnik *shkohd-n'eek*
pet zwierzę (domowe) *zvyeh-zheh (doh-moh-veh)*
petrol benzyna *behn-zyh-nah*
pharmacy apteka *ahp-teh-kah*
phone telefon *teh-leh-fohn*
phone booth budka telefoniczna *buht-kah teh-leh-foh-n'eech-nah*
phone card karta telefoniczna *kahr-tah teh-leh-foh-n'eech-nah*
phone number numer telefonu *nuh-mehr teh-leh-foh-nuh*
photograph zdjęcie *zdyehn'-ch'yeh*
phrase zwrot *zvroht*
physician lekarz *leh-kahzh*

piano fortepian *fohr-teh-pyahn*
pick (select) wybierać *vyh-byeh-rahch'*; **(pluck, gather)**
  zrywać, zbierać *zryh-vahch', zbyeh-rahch'*
picnic piknik *peek-n'eek*
picture obrazek *oh-brah-zehk*
pie ciasto, placek *ch'yah-stoh, plah-tsehk*
piece kawałek *kah-vah-wehk*
pig świnia *sh'fee-n'yah*
pigeon gołąb *goh-wohmp*
pill tabletka *tah-bleht-kah*
pillow poduszka *poh-duhsh-kah*
pipe (smoking) fajka *fahy-kah*; **(conduit)** rura *ruh-rah*
place miejsce *myehy-stseh*
plain prosty *proh-styh*
plan (*n.*) plan *plahn*
plan (*v.*) planować *plah-noh-vahch'*
plane samolot *sah-moh-loht*
plant (*n.*) roślina *roh-sh'lee-nah*
plastic plastikowy *plah-stee-koh-vyh*
plate talerz *tah-lehsh*
platform peron *peh-rohn*
play (*n.*) **(theater)** sztuka *shtuh-kah*
play (*v.*) grać *grahch'*
pleasant przyjemny *pshyh-yehm-nyh*
please proszę *proh-sheh*
plug zatyczka *zah-tyhch-kah*
pocket kieszeń *kyeh-shehn'*
poem wiersz *vyehrsh*
point (*v.*) wskazać *fskah-zahch'*
poison trucizna *truh-ch'eez-nah*
police policja *poh-lee-tsyah*
police station posterunek policji *poh-steh-ruh-nehk poh-lee-tsyee*
polite uprzejmy *uh-pshehy-myh*
politics polityka *poh-lee-tyh-kah*
pollution zanieczyszczenie *zah-n'yeh-chyhsh-cheh-n'yeh*
pool basen *bah-sehn*
population ludność *luhd-nohsh'ch'*
pork wieprzowina *vyehp-shoh-vee-nah*
portable (*adj.*) przenośny *psheh-nohsh'-nyh*
possibly (*adv.*) być może; możliwe (że) *byhch' moh-zheh; moh-zhlee-veh (zheh)*
post office poczta *pohch-tah*
postage opłata pocztowa *oh-pwah-tah pohch-toh-vah*
postal code kod pocztowy *kohd pohch-toh-vyh*

postbox skrzynka pocztowa _skshyhn-kah pohch-toh-vah_
postcard pocztówka _pohch-tuhf-kah_
postpone odkładać; odraczać _oht-kwah-dahch'; ohd-rah-chahch'_
pot garnek _gahr-nehk_
potato ziemniak _zh'yehm-n'yahk_
pottery ceramika _tseh-rah-mee-kah_
poultry drób _druhp_
pound (_n._) funt _fuhnt_
pour lać; nalewać _lahch'; nah-leh-vahch'_
poverty bieda _byeh-dah_
power (electricity) prąd _prohnt_
pray modlić się _mohd-leech' sh'yeh_
prefer woleć, preferować _voh-lehch', preh-feh-roh-vahch'_
pregnant w ciąży _fch'yohn-zhyh_
prescription recepta _reh-tsehp-tah_
president (of State) prezydent _preh-zyh-dehnt;_ (**of company**) prezes _preh-zehs_
price cena _tseh-nah_
priest ksiądz _ksh'yohndz_
printer drukarka _druh-kahr-kah_
prison więzienie _vyehn-zh'yeh-n'yeh_
prisoner więzień _vyehn-zh'yehn'_
privacy prywatność _pryh-vaht-nohsh'ch'_
private (_adj._) prywatny _pryh-vaht-nyh_
private property własność prywatna _vwahs-nohsh'ch' pryh-vaht-nah_
private room własny pokój _vwahs-nyh poh-kuhy_
prize nagroda _nah-groh-dah_
probably prawdopodobnie _prahv-doh-poh-dohb-n'yeh_
problem problem _prohb-lehm_
product produkt _proh-duhkt_
professional (_adj._) zawodowy; profesjonalny _zah-voh-doh-vyh; proh-feh-syoh-nahl-nyh_
professor profesor _proh-feh-sohr_
profile (side view of face) profil _proh-feel;_ (**biographical sketch**) sylwetka _syhl-veht-kah_
profit (_n._) zysk _zyhsk_
program program _proh-grahm_
prohibit zabraniać _zah-brah-n'yahch'_
project (_n._) projekt, plan _proh-yehkt, plahn_
promise (_v._) obiecywać _oh-byeh-tsyh-vahch'_
promotion awans _ah-vahns_
pronounce wymawiać _vyh-mah-vyahch'_
proper właściwy _vwahsh'-ch'ee-vyh_

property własność _vwahs_-nohsh'ch'
prosecute wnosić oskarżenie _vnoh_-sh'eech' ohs-kahr-_zheh_-n'yeh
protect chronić _hroh_-n'eech'
protest (_n._) protest _proh_-tehst
protest (_v._) protestować proh-tehs-_toh_-vahch'
Protestant protestant (_masc._)/protestantka (_fem._) proh-tehs-tahnt/proh-tehs-_tahnt_-kah
province prowincja proh-_veen_-tsyah
psychologist psycholog psyh-_hoh_-lohg
public (_adj._) publiczny puh-_bleech_-nyh
public (_n._) publiczność puh-_bleech_-nohsh'ch'
public telephone telefon publiczny teh-_leh_-fohn puh-_bleech_-nyh
public toilet toaleta publiczna toh-ah-_leh_-tah puh-_bleech_-nah
public transportation publiczne środki transportu puh-_bleech_-neh _sh'rohd_-kee trahns-_pohr_-tuh
pull ciągnąć _ch'yohng_-nohnch'
pulse tętno _tehnt_-noh
pump (_n._) pompa _pohm_-pah
pump (_v._) pompować pohm-_poh_-vahch'
punch (_n._) (**beverage**) poncz pohnch
punch (_v._) (**to hit**) uderzać pięścią uh-_deh_-zhahch' _pyehn'sh'_-ch'yohm
puncture (_n._) przebicie psheh-_bee_-ch'yeh
punish karać _kah_-rahch'
purchase (_n._) zakup _zah_-kuhp
purchase (_v._) kupować kuh-_poh_-vahch'
pure czysty _chyhs_-tyh
purple fioletowy fyoh-leh-_toh_-vyh
purpose cel tsehl
purse torebka toh-_rehp_-kah
push pchać phahch'
puzzle (jigsaw) układanka uh-kwah-_dahn_-kah
pyramid piramida pee-rah-_mee_-dah

Q

qualify kwalifikować (się) kfah-lee-fee-_koh_-vahch' (sh'yeh)
quality jakość _yah_-kohsh'ch'
quantity ilość _ee_-lohsh'ch'
quarantine (_n._) kwarantanna kfah-rahn-_tahn_-nah
quarter ćwierć; kwadrans (time) ch'fyehrch'; _kfah_-drahns

question (*n.*) pytanie *pyh-tah-n'yeh*
queue (*n.*) kolejka *koh-lehy-kah*
queue (*v.*) stać w kolejce *stahch' fkoh-lehy-tseh*
quick szybki *shyhp-kee*
quiet cichy *ch'ee-hyh*

R

radio radio *rah-dyoh*
rail (for protection, support) barierka *bah-ryehr-kah;*
  (handrail) poręcz *poh-rehnch;* **(transportation)** szyna
  shyh-nah
railroad kolej *koh-lehy*
rain (*n.*) deszcz *dehshch*
rain (*v.*) padać *pah-dahch'*
ramp wjazd *vyahst*
rape (*n.*) gwałt *gvahwt*
rape (*v.*) zgwałcić *zgvahw-ch'eech'*
rapid szybki *shyhp-kee*
rare (meat) krwisty *krfee-styh;* **(unusual)** rzadki *zhaht-kee*
rat szczur *shchuhr*
rate (speed) poziom *poh-zh'yohm;* **(level)** tempo *tehm-
  poh*
ratio stosunek *stoh-suh-nehk*
ration przydział *pshyh-dj'yahw*
raw surowy *suh-roh-vyh*
razor maszynka do golenia *mah-shyhn-kah doh goh-leh-
  n'yah*
read czytać *chyh-tahch'*
ready gotowy *goh-toh-vyh*
rear (*adj.*) tylny *tyhl-nyh*
reason (*n.*) powód *poh-vuht*
reasonable rozsądny *rohz-sohn-dnyh*
rebel (*n.*) buntownik *buhn-tohv-n'eek*
rebel (*v.*) buntować się *buhn-toh-vahch' sh'yeh*
rebellion bunt *buhnt*
receipt paragon *pah-rah-gohn*
receive otrzymywać *oh-tshyh-myh-vahch'*
recognize rozpoznawać *rohz-pohz-nah-vahch'*
recommend polecić *poh-leh-ch'eech'*
record (*n.*) **(audio)** płyta *pwyh-tah;* **(sports)** rekord *reh-
  kohrt*
record (*v.*) **(on a disc, tape)** nagrywać *nah-gryh-vahch'*
rectangle prostokąt *prohs-toh-kohnt*

recycle przetwarzać *pzheh-tfah-zhahch'*
red czerwony *chehr-voh-nyh*
referee (*n.*) sędzia *sehn'-dj'yah*
reference świadectwo pracy; referencje *sh'fyah-dehts-tfoh prah-tsyh; reh-feh-rehn-tsyeh*
refrigerator lodówka *loh-duhf-kah*
refuge schronienie, azyl *s-hroh-n'yeh-n'yeh, ah-zyhl*
refugee uchodźca *uh-hohdj'-tsah*
refund zwrot pieniędzy *zvroht pyeh-n'yehn-dzyh*
regime reżim *reh-zheem*
region region *reh-gyohn*
registration rejestracja *reh-yeh-strah-tsyah*
regular regularny *reh-guh-lahr-nyh*
relationship związek *zvyohn-zehk*
relative (*n.*) krewny (*masc.*)/krewna (*fem.*) *kreh-vnyh/kreh-vnah*
reliable (person, equipment, memory, etc.) niezawodny *n'yeh-zah-vohd-nyh;* **(witness, account, information, etc.)** wiarygodny *vyah-ryh-gohd-nyh*
religion religia *reh-lee-gyah*
remedy (medicine) lekarstwo *leh-kahr-stfoh;* **(legal)** zadośćuczynienie *zah-dohsh'ch'-uh-chyh-n'yeh-n'yeh*
remember pamiętać *pah-myehn-tahch'*
remind przypominać *pshyh-poh-mee-nahch'*
remove usuwać *uhu-suh-vahch'*
rent (*v.*) wynająć *vyh-nah-yohn'ch'*
repair (*n.*) naprawa *nah-prah-vah*
repair (*v.*) naprawiać *nah-prah-vyahch'*
repair shop warsztat naprawczy *vahrsh-taht nah-prahv-chyh*
repay spłacać; zwracać *spwah-tsahch'; zvrah-tsahch'*
repeat powtarzać *pohf-tah-zhahch'*
replace zastępować *zah-stehm-poh-vahch'*
reply (*n.*) odpowiedź *oht-poh-vyehdj'*
reply (*v.*) odpowiadać *oht-poh-vyah-dahch'*
report (*v.*) zgłosić *zgwoh-sh'eech'*
reporter reporter *reh-pohr-tehr*
republic republika *reh-puh-blee-kah*
request prośba *prohsh'-bah*
require wymagać *vyh-mah-gahch'*
rescue ratować *rah-toh-vahch'*
reservation rezerwacja *reh-zehr-vah-tsyah*
reserve rezerwować *reh-zehr-voh-vahch'*
reservoir zbiornik *zbyohr-n'eek*
respect (*n.*) szacunek *shah-tsuh-nehk*

respect (*v.*) szanować *shah-noh-vahch'*
rest (*v.*) odpoczywać *oht-poh-chyh-vahch'*
restaurant restauracja *rehs-tahw-rah-tsyah*
restricted ograniczony *oh-grah-n'ee-choh-nyh*
resume (*n.*) CV, życiorys *see vee, zhyh-ch'yoh-ryhs*
retrieve odzyskiwać *ohd-zyhs-kee-vahch'*
return (*v.*) wrócić; zwrócić (give back) *vruh-ch'eech';*
    zvruh-ch'eech'
reverse (*v.*) odwrócić (invert) *oht-vruh-ch'eech'*
revive (*v.*) wskrzesić (fig.: custom, language) *fsksheh-*
    sh'eech'
revolution rewolucja *reh-voh-luh-tsyah*
rib żebro *zheh-broh*
ribbon wstążka *fstohn-zhkah*
rice ryż *ryhzh*
ride (*v.*) jeździć (na) *yehzh'-dj'eech' (nah)*
right (*adj.*) (**direction**) prawy *prah-vyh;* (**correct**)
    dobry, właściwy *doh-bryh, vwahsh'-ch'ee-vyh;* (**good**)
    dobry *doh-bryh*
ring pierścionek *pyehr-sh'ch'yoh-nehk*
riot zamieszki *zah-myehsh-kee*
rip (*n.*) rozdarcie *rohz-dahr-ch'yeh*
rip (*v.*) rozdzierać *rohz-dj'yeh-rahch'*
risk (*n.*) ryzyko *ryh-zyh-koh*
risk (*v.*) ryzykować *ryh-zyh-koh-vahch'*
river rzeka *zheh-kah*
road droga *droh-gah*
road map mapa drogowa *mah-pah droh-goh-vah*
roasted pieczony *pyeh-choh-nyh*
rob okraść, obrabować *oh-krahsh'ch', oh-brah-boh-vahch'*
rock (music) rock *rohk;* (**stone**) skała *skah-wah*
romance romans *roh-mahns*
romantic romantyczny *roh-mahn-tyhchnyh*
roof dach *dahh*
room pokój *poh-kuhy*
room rate cena pokoju (za dzień / za dobę) *tseh-nah*
    poh-koh-yuh (zah dj'yehn' / zah doh-beh)
room service obsługa pokoi *ohp-swuh-gah poh-koh-yee*
rope lina *lee-nah*
rot (*v.*) gnić *gn'eech'*
rotten zepsuty, zgniły *zehp-suh-tyh, zgn'ee-wyh*
rough szorstki, nierówny *shohr-stkee, n'yeh-ruhv-nyh*
round-trip podróż tam i z powrotem *pohd-ruhzh tahm*
    ee z poh-vroh-tehm
round-trip ticket bilet powrotny *bee-leht poh-vroh-tnyh*

route trasa *trah-sah*
royalty członek (pl.członkowie) rodziny królewskiej *chwoh-nehk (pl. chwohn-koh-vyeh) roh-djee-nyh kruh-lehf-skyehy*
rubber guma *guh-mah*
rude niegrzeczny *n'yeh-gzheh-chnyh*
rug dywanik *dyh-vah-n'eek*
rugby rugby *rahg-bee*
ruins ruiny *ruh-yee-nyh*
rule (*n.*) zasada *zah-sah-dah*
rule (*v.*) rządzić *zhohn-dj'eech'*
run biec, biegać *byehts, byeh-gahch'*

S

sacred święty *sh'fyehn-tyh*
sad smutny *smuht-nyh*
saddle siodło *sh'yoh-dwoh*
safe (*adj.*) bezpieczny *behs-pyeh-chnyh*
safe (*n.*) sejf *sehyf*
safety bezpieczeństwo *behs-pyeh-chehn'-stfoh*
sail (*v.*) żeglować *zheh-gloh-vahch'*
salad sałatka *sah-waht-kah*
salary pensja *pehn-syah*
sale (selling) sprzedaż *spsheh-dahzh;* **(seasonal, clearance)** obniżka, wyprzedaż *ohb-neezh-kah, vyh-psheh-dahzh*
sales receipt paragon; rachunek *pah-rah-gohn; rah-huh-nehk*
sales tax podatek obrotowy, podatek od sprzedaży *poh-dah-tehk oh-broh-toh-vyh, poh-dah-tehk oht spsheh-dah-zhyh*
salon (beauty) salon kosmetyczny *sah-lohn kohs-meh-tyhch-nyh;* **(hair)** salon fryzjerski *sah-lohn fryh-zyehr-skee*
salt sól *suhl*
same taki sam *tah-kee sahm*
sample (*n.*) próbka *pruhb-kah*
sanction (*n.*) sankcja *sahnk-tsyah*
sanction (*v.*) sankcjonować *sahnk-tsyoh-noh-vahch'*
sanctuary sanktuarium (holy place) *sahn-ktuh-ah-ryuhm*
sand piasek *pyah-sehk*
sandals sandały *sahn-dah-wyh*

sandwich kanapka *kah-nahp-kah*
sanitary napkin podpaska *poht-pahs-kah*
satellite satelita; antena satelitarna *sah-teh-lee-tah; ahn-teh-nah sah-teh-lee-tahr-nah*
Saturday sobota *soh-boh-tah*
sauce sos *sohs*
sausage kiełbasa *kyehw-bah-sah*
save (rescue) ratować *rah-toh-vahch'*; **(put away)** oszczędzać *ohsh-chehn-dzahch'*
saw piła *pee-wah*
say powiedzieć *poh-vyeh-dj'yehch'*
scanner skaner *skah-nehr*
scar blizna *blee-znah*
scarf szalik *shah-leek*
scary przerażający *psheh-rah-zhah-yohn-tsyh*
scene scena *stseh-nah*
scenery sceneria; otoczenie *stseh-neh-ryah; oh-toh-cheh-n'yeh*
schedule (*n.*) plan, rozkład *plahn, rohz-kwaht*
school szkoła *shkoh-wah*
science nauka *nah-uh-kah*
scissors nożyczki *noh-zhyhch-kee*
score wynik *vyh-n'eek*
screen ekran *eh-krahn*
screw śruba *sh'ruh-bah*
screwdriver śrubokręt *sh'ruh-boh-krehnt*
sculpture rzeźba *zhehzh'-bah*
sea morze *moh-zheh*
seafood owoce morza *oh-voh-tseh moh-zhah*
seasick (to be/feel ~) cierpieć na chorobę morską *ch'yehr-pyehch' nah hoh-roh-beh mohr-skohm*
season pora roku *poh-rah roh-kuh*
seasonal sezonowy *seh-zoh-noh-vyh*
seat miejsce *myehy-stseh*
seat belt pas bezpieczeństwa *pahs behs-pyeh-chehn'-stfah*
seat number numer miejsca *nuh-mehr myehy-stsah*
second (not first) drugi *druh-gee*; **(time unit)** sekunda *seh-kuhn-dah*
secondhand store sklep z używaną odzieżą *sklehp zuh-zyh-vah-nohm oh-dj'yeh-zhohm*
secret tajemnica *tah-yehm-n'ee-tsah*
secretary sekretarz (*masc.*)/sekretarka (*fem.*) *seh-kreh-tahsh/seh-kreh-tahr-kah*
section sekcja; część *sehk-tsyah; chehnsh'ch'*

secular świecki *sh'fyeh-tskee*
security bezpieczeństwo; ochrona *behs-pyeh-chehn'-stfoh; oh-hroh-nah*
sedative środek uspokajający *sh'roh-dehk uhs-poh-kah-yah-yohn-tsyh*
see (notice) zobaczyć *zoh-bah-chyhch';* **(inspect)** sprawdzić *sprahv-dj'eech';* **(witness)** widzieć *vee-dj'yehch'*
seed nasienie, ziarno *nah-sh'yeh-n'yeh, zh'yahr-noh*
seek szukać *shuh-kahch'*
seem wydawać się *vyh-dah-vahch' sh'yeh*
select (*v.*) wybierać *vyh-byeh-rahch'*
selection wybór *vyh-buhr*
self-service samoobsługa *sah-moh-ohb-swuh-gah*
sell sprzedawać *spsheh-dah-vahch'*
seminar seminarium *seh-mee-nah-ryuhm*
senate senat *seh-naht*
senator senator *seh-nah-tohr*
send wysyłać *vyh-syh-wahch'*
senior (*adj.*) starszy *stahr-shyh*
senior (*n.*) senior *seh-n'yohr*
sensitive wrażliwy *vrah-zhlee-vyh*
sentence zdanie *zdah-n'yeh*
separate (*adj.*) oddzielny *oht-dj'yehl-nyh*
separate (*v.*) **(to set apart)** rozdzielić *rohz-dj'yeh-leech'*
September wrzesień *vzheh-sh'yehn'*
serious poważny *poh-vahzh-nyh*
servant służący (*masc.*)/służąca (*fem.*) *swuh-zhohn-tsyh/swuh-zhohn-tsah*
serve obsługiwać *ohb-swuh-gee-vahch'*
server (computer) serwer *sehr-vehr;* **(waiter)** kelner (*masc.*)/kelnerka (*fem.*) *kehl-nehr/kehl-nehr-kah*
service (restaurant) obsługa *ohb-swuh-gah;* **(religious)** nabożeństwo *nah-boh-zhehn'-stfoh*
settlement ugoda (agreement) *uh-goh-dah*
seven siedem *sh'yeh-dehm*
seventeen siedemnaście *sh'yeh-dehm-nahsh'-ch'yeh*
seventy siedemdziesiąt *sh'yeh-dehm-dj'yeh-sh'yohnt*
sew szyć *shyhch'*
sex seks *sehks;* **(gender)** płeć *pwehch'*
shampoo szampon *shahm-pohn*
share dzielić (się) *dj'yeh-leech' (sh'yeh)*
shark rekin *reh-keen*
sharp ostry *ohs-tryh*
shave golić (się) *goh-leech' (sh'yeh)*

shaving cream krem do golenia *krehm doh goh-leh-n'yah*

she ona *oh-nah*

sheep owca *ohf-tsah*

sheets prześcieradło *pshehsh'-ch'yeh-rahd-woh*

shellfish skorupiak *skoh-ruh-pyahk*

shelter (*n.*) schronienie *s-hroh-n'yeh-n'yeh*

ship (*n.*) statek *stah-tehk*

shirt (man's) koszula *koh-shuh-lah*; **(woman's)** bluzka *bluhs-kah*

shoe but *buht*

shoot strzelać *stsheh-lahch'*

shop (*n.*) **(store)** sklep *sklehp*; **(workshop)** warsztat *vahrsh-taht*

shopkeeper sklepikarz *skleh-pee-kahsh*

shoplifting kradzież sklepowa *krah-dj'yehsh skleh-poh-vah*

shopping basket koszyk na zakupy *koh-shyhk nah zah-kuh-pyh*

shopping center centrum handlowe *tsehn-truhm hahn-dloh-veh*

shore brzeg *bzhehg*

short (of length) krótki *kruht-kee;* **(of person)** niski *n'ees-kee*

shot (*n.*) **(medicine)** zastrzyk *zahs-tshyhk*

shoulder bark, ramię *bahrk, rah-myeh*

shout (*n.*) krzyk *kshyhk*

shout (*v.*) krzyczeć *kshyh-chehch'*

show (*n.*) sztuka *shtuh-kah*

show (*v.*) pokazywać *poh-kah-zyh-vahch'*

shower prysznic *pryhsh-n'eets*

shut (*v.*) zamykać *zah-myh-kahch'*

sick chory *hoh-ryh*

side strona; bok *stroh-nah; bohk*

sight wzrok *vzrohk*

sightseeing zwiedzanie *zvyeh-dzah-n'yeh*

sign znak *znahk*

signal (*n.*) sygnał *syhg-nahw*

signal (*v.*) sygnalizować *syhg-nah-lee-zoh-vahch'*

signature podpis *poht-pees*

silver (*adj.*) srebrny *sreh-brnyh*

silver (*n.*) srebro *sreh-broh*

sing śpiewać *sh'pyeh-vahch'*

single (*n.*) kawaler (*n.* masc), panna (*n.* fem) *kah-vah-lehr, pahn-nah*

single (*adj.*) **(not double)** jednoosobowy *yehd-noh-oh-soh-boh-vyh;* **(unmarried)** stanu wolnego *stah-nuh vohl-neh-goh*

sink (in kitchen) zlew *zlehf;* **(in bathroom)** umywalka *uh-myh-vahl-kah*

sir pan; proszę pana *pahn; proh-sheh pah-nah*

siren syrena *syh-reh-nah*

sister siostra *sh'yoh-strah*

sit siadać *sh'yah-dahch'*

six sześć *shehsh'ch'*

sixteen szesnaście *shehs-nahsh'-ch'yeh*

sixty sześćdziesiąt *shehsh'ch'-dj'yeh-sh'yohnt*

size rozmiar *rohz-myahr*

skate (*n.*) łyżwa *wyhzh-vah*

skate (*v.*) jeździć na łyżwach *yehzh'-dj'eech' nah wyhzh-vahh*

ski (*n.*) narta *nahr-tah*

ski (*v.*) jeździć na nartach *yehzh'-dj'eech' nah nahr-tahh*

skin skóra *skuh-rah*

skirt spódnica *spuhd-n'ee-tsah*

skull czaszka *chahsh-kah*

sky niebo *n'yeh-boh*

sleep spać *spahch'*

sleeping bag śpiwór *sh'pee-vuhr*

sleeping car wagon sypialny *vah-gohn syh-pyahl-nyh*

sleeping pills tabletki nasenne *tah-bleht-kee nah-sehn-neh*

slow wolny *vohl-nyh*

small mały *mah-wyh*

smell (*v.*) **(sniff)** wąchać *vohn-hahch';* **(emit odor)** pachnieć *pahh-n'yehch'*

smile uśmiechać się *uhsh'-myeh-hahch' sh'yeh*

smoke (*v.*) palić *pah-leech'*

smoking dla palących *dlah pah-lohn-tsyhh*

smooth równy, gładki *ruhv-nyh, gwaht-kee*

snack (*n.*) przekąska *psheh-kohn-skah*

snake wąż *vohnzh*

snow (*n.*) śnieg *sh'n'yehg*

snow (*v.*) **(it's ~ing)** pada śnieg *pah-dah sh'n'yehg*

soap mydło *myh-dwoh*

soccer piłka nożna *peew-kah nohzh-nah*

sock skarpetka *skahr-peht-kah*

soft miękki *myehn-kee*

sold sprzedany *spsheh-dah-nyh*

sold out wyprzedany *vyh-psheh-dah-nyh*

soldier żołnierz _zhohw_-n'yehzh
some trochę, kilka, parę _troh_-heh, _keel_-kah, _pah_-reh
someone ktoś _ktohsh'_
something coś _tsohsh'_
son syn _syhn_
song piosenka _pyoh-_sehn_-kah_
soon (_adv._) niedługo n'yeh-_dwuh_-goh
sore (_adj._) obolały oh-boh-_lah_-wyh
sorry przepraszam psheh-_prah_-shahm
sound dźwięk _dj'vyehnk_
soup zupa _zuh_-pah
sour kwaśny _kfah_-sh'nyh
source źródło _zh'ruh_-dwoh
south południe poh-_wuhd_-n'yeh
soy soja _soh_-yah
spare (_adj._) zapasowy zah-pah-_soh_-vyh
spare part część zapasowa chehn'sh'ch' zah-pah-_soh_-vah
speak mówić _muh_-veech'
special specjalny speh-_tsyahl_-nyh
speed prędkość _prehnt_-kohsh'ch'
speed limit ograniczenie prędkości oh-grah-n'ee-_cheh_-n'yeh prehnt-_kohsh'_-ch'ee
speedometer prędkościomierz prehnt-kohsh'-_ch'yoh_-myehzh
spell przeliterować psheh-lee-teh-_roh_-vahch'
spend (**time**) spędzać _spehn_-dzahch'; (**money**) wydawać vyh-_dah_-vahch'
spicy ostry _ohs_-tryh
spider pająk _pah_-yohnk
spine kręgosłup krehn-_goh_-swuhp
spoon łyżka _wyhsh_-kah
sport sport _spohrt_
sports (_n.pl._) sporty _spohr_-tyh
spring wiosna _vyoh_-snah
square (**shape**) kwadrat _kfah_-draht; (**landmark**) plac _plahts_
stadium stadion _stah_-dyohn
staff personel pehr-_soh_-nehl
stairs schody _s-hoh_-dyh
stamp (**postal**) znaczek _znah_-chehk; (**official**) pieczęć _pyeh_-chehnch'
stand (_v._) stać _stahch'_
standard (_n._) standard, norma _stahn_-dahrt, _nohr_-mah
start (_v._) zaczynać (się) zah-_chyh_-nahch' (sh'yeh); (**of a car**) zapalić zah-_pah_-leech'

state (*n.*) państwo *pahn'-stfoh*
station stacja, dworzec *stah-tsyah, dvoh-zhehts*
statue pomnik *pohm-n'eek*
stay (*n.*) pobyt *poh-byht*
stay (*v.*) zostać *zoh-stahch'*; (**in a hotel**) zatrzymać się
   zah-tshyh-mahch' sh'yeh
steak stek *stehk*
steal kraść *krahsh'ch'*
step (*n.*) krok *krohk*
sterile sterylny *steh-ryhl-nyh*
stitch szew (med) *shehf*
stolen ukradziony *uh-krah-dj'yoh-nyh*
stomach (belly) brzuch *bzhuhh;* (**organ**) żołądek *zhoh-*
   wohn-dehk
stone kamień *kah-myehn'*
stop (*n.*) przystanek *pshyh-stah-nehk*
stop (*v.*) (**bring/come to a halt**) zatrzymać, zatrzymać
   się *zah-tshyh-mahch', zah-tshyh-mahch' sh'yeh;* (**cease**)
   przerywać *psheh-ryh-vahch'*
store (*n.*) sklep *sklehp*
storm (*n.*) burza *buh-zhah*
stove kuchenka *kuh-hehn-kah*
straight prosty *proh-styh*
stranger obcy,nieznajomy *ohp-tsyh, n'yeh-znah-yoh-myh*
street ulica *uh-lee-tsah*
student (college, university) student *stuh-dehnt;*
   (**primary, secondary**) uczeń *uh-chehn'*
study (*v.*) studiować, uczyć się *stuh-dyoh-vahch', uh-chy-*
   hch' sh'yeh
substitute (*v.*) zastępować *zahs-tehm-poh-vahch'*
suburb przedmieście *psheht-myehsh'-ch'yeh*
subway metro *meh-troh*
sugar cukier *tsuh-kyehr*
suit (man's) garnitur *gahr-n'ee-tuhr;* (**woman's**)
   kostium *kohs-tyuhm*
suitcase walizka *vah-leez-kah*
suite apartament *ah-pahr-tah-mehnt*
summer lato *lah-toh*
summon (*v.*) wzywać *vzyh-vahch'*
sun słońce *swohn'-tseh*
sunblock krem z filtrem przeciwsłonecznym *krehm*
   sfeel-trehm psheh-ch'eef-swoh-nehch-nyhm
sunburn oparzenie słoneczne *oh-pah-zheh-n'yeh swoh-*
   nehch-neh
supermarket supermarket *suh-pehr-mahr-keht*

supplies zaopatrzenie, zapasy *zah-oh-pah-<u>tsheh</u>-n'yeh,*
  zah-<u>pah</u>-syh
surgeon chirurg <u>hee</u>-ruhrg
surgery operacja, zabieg *oh-peh-<u>rah</u>-tsyah, <u>zah</u>-byehg*
surname nazwisko *nahz-<u>vees</u>-koh*
surprise (*n.*) niespodzianka *n'yeh-spoh-<u>dj'yahn</u>-kah*
surprise (*v.*) zaskakiwać *zahs-kah-<u>kee</u>-vahch'*
surrender (*v.*) poddawać (się) *pohd-<u>dah</u>-vahch' (sh'yeh)*
suspect (*n.*) podejrzany (*masc.*)/podejrzana (*fem.*)
  poh-dehy-<u>zhah</u>-nyh/poh-dehy-<u>zhah</u>-nah
swallow (*v.*) połykać *poh-<u>wyh</u>-kahch'*
swear (take an oath) przysięgać *pshyh-<u>sh'yehn</u>-gahch';*
  (curse) przeklinać *psheh-<u>klee</u>-nahch'*
sweat (*n.*) pot *poht*
sweat (*v.*) pocić się *<u>poh</u>-ch'eech' sh'yeh*
sweet słodki (taste) *<u>swoht</u>-kee*
swelling opuchlizna *oh-puh-<u>hleez</u>-nah*
swim (*v.*) pływać *<u>pwyh</u>-vahch'*
symbol symbol *<u>syhm</u>-bohl*
symptom objaw *<u>ohb</u>-yahf*
synagogue synagoga *syh-nah-<u>goh</u>-gah*
syringe strzykawka *stshyh-<u>kahf</u>-kah*
system system *<u>syhs</u>-tehm*

T

table stół *stuhw*
tag etykietka, metka *eh-tyh-<u>kyeht</u>-kah, <u>meht</u>-kah*
take brać *brahch'*
talk rozmawiać *rohz-<u>mah</u>-vyahch'*
tall wysoki *vyh-<u>soh</u>-kee*
tampon tampon *<u>tahm</u>-pohn*
tape (*n.*) taśma *<u>tahsh'</u>-mah*
taste (*n.*) smak *smahk*
taste (*v.*) kosztować *kohsh-<u>toh</u>-vahch'*
tax podatek *poh-<u>dah</u>-tehk*
taxi taksówka *tahk-<u>suhf</u>-kah*
tea herbata *hehr-<u>bah</u>-tah*
teacher nauczyciel (*masc.*)/nauczycielka (*fem.*) *nah-*
  uh-<u>chyh</u>-ch'yehl/nah-uh-chyh-<u>ch'yehl</u>-kah
telephone telefon *teh-<u>leh</u>-fohn*
television telewizja *teh-leh-<u>vee</u>-zyah*
tell powiedzieć *poh-<u>vyeh</u>-dj'yehch'*
temperature temperatura *tehm-peh-rah-<u>tuh</u>-rah*

temple świątynia *sh'fyohn-tyh-n'yah*
temporary tymczasowy *tyhm-chah-soh-vyh*
ten dziesięć *dj'yeh-sh'yehn'ch'*
tenant lokator *(masc.)*/lokatorka *(fem.)* *loh-kah-tohr/loh-kah-tohr-kah*
tent namiot *nah-myoht*
territory terytorium *teh-ryh-toh-ryuhm*
terrorist terrorysta *tehr-roh-ryhs-tah*
test (exam) test *tehst;* **(trial, attempt)** próba *pruh-bah;*
  (medical) badanie *bah-dah-n'yeh*
thank you dziękuję *dj'yehn-kuh-yeh*
that to, tamto *toh, tahm-toh*
theater teatr *teh-ahtr*
then *(adv.)* wtedy (time) *fteh-dyh*
there tam *tahm*
they oni *(masc.)*/one *(fem.)* *oh-n'ee/oh-neh*
thief złodziej *zwoh-dj'yehy*
thigh udo *uh-doh*
thin chudy *huh-dyh*
thing rzecz *zhehch*
think myśleć *myhsh'-lehch'*
thirsty spragniony *sprahg-n'yoh-nyh*
thirty trzydzieści *tshyh-dj'yehsh'-ch'ee*
this ten *(masc.)*/ta *(fem.)*/to *(neut.)* *tehn/tah/toh*
thought *(n.)* myśl *myhsh'l*
thousand tysiąc *tyh-sh'yohnts*
threat groźba *grohzh'-bah*
three trzy *tshyh*
throat gardło *gahr-dwoh*
through przez *pshehz*
throw *(v.)* rzucać *zhuh-tsahch'*
thumb kciuk *kch'yuhk*
thunder grzmot, piorun *gzhmoht, pyoh-ruhn*
Thursday czwartek *chfahr-tehk*
ticket bilet *bee-leht*
tie *(n.)* krawat *krah-vaht*
time czas *chahs*
tip (gratuity) napiwek *nah-pee-vehk*
tire *(n.)* opona *oh-poh-nah*
today dzisiaj *dj'ee-sh'yahy*
together razem *rah-zehm*
toilet toaleta *toh-ah-leh-tah*
toilet paper papier toaletowy *pah-pyehr toh-ah-leh-toh-vyh*
toll opłata za przejazd (autostradą) *oh-pwah-tah zah*
  psheh-yahst (ahw-toh-strah-dohm)

tomato pomidor *poh-<u>mee</u>-dohr*
tomorrow jutro *<u>yuh</u>-troh*
tonight dziś wieczorem *dj'eesh' vyeh-<u>choh</u>-rehm*
tool narzędzie *nah-<u>zhehn</u>-dj'yeh*
tooth ząb *zohmp*
toothache ból zęba *buhl <u>zehm</u>-bah*
toothbrush szczoteczka do zębów *shchoh-<u>tehch</u>-kah doh <u>zehm</u>-buhf*
toothpaste pasta do zębów *<u>pahs</u>-tah doh <u>zehm</u>-buhf*
top góra *<u>guh</u>-rah*
torture (*n.*) ból, tortura *buhl, tohr-<u>tuh</u>-rah*
torture (*v.*) torturować *tohr-tuh-<u>roh</u>-vahch'*
total całkowity *tsahw-koh-<u>vee</u>-tyh*
touch (*n.*) **(one of the senses)** dotyk *<u>doh</u>-tyhk*
touch (*v.*) dotykać *doh-<u>tyh</u>-kahch'*
tourist turysta (*masc.*)/turystka (*fem.*) *tuh-<u>ryhs</u>-tah/tuh-<u>ryhst</u>-kah*
towel ręcznik *<u>rehnch</u>-n'eek*
town miasto *<u>myah</u>-stoh*
trade (*n.*) **(commerce)** handel *<u>hahn</u>-dehl*
trade (*v.*) handlować *hahn-<u>dloh</u>-vahch'*
tradition tradycja *trah-<u>dyh</u>-tsyah*
traditional tradycyjny *trah-dyh-<u>tsyhy</u>-nyh*
traffic ruch uliczny *ruhh uh-<u>leech</u>-nyh*
trail szlak *shlahk*
train pociąg *<u>poh</u>-ch'yohng*
train station dworzec kolejowy *<u>dvoh</u>-zhehts koh-leh-<u>yoh</u>-vyh*
transfer (*v.*) przesiadać się *psheh-<u>sh'yah</u>-dahch' sh'yeh*
translate tłumaczyć *twuh-<u>mah</u>-chyhch'*
translator tłumacz *<u>twuh</u>-mahch*
transplant (*n.*) transplantacja *trahns-plahn-<u>tah</u>-tsyah*
transport (*v.*) przewozić, transportować *psheh-<u>voh</u>-zh'eech', trahns-pohr-<u>toh</u>-vahch'*
transportation transport *<u>trahns</u>-pohrt*
trap (*v.*) łapać w pułapkę/sidła *<u>wah</u>-pahch' fpuh-<u>wahp</u>-keh/<u>sh'ee</u>-dwah*
trash (*n.*) śmieci *<u>sh'myeh</u>-ch'ee*
travel (*n.*) podróż *<u>poh</u>-druhzh*
travel (*v.*) podróżować *poh-druh-<u>zhoh</u>-vahch'*
tray taca *<u>tah</u>-tsah*
treat (*v.*) **(behave towards)** traktować *trahk-<u>toh</u>-vahch'*; **(give medical care to)** leczyć *<u>leh</u>-chyhch'*
trespassing wtargnięcie, naruszenie własności *ftahrg-<u>n'yehn</u>'-ch'yeh, nah-ruh-<u>sheh</u>-n'yeh vwahs-<u>nohsh</u>'-ch'ee*

trial rozprawa, proces *rohz-prah-vah, proh-tsehs*
triangle trójkąt *truhy-kohnt*
tribe plemię *pleh-myeh*
trick (*n.*) podstęp, kawał *poht-stehmp, kah-vahw*
trip (*n.*) wycieczka; podróż *vyh-ch'yehch-kah; pohd-ruhzh*
trolley wózek *vuh-zehk*
trouble problem *proh-blehm*
truck ciężarówka *ch'yehn-zhah-ruhf-kah*
trunk (car) bagażnik *bah-gahzh-n'eek;* **(tree)** pień *pyehn'*
trust (*n.*) zaufanie *zah-uh-fah-n'yeh*
trust (*v.*) ufać *uh-fahch'*
truth prawda *prahv-dah*
try (*v.*) próbować *pruh-boh-vahch'*
true prawdziwy *prahv-dj'ee-vyh*
Tuesday wtorek *ftoh-rehk*
tunnel tunel *tuh-nehl*
turn skręcić *skrehn-ch'eech'*
tutor (*n.*) nauczyciel (prywatny) *nah-uh-chyh-ch'yehl (pryh-vaht-nyh)*
tutor (*v.*) udzielać lekcji (prywatnych) *uh-dj'yeh-lahch' lehk-tsyee (pryh-vaht-nyhh)*
twelve dwanaście *dvah-nahsh'-ch'yeh*
twenty dwadzieścia *dvah-dj'yehsh'-ch'yah*
twice (*adv.*) dwa razy *dvah rah-zyh*
twin bliźniak (*masc.*)/bliźniaczka (*fem.*) *bleezh'-n'yahk/ bleezh'-n'yah-chkah*
type (*n.*) rodzaj (sort) *roh-dzahy*

U

umbrella parasol *pah-rah-sohl*
uncle wujek *vuh-yehk*
uncomfortable niewygodny *n'yeh-vyh-gohd-nyh*
unconscious nieprzytomny *n'yeh-pshyh-tohm-nyh*
under pod *poht*
underground (*adj.*) podziemny *poht-zh'yehm-nyh*
underground (*adv.*) pod ziemią *poht zh'yeh-myohm*
understand rozumieć *roh-zuh-myehch'*
underwear bielizna *byeh-leez-nah*
undo rozpinać *rohz-pee-nahch'*
unfamiliar nieznany *n'yeh-znah-nyh*
unhappy nieszczęśliwy *n'yeh-shchehn-sh'lee-vyh*
uniform mundur, uniform *muhn-duhr, uh-n'ee-fohrm*

union unia; związek _uh_-n'yah; _zvyohn_-zehk

United States Stany Zjednoczone _stah_-nyh zyehd-noh-_choh_-neh

university uniwersytet uh-n'ee-vehr-_syh_-teht

unlock otworzyć oht-_foh_-zhyhch'

until (to a given point) (aż) do _(ahzh) doh;_ **(before fulfillment of condition)** dopóki nie, zanim doh-_puh_-kee n'yeh, _zah_-n'eem

unusual niezwykły n'yeh-_zvyh_-kwyh

up w górę; do góry; wzwyż w _guh_-reh; doh _guh_-ryh; vzvy-hzh

use (_v._) używać uh-_zhyh_-vahch'

usual zwykły _zvyh_-kwyh

V

vacancy wolny pokój _vohl_-nyh _poh_-kuhy

vacation (from school) wakacje vah-_kah_-tsyeh; **(from a job)** urlop _uhr_-lohp

vaccinate szczepić _shcheh_-peech'

vanilla (_n._) wanilia vah-_n'ee_-lyah

vegetable warzywo vah-_zhyh_-voh

vegetarian (_adj._) wegetariański veh-geh-tah-_ryahn'_-skee

vegetarian (_n._) wegetarianin (_masc._)/wegetarianka (_fem._) veh-geh-tah-_ryah_-n'een/veh-geh-tah-_ryahn_-kah

vehicle pojazd _poh_-yahst

veil (_n._) welon _veh_-lohn

vein żyła _zhyh_-wah

verb czasownik chah-_sohv_-n'eek

very (_adj._) właśnie ten (_masc._)/właśnie ta (_fem._) _vwahsh'_-n'yeh tehn/_vwahsh'_-n'yeh tah

very (_adv._) bardzo _bahr_-dzoh

view (_n._) widok _vee_-dohk

village wieś _vyehsh'_

violence przemoc _psheh_-mohts

virus wirus _vee_-ruhs

visa wiza _vee_-zah

visit (_n._) wizyta vee-_zyh_-tah

visit (_v._) odwiedzać ohd-_vyeh_-dzahch'

visitor (guest) gość _gohsh'ch';_ **(tourist)** turysta tuh-_ryh_-stah

voice głos gwohs

volunteer (_n._) ochotnik oh-_hoht_-n'eek

vomit (_v._) wymiotować vyh-myoh-_toh_-vahch'

vote (*v.*) głosować *gwoh-soh-vahch'*

W

wait (*v.*) czekać *cheh-kahch'*
wake (*v.*) budzić (się) *buh-dj'eech' (sh'yeh)*
walk (*n.*) spacer *spah-tsehr*
walk (*v.*) chodzić, spacerować, iść *hoh-dj'eech', spah-tseh-roh-vahch', eesh'ch'*
wall ściana *sh'ch'yah-nah*
wallet portfel *pohrt-fehl*
want chcieć *hch'yehch'*
war wojna *vohy-nah*
warm ciepły *ch'yeh-pwyh*
warn ostrzegać *ohs-tsheh-gahch'*
warning ostrzeżenie *ohs-tsheh-zheh-n'yeh*
wash (to clean oneself) myć się *myhch' sh'yeh;* (to do laundry) prać *prahch'*
washing machine pralka *prahl-kah*
watch (*n.*) zegarek *zeh-gah-rehk*
watch (*v.*) oglądać, obserwować *oh-glohn-dahch', ohp-sehr-voh-vahch'*
water woda *voh-dah*
we my *myh*
wear ubierać, nosić (of garments) *uh-byeh-rahch', noh-sh'eech'*
weather pogoda *poh-goh-dah*
wedding ślub, wesele *sh'luhp, veh-seh-leh*
Wednesday środa *sh'roh-dah*
week tydzień *tyh-dj'yehn'*
weekday dzień powszedni *dj'yehn' pohf-shehd-n'ee*
weekend weekend *wee-kehnt*
weigh ważyć *vah-zhyhch'*
welcome witaj (*sing.*)/witajcie (*plural*) *vee-tahy/vee-tahy-ch'yeh*
well (*interjection*) (expressing hesitation) no cóż *noh tsuhsh;* (expressing surprise) no proszę *noh proh-sheh*
west zachód *zah-huht*
what co *tsoh*
wheat pszenica *psheh-n'ee-tsah*
wheel koło *koh-woh*
wheelchair wózek inwalidzki *vuh-zehk een-vah-leedz-kee*
when kiedy *kyeh-dyh*
where gdzie *gdj'yeh*

whistle (*v.*) gwizdać *gveez-dahch'*
white biały *byah-wyh*
who (**interrogative**) kto *ktoh;* (**relative**) który *ktuh-ryh*
why dlaczego *dlah-cheh-goh*
wife żona *zhoh-nah*
wild dziki *dj'ee-kee*
win wygrywać *vyh-gryh-vahch'*
wind wiatr *vyahtr*
window okno *ohk-noh*
wine wino *vee-noh*
wing skrzydło *skshyh-dwoh*
winter zima *zh'ee-mah*
wipe (*v.*) wycierać *vyh-ch'yeh-rahch'*
wire kabel *kah-behl*
wireless internet bezprzewodowy internet *behs-psheh-voh-doh-vyh een-tehr-neht*
wisdom mądrość *mohn-drohsh'ch'*
withdraw wycofywać (się) *vyh-tsoh-fyh-vahch' (sh'yeh)*
withdrawal wycofanie (się) *vyh-tsoh-fah-n'yeh (sh'yeh)*
without bez *behs*
woman kobieta *koh-byeh-tah*
wood drzewo, drewno *djeh-voh, drehv-noh*
wool wełna *vehw-nah*
word słowo *swoh-voh*
work (*v.*) pracować *prah-tsoh-vahch'*
world świat *sh'fyaht*
worm robak *roh-bahk*
worry (*v.*) martwić (się) *mahrt-feech' (sh'yeh)*
wrap (*v.*) zawinąć *zah-vee-nohn'ch'*
wrist nadgarstek *nahd-gahr-stehk*
write pisać *pee-sahch'*
wrong (*adj.*) zły *zwyh*
wrong (*adv.*) źle *zh'leh*

X

x-ray (*n.*) zdjęcie rentgenowskie *zdyehn'-ch'yeh rehnt-geh-nohfs-kyeh*
x-ray (*v.*) prześwietlić *pshehsh'-fyeht-leech'*

Y

year rok *rohk*
yeast drożdże <u>*drohzh*</u>-*djeh*
yell (*v.*) wrzeszczeć <u>*vzhehsh*</u>-*chehch'*
yellow żółty <u>*zhuhw*</u>-*tyh*
yes tak *tahk*
yesterday wczoraj <u>*fchoh*</u>-*rahy*
yogurt jogurt <u>*yoh*</u>-*guhrt*
you ty (*sing.*); wy (*plural*); pan (*Sir*), pani
  (*Ms/Madam*), państwo (*plural formal*) *tyh; vyh; pahn,*
  <u>*pah*</u>-*n'ee,* <u>*pahn'*</u>-*stfoh*
young młody <u>*mwoh*</u>-*dyh*

Z

zero zero <u>*zeh*</u>-*roh*
zipper zamek błyskawiczny <u>*zah*</u>-*mehk bwyhs-kah-*<u>*veech*</u>-
  nyh
zoo zoo *zoh*

Phrasebook

BASIC LANGUAGE

Essentials

Hello.
Dzień dobry.
dj'yehn' <u>dohb</u>-ryh

Goodbye.
Do widzenia.
doh vee-<u>dzeh</u>-n'yah

Yes.	No.
Tak.	**Nie.**
tahk	n'yeh

Do you speak English?
Czy mówi pan/pani po angielsku? (*fml*)
chyh <u>muh</u>-vee pahn/<u>pah</u>-nee poh
ahn-<u>gyehl</u>- skuh

Excuse me. (*to get attention or to pass*)
Przepraszam.
psheh-<u>prah</u>-shahm

Okay.
Dobrze.
<u>dohb</u>-zheh

Please.
Proszę.
<u>proh</u>-sheh

Thank you.
Dziękuję.
dj'yehn-<u>kuh</u>-yeh

You're welcome.
Proszę bardzo.
<u>proh</u>-sheh <u>bahr</u>-dzoh

Sorry.
Przepraszam.
psheh-<u>prah</u>-shahm

It doesn't matter.
Nie szkodzi.
n'yeh <u>shkoh</u>-dj'ee

I need …
Potrzebuję …
poh-tsheh-<u>buh</u>-yeh …

Help!
Pomocy!
poh-<u>moh</u>-tsyh

Where is the bathroom?
Gdzie jest toaleta?
gdj'yeh yehst toh-ah-<u>leh</u>-tah

Who?	What?	Where?
Kto?	**Co?**	**Gdzie?**
ktoh	tsoh	gdj'yeh

When?	Why?
Kiedy?	**Dlaczego?**
<u>kyeh</u>-dyh	dlah-<u>cheh</u>-goh
entrance	exit
wejście	**wyjście**
<u>vehy</u>-sh'ch'yeh	<u>vyhy</u>-sh'ch'yeh
open	closed
otwarte	**zamknięte**
oh-<u>tfahr</u>-teh	zahm-<u>kn'yehn</u>-teh
good	bad
dobry	**zły/zła**
<u>doh</u>-bryh	zwyh/zwah
this	that
to	**tamto**
toh	<u>tahm</u>-toh
here	there
tu/tutaj	**tam**
tuh/<u>tuh</u>-tahy	tahm

Greetings

Good morning.
Dzień dobry.
dj'yehn' <u>dohb</u>-ryh

Good afternoon.
Dzień dobry.
dj'yehn' <u>dohb</u>-ryh

Good evening.
Dobry wieczór.
<u>dohb</u>-ryh <u>vyeh</u>-chuhr

Good night.
Dobranoc.
doh-<u>brah</u>-nohts

Welcome!
Witaj! (*singular*) / **Witajcie!** (*plural*)
<u>vee</u>-tahy / vee-<u>tahy</u>-ch'yeh

How are you? (*to a man*)
Jak się pan/pani ma?
yahk sh'yeh pahn/<u>pah</u>-nee mah

How are you? (*to a woman*)
Jak się pan/pani ma?
yahk sh'yeh pahn/<u>pah</u>-nee mah

I'm fine, thank you.
Dobrze, dziękuję.
<u>dohb</u>-zheh dj'yehn-<u>kuh</u>-yeh

And you?
A pan/pani?
ah pahn/<u>pah</u>-nee

See you soon.
Do zobaczenia wkrótce.
doh zoh-bah-<u>cheh</u>-n'yah <u>fkruht</u>-tseh

See you later.
Na razie.
nah <u>rah</u>-zh'yeh

See you tomorrow.
Do jutra.
doh <u>yuh</u>-trah

Take care!
Trzymaj się!
<u>tshyh</u>-mahy sh'yeh

Language Difficulties

Do you speak English?
Czy mówi pan/pani po angielsku?
chyh <u>muh</u>-vee pahn/<u>pah</u>-nee poh
ahn-<u>gyehl</u>-skuh

Does anyone here speak English?
Czy ktoś tu mówi po angielsku?
chyh ktohsh'tuh <u>muh</u>-vee poh ahn-<u>gyehl</u>-skuh

I don't speak Polish.
Nie mówię po polsku.
n'yeh <u>muh</u>-vyeh poh <u>pohl</u>-skuh

I speak only a little Polish.
Tylko trochę mówię po polsku.
<u>tyhl</u>-koh <u>troh</u>-heh <u>muh</u>-vyeh poh <u>pohl</u>-skuh

I speak only English.
Mówię tylko po angielsku.
<u>muh</u>-vyeh <u>tyhl</u>-koh poh ahn-<u>gyehl</u>-skuh

Do you understand?
Czy pan/pani rozumie?
chyh pahn/<u>pah</u>-nee roh-<u>zuh</u>-myeh

I understand.
Rozumiem.
roh-<u>zuh</u>-myehm

I don't understand.
Nie rozumiem.
n'yeh roh-<u>zuh</u>-myehm

Could you please …?
Czy mógłby pan …?
chyh <u>muhg</u>-byh pahn …
or
Czy mogłaby pani …?
chyh moh-<u>gwah</u>-byh <u>pah</u>-nee …

repeat that
to powtórzyć
toh pohf-<u>tuh</u>-zhyhch'

speak more slowly
mówić wolniej
<u>muh</u>-veech' <u>vohl</u>-n'yehy

speak louder
mówić głośniej
<u>muh</u>-veech' <u>gwohsh</u>'-n'yehy

point out the word for me
pokazać mi to słowo
poh-<u>kah</u>-zahch' mee toh <u>swoh</u>-voh

write that down
zapisać mi to
zah-<u>pee</u>-sahch' mee toh

wait while I look it up
poczekać aż to sprawdzę w słowniku
poh-<u>cheh</u>-kahch' ahsh toh <u>sprah</u>-vdzeh
fswoh-<u>vnee</u>-kuh

What does ... mean?
Co znaczy ...?
tsoh <u>znah</u>-chyh ...

How do you say ... in Polish?
Jak się mówi ... po polsku?
yahk sh'yeh <u>muh</u>-vee ... poh <u>pohl</u>-skuh

How do you spell ... ?
Jak się pisze ... ?
yahk sh'yeh <u>pee</u>-sheh ...

TRAVEL & TRANSPORTATION

Arrival, Departure, and Clearing Customs

I'm here …
Przyjechałem/Przyjechałam tu …
pshyh-yeh-<u>hah</u>-wehm/pshyh-yeh-<u>hah</u>-wahm
tuh …

> on vacation
> **na wakacje** (*students*)
> nah vah-<u>kah</u>-tsyeh
> **urlop** (*working adults*)
> nah <u>uhr</u>-lohp

> for business
> **w interesach**
> veen-teh-<u>reh</u>-sahh

> to visit relatives
> **z wizytą do krewnych**
> zvee-<u>zyh</u>-tohm doh <u>krehv</u>-nyhh

> to study
> **na studia**
> nah <u>stuh</u>-dyah

I'm just passing through.
Jestem przejazdem.
<u>yehs</u>-tehm psheh-<u>yahz</u>-dehm

I'm going to …
Jadę do …
<u>yah</u>-deh doh …

You Might Hear

Czy ma pan/pani coś do oclenia?
chyh mah pahn/<u>pah</u>-n'ee tsohsh'doh ohts-<u>leh</u>-n'yah
Do you have anything to declare?

Czy pan się sam pakował?
chyh pahn sh'yeh sahm pah-<u>koh</u>-vahw
or
Czy pani się sama pakowała?
chyh <u>pah</u>-n'ee sh'yeh <u>sah</u>-mah pah-koh-<u>vah</u>-wah
Did you pack this on your own?

Proszę otworzyć tę torbę.
<u>proh</u>-sheh oht-<u>foh</u>-zhyhch'teh <u>tohr</u>-beh
Please open this bag.

Musi pan/pani zapłacić za to cło.
<u>muh</u>-sh'ee pahn/<u>pah</u>-n'ee zah-<u>pwah</u>-ch'eech'zah toh tswoh
You must pay duty on this.

Na jak długo pan przyjechał / pani przyje-chała?
nah yahk <u>dwuh</u>-goh pahn pshyh-<u>yeh</u>-hahw /
<u>pah</u>-n'ee pshyh-yeh-<u>hah</u>-wah
How long are you staying?

Gdzie się pan/pani zatrzyma?
gdj'yeh sh'yeh pahn/<u>pah</u>-n'ee zah-<u>tshyh</u>-mah
Where are you staying?

I'm staying at …
Zatrzymałem/Zatrzymałam się w …
zah-tshyh-<u>mah</u>-wehm sh'yeh/zah-tshyh-
<u>mah</u>-wahm sh'yeh v …

I'm staying for X …
Przyjechałem/Przyjechałam na X …
pshyh-yeh-<u>hah</u>-wehm/pshyh-yeh-<u>hah</u>-
wahm nah X …

> days
> **dni**
> dn'ee

> weeks
> **tygodni**
> tyh-<u>goh</u>-dn'ee

> months
> **miesięcy**
> myeh-<u>sh'yehn</u>-tsyh

I have nothing to declare.
Nie mam nic do oclenia.
n'yeh mahm n'eets doh ohts-<u>leh</u>-n'yah

I'd like to declare …
**Chciałbym/Chciałabym zgłosić do
oclenia …**
<u>hch'yahw</u>-byhm/hch'yah-<u>wah</u>-byhm
<u>zgwoh</u>-sh'eech' doh ohts-<u>leh</u>-n'yah …

Do I have to declare this?
Czy muszę to zgłaszać do oclenia?
chyh <u>muh</u>-sheh toh <u>zgwah</u>-shahch' doh
ohts-<u>leh</u>-n'yah

You Might See

Kontrola imigracyjna
Immigration

Odprawa celna
Customs

Kontrola paszportowa
Passport control

Kwarantanna
Quarantine

**Obywatele Unii Europejskiej/
UE (…)**
EU citizens

**Podróżni spoza Unii
Europejskiej/UE**
non-EU citizens

Odbiór bagażu
Baggage Claim

Stanowisko odprawy
Check-in

Policja
Police

Kontrola bezpieczeństwa
Security Check

That is mine.
To moje.
toh <u>moh</u>-yeh

That is not mine.
To nie moje.
toh n'yeh <u>moh</u>-yeh

This is for personal use.
To jest do użytku osobistego.
toh yehst doh uh-<u>zhyht</u>-kuh oh-soh-bees-<u>teh</u>-goh

This is a gift.
To prezent.
toh <u>preh</u>-zehnt

I'm with a group.
Przyjechałem/Przyjechałam z grupą.
pshyh-yeh-<u>hah</u>-wehm/pshyh-yeh-<u>hah</u>-wahm <u>zgruh</u>-pohm

I'm on my own.
Przyjechałem sam. / Przyjechałam sama.
pshyh-yeh-<u>hah</u>-wehm sahm /
pshyh-yeh-<u>hah</u>-wahm <u>sah</u>-mah

Here is my …
Oto mój/moja …
<u>oh</u>-toh muhy/<u>moh</u>-yah …

> boarding pass
> **karta pokładowa**
> <u>kahr</u>-tah poh-kwah-<u>doh</u>-vah

ID
dowód tożsamości
<u>doh</u>-vuht tosh-sah-<u>mohsh</u>'-ch'ee

passport
paszport
<u>pahsh</u>-pohrt

ticket
bilet
<u>bee</u>-leht

visa
wiza
<u>vee</u>-zah

Buying Tickets

Where can I buy a ... ticket?
Gdzie mogę kupić bilet na ...?
gdj'yeh <u>moh</u>-geh <u>kuh</u>-peech' <u>bee</u>-leht nah ...

bus
autobus
ahw-<u>toh</u>-buhs

plane
samolot
sah-<u>moh</u>-loht

train
pociąg
<u>poh</u>-ch'yohng

subway
metro
<u>meh</u>-troh

I'd like a … ticket.
Poproszę bilet …
poh-<u>proh</u>-sheh <u>bee</u>-leht …

> one-way
> **w jedną stronę**
> <u>vyehd</u>-nohm <u>stroh</u>-neh

> round-trip
> **tam i z powrotem**
> tahm eez poh-<u>vroh</u>-tehm

> first class
> **w pierwszej klasie**
> <u>fpyehr</u>-fshehy <u>klah</u>-sh'yeh

> economy class
> **w klasie turystycznej**
> <u>fklah</u>-sh'yeh tuh-ryhs-<u>tyhch</u>-nehy

> business class
> **w klasie biznes**
> <u>fklah</u>-sh'yeh <u>beez</u>-nehs

A ticket to … please.
Poproszę bilet do …
poh-<u>proh</u>-sheh <u>bee</u>-leht doh …

One ticket, please. / Two tickets, please.
Poproszę jeden bilet. / Poproszę dwa bilety.
poh-<u>proh</u>-sheh <u>yeh</u>-dehn <u>bee</u>-leht /
poh-<u>proh</u>-shehdvah bee-<u>leh</u>-tyh

How much?
Ile płacę?
<u>ee</u>-leh <u>pwah</u>-tseh

Is there a discount for …?
Czy mają państwo zniżkę dla …?
chyh <u>mah</u>-yohm <u>pahn'</u>-stfoh <u>zn'eesh</u>-keh
dlah …

> children
> **dzieci**
> <u>dj'yeh</u>-ch'ee

> senior citizens
> **emerytów**
> eh-meh-<u>ryh</u>-tuhf

> students
> **uczniów** (*elementary, high school*)
> <u>uhch</u>-n'yuhf
> **studentów** (*college, university*)
> stuh-<u>dehn</u>-tuhf

> tourists
> **turystów**
> tuh-<u>ryhs</u>-tuhf

I have an e-ticket.
Mam bilet elektroniczny.
mahm <u>bee</u>-leht eh-lehk-troh-<u>n'eech</u>-nyh

Can I buy a ticket on the …?
Czy można kupić bilet w …?
chyh <u>mohzh</u>-nah <u>kuh</u>-peech' <u>bee</u>-leht v …

> bus
> **autobusie**
> ahw-toh-<u>buh</u>-sh'yeh

train
pociągu
poh-<u>ch'yohn</u>-guh

tram
tramwaju
trahm-<u>vah</u>-yuh

Do I need to stamp the ticket?
Czy muszę skasować bilet?
chyh <u>muh</u>-sheh skah-<u>soh</u>-vahch' <u>bee</u>-leht

I'd like to … my reservation.
Chciałbym/Chciałabym … rezerwację.
<u>hch'yahw</u>-byhm/hch'yah-<u>wah</u>-byhm …
reh-zehr-<u>vah</u>-tsyeh

change
zmienić
<u>zmyeh</u>-n'eech'

cancel
odwołać
ohd-<u>voh</u>-wahch'

confirm
potwierdzić
poht-<u>fyehr</u>-dj'eech'

How long is this ticket valid for?
Jak długo ważny jest ten bilet?
yahk <u>dwuh</u>-goh <u>vahzh</u>-nyh yehst tehn
<u>bee</u>-leht

I'd like to leave …
Chciałbym/Chciałabym wyjechać …
hch'<u>yahw</u>-byhm/hch'yah-<u>wah</u>-byhm vyh-<u>yeh</u>-hahch' …

I'd like to arrive …
Chciałbym/Chciałabym przyjechać …
hch'<u>yahw</u>-byhm/hch'yah-<u>wah</u>-byhm pshyh-<u>yeh</u>-hahch' …

today
dzisiaj
<u>dj'ee</u>-sh'yahy

tomorrow
jutro
<u>yuh</u>-troh

next week
w przyszłym tygodniu
<u>fpshyh</u>-shwyhm tyh-<u>goh</u>-dn'yuh

in the morning
rano
<u>rah</u>-noh

in the afternoon
po południu
poh poh-<u>wuhd</u>-n'yuh

in the evening
wieczorem
vyeh-<u>choh</u>-rehm

late at night
późno w nocy
<u>puhzh'</u>-noh <u>vnoh</u>-tsyh

You Might See

Kasa biletowa
Ticket window

Rezerwacje
Reservations

By Airplane

When is the next flight to …?
Kiedy będzie następny lot do …?
kyeh-dyh behn-dj'yeh nahs-tehm-pnyh
loht doh …

Is there a bus/train to the airport?
**Czy na lotnisko można dostać się
autobusem/pociągiem?**
chyh na loht-n'ee-skoh mohzh-nah dohs-
tahch' sh'yeh ahw-toh-buh-sehm/poh-ch'y-
ohn-gyehm

How much is a taxi to the airport?
Ile kosztuje taksówka na lotnisko?
ee-leh koh-shtuh-yeh tahk-suhf-kah nah
loht-n'ees-koh

Airport, please.
Na lotnisko proszę.
nah loht-n'ees-koh proh-sheh

My airline is …
Lecę liniami …
leh-tseh lee-n'yah-mee …

My flight leaves at …
Mam samolot o …
mahm sah-<u>moh</u>-loht oh …

My flight number is …
Numer mojego lotu to …
<u>nuh</u>-mehr moh-<u>yeh</u>-goh <u>loh</u>-tuh toh …

What terminal? / What gate?
Który to terminal? / Które wyjście?
<u>ktuh</u>-ryh toh tehr-<u>mee</u>-nahl / <u>ktuh</u>-reh <u>vy</u>-<u>hysh'</u>-ch'yeh

Where is the check-in desk?
Gdzie jest stanowisko odprawy?
gdj'yeh yehst stah-noh-<u>vee</u>-skoh oht-<u>prah</u>-vyh

My name is …
Nazywam się …
nah-<u>zyh</u>-vahm sh'yeh …

I'm going to …
Lecę do …
<u>leh</u>-tseh doh …

Is there a connecting flight?
Czy jest połączenie z przesiadką?
chyh yehst poh-wohn-<u>cheh</u>-n'yeh spsheh-<u>sh'yaht</u>-kohm

I'd like … flight.
Chciałbym/Chciałabym lot …
<u>hch'yahw</u>-byhm/hch'yah-<u>wah</u>-byhm loht …

a direct
bezpośredni
behz-poh-<u>sh'rehd</u>-n'ee

a connecting
z przesiadką
spsheh-<u>sh'yaht</u>-kohm

an overnight
nocny
<u>nohts</u>-nyh

How long is the layover?
Jak długa będzie przerwa w podróży?
yahk <u>dwuh</u>-gah <u>behn</u>-dj'yeh <u>pshehr</u>-vah
fpohd-<u>ruh</u>-zhyh

I have …
Mam …
mahm …

one suitcase
jedną walizkę
<u>yehd</u>-nohm vah-<u>leez</u>-keh

two suitcases
dwie walizki
dvyeh vah-<u>leez</u>-kee

one carry-on item
jedną sztukę bagażu podręcznego
<u>yehd</u>-nohm <u>shtuh</u>-keh bah-<u>gah</u>-zhuh
pohd-rehnch-<u>neh</u>-goh

two carry-on items
dwie sztuki bagażu podręcznego
dvyeh <u>shtuh</u>-kee bah-<u>gah</u>-zhuh pohd-
rehnch-<u>neh</u>-goh

Do I have to check this bag?
Czy muszę nadać tę torbę?
chyh <u>muh</u>-sheh <u>nah</u>-dahch' teh <u>tohr</u>-beh

How much luggage is allowed?
Ile bagażu mogę wziąć?
<u>ee</u>-leh bah-<u>gah</u>-zhuh <u>moh</u>-geh vzh'yohnch'

I'd like … seat.
Chciałbym/Chciałabym miejsce …
hch'<u>yahw</u>-byhm/hch'yah-<u>wah</u>-byhm
<u>myehy</u>-stseh …

> a window
> **przy oknie**
> pshyh <u>ohk</u>-n'yeh

> an aisle
> **przy przejściu**
> pshyh <u>pshehy</u>-sh'ch'yuh

> an exit row
> **w rzędzie przy wyjściu**
> <u>vzhehn</u>-dj'yeh pshyh <u>vyhy</u>-sh'ch'yuh

Can you seat us together?
Czy może nas pan/pani posadzić obok siebie?
chyh <u>moh</u>-zheh nahs pahn/<u>pah</u>-n'ee poh-<u>sah</u>-dj'eech' <u>oh</u>-bohk <u>sh'yeh</u>-byeh

Is the flight …?
Czy lot jest …?
chyh loht yehst …

You Might Hear

Następny proszę!
nahs-<u>tehm</u>-pnyh <u>proh</u>-sheh
Next!

Poproszę paszport/kartę pokładową.
poh-<u>proh</u>-sheh <u>pahsh</u>-pohrt/<u>kahr</u>-teh poh-kwah-
<u>doh</u>-vohm
Your passport/boarding pass, please.

Proszę opróżnić kieszenie.
<u>proh</u>-sheh oh-<u>pruhzh</u>-n'eech' kyeh-<u>sheh</u>-n'yeh
Empty your pockets.

Proszę zdjąć obuwie.
<u>proh</u>-sheh zdyohnch' oh-<u>buh</u>-vyeh
Take off your shoes.

**Proszę umieścić wszystkie metalowe przed-
mioty w pojemniku.**
<u>proh</u>-sheh uh-<u>myehsh'</u>-ch'eech' <u>vshyhs</u>-tkyeh meh-
tah-<u>loh</u>-veh pshet-<u>myoh</u>-tyh fpoh-yehm-<u>n'ee</u>-kuh
Place all metal items in the tray.

Lot numer …	**Wyjście numer…**
loht <u>nuh</u>-mehr …	<u>vyhy</u>-sh'ch'yeh <u>nuh</u>-mehr …
Flight number …	Gate number …

Zapraszamy pasażerów na pokład samolotu …
zah-prah-<u>shah</u>-myh pah-sah-<u>zheh</u>-ruhf nah <u>poh</u>-
kwahd sah-moh-<u>loh</u>-tuh …
Now boarding …

on time
punktualnie
puhn-ktuh-<u>ahl</u>-n'yeh

delayed
opóźniony
oh-puhzh'-<u>n'yoh</u>-nyh

cancelled
odwołany
ohd-voh-<u>wah</u>-nyh

Where is the baggage claim?
Gdzie jest odbiór bagażu?
gdj'yeh yehst <u>ohd</u>-byuhr bah-<u>gah</u>-zhuh

I've lost my luggage.
Zgubiłem/Zgubiłam bagaż.
zguh-<u>bee</u>-wehm/zguh-<u>bee</u>-wahm <u>bah</u>-gahsh

My luggage has been stolen.
Ukradziono mi bagaż.
uh-krah-<u>dj'yoh</u>-noh mee <u>bah</u>-gahsh

My suitcase is damaged.
Moja walizka jest uszkodzona.
<u>moh</u>-yah vah-<u>lecz</u>-kah yehst uhsh-koh-<u>dzoh</u>-nah

You Might See

Stanowisko odprawy
Check-in

**Stanowisko odprawy dla pasażerów
z biletami elektronicznymi**
E-ticket check-in

Karta pokładowa
Boarding pass

Wejście na pokład
Boarding

Ochrona
Security

Odbiór bagażu
Baggage claim

Międzynarodowy (*airport, terminal*)
Zagraniczny (*flight*)
International

Krajowy
Domestic

Przyloty
Arrivals

Odloty
Departures

Transfery
Connections

By Train

Which line goes to … station?
Która linia jedzie do stacji …?
<u>ktuh</u>-rah <u>lee</u>-n'yah <u>yeh</u>-dj'yeh doh <u>stah</u>-tsyee …

Is it direct?
Czy to bezpośrednie połączenie?
chyh toh behz-pohsh'-<u>rehd</u>-n'yeh poh-wohn-<u>cheh</u>-n'yeh

Is it an express/local train?
Czy to ekspres/pociąg miejscowy?
chyh toh <u>ehks</u>-prehs/<u>poh</u>-ch'yohng myehy-<u>stsoh</u>-vyh

I'd like to take the high-speed train.
Chciałbym/Chciałabym pojechać pociągiem szybkobieżnym.
hch'<u>yahw</u>-byhm/hch'yah-<u>wah</u>-byhm poh-<u>yeh</u>-hahch' poh-<u>ch'yohn</u>-gyehm shyhp-koh-<u>byehzh</u>-nyhm

Do I have to change trains?
Czy muszę się przesiadać?
chyh <u>muh</u>-sheh sh'yeh psheh-<u>sh'yah</u>-dahch'

Can I have a schedule?
Czy mogę prosić o rozkład jazdy?
chyh <u>moh</u>-geh <u>proh</u>-sh'eech' oh <u>rohz</u>-kwahd <u>yahz</u>-dyh

When is the last train back?
Kiedy odchodzi ostatni pociąg powrotny?
kyeh-dyh oht-hoh-dj'yee ohs-taht-n'yee
poh-ch'yohng poh-vroh-tnyh

Which track?
Z którego peronu?
sktuh-reh-goh peh-rohn-nuh

Where is track …?
Gdzie jest peron …?
gdj'yeh yehst peh-rohn …

Where is/are the …?
Gdzie jest/są …?
gdj'yeh yehst/sohm …

dining car
wagon restauracyjny
vah-gohn rehs-tahw-rah-tsyhy-nyh

information desk
informacja
een-fohr-mah-tsyah

luggage lockers
skrytki bagażowe
skryh-tkee bah-gah-zhoh-veh

reservations desk
rezerwacje
reh-zehr-vah-tsyeh

ticket machine
automat biletowy
ahw-toh-maht bee-leh-toh-vyh

ticket office
kasa biletowa
<u>kah</u>-sah bee-leh-<u>toh</u>-vah

waiting room
poczekalnia
poh-cheh-<u>kahl</u>-n'yah

This is my seat.
To moje miejsce.
toh <u>moh</u>-yeh <u>myehy</u>-stseh

Here is my ticket.
Oto mój bilet.
<u>oh</u>-toh muhy <u>bee</u>-leht

Can I change seats?
Czy mogę się przesiąść?
chyh <u>moh</u>-geh sh'yeh <u>psheh</u>-sh'yohn'sh'ch'

What station is this?
Co to za stacja?
tsoh toh zah <u>stah</u>-tsyah

What is the next station?
Jaka będzie następna stacja?
<u>yah</u>-kah <u>behn</u>-dj'yeh nahs-<u>tehm</u>-pnah
<u>stah</u>-tsyah

Does this train stop at …?
Czy ten pociąg zatrzymuje się w …?
chyh tehn <u>poh</u>-ch'yohng zah-tshyh-<u>muh</u>-
yeh sh'yeh v …

By Bus and Subway

Which bus do I take for …?
Którym autobusem dojadę do …?
ktuh-ryhm ahw-toh-buh-sehm doh-yah-
deh doh …

Which subway do I take for …?
Którą linią metra dojadę do …?
ktuh-rohm lee-n'yohm meh-trah doh-yah-
deh doh …

Which …?
Który/Która/Które …?
ktuh-ryh/ktuh-rah/ktuh-reh …

> gate
> **wyjście**
> vyhy-sh'ch'yeh

> line
> **linia**
> lee-n'yah

> station
> **stacja**
> stah-tsyah

> stop
> **przystanek**
> pshyh-stah-nehk

Where is the nearest bus stop?
**Gdzie jest najbliższy przystanek
autobusowy?**
gdj'yeh yehst nahy-bleesh-shyh pshyh-
stah-nehk ahw-toh-buh-soh-vyh

Where is the nearest subway station?
Gdzie jest najbliższa stacja metra?
gdj'yeh yehst nahy-<u>bleesh</u>-shah <u>stah</u>-tsyah
<u>meh</u>-trah

Can I have a bus/subway map?
**Czy mogę prosić mapę linii autobuso-
wych/metra?**
chyh <u>moh</u>-geh <u>proh</u>-sh'eech' <u>mah</u>-peh <u>lee</u>-n'ee
ahw-toh-buh-<u>soh</u>-vyhh/<u>meh</u>-trah

How far is it?
Czy to daleko?
chyh toh dah-<u>leh</u>-koh

How do I get to …?
Jak mam dojechać do …?
yahk mahm doh-<u>yeh</u>-hahch' doh …

Is this the bus/subway to …?
Czy ten autobus/to metro jedzie do …?
chyh tehn ahw-<u>toh</u>-buhs/toh <u>meh</u>-troh
<u>yeh</u>-dj'yeh doh …

When is the … bus to …?
Kiedy odchodzi … autobus do …?
<u>kyeh</u>-dyh oht-<u>hoh</u>-dj'yee … ahw-<u>toh</u>-buhs doh

first
pierwszy
<u>pyehr</u>-fshyh

next
następny
nahs-<u>tehm</u>-pnyh

last
ostatni
ohs-<u>taht</u>-n'yee

Do I have to change buses/trains?
Czy muszę się przesiadać?
chyh <u>muh</u>-sheh sh'yeh psheh-<u>sh'yah</u>-dahch'

Where do I transfer?
Gdzie mam się przesiąść?
gdj'yeh mahm sh'yeh <u>psheh</u>-sh'yohn'sh'ch'

Can you tell me when to get off?
**Czy może mi pan/pani powiedzieć,
kiedy mam wysiąść?**
chyh <u>moh</u>-zheh mee pahn/<u>pah</u>-n'ee
poh-<u>vyeh</u>-dj'yehch' <u>kyeh</u>-dyh mahm
<u>vyh</u>-sh'yohn'sh'ch'

You Might See

Przystanek autobusowy
Bus stop

Stacja metra
Subway station

wejście
entrance

wyjście
exit

How many stops to …?
Ile przystanków jest do …?
<u>ee</u>-leh pshyh-<u>stahn</u>-kuhf yehst doh …

Where are we?
Gdzie jesteśmy?
gdj'yeh yehs-<u>tehsh</u>'-myh

Stop here, please!
Proszę się zatrzymać!
<u>proh</u>-sheh sh'yeh zah-<u>tshyh</u>-mahch'!

By Taxi

Taxi!
Taxi!
<u>tah</u>-ksee

Where can I get a taxi?
Gdzie mogę złapać taksówkę?
gdj'yeh <u>moh</u>-geh <u>zwah</u>-pahch' tahk-<u>suhf</u>-keh

Can you call a taxi?
Czy może pan/pani zamówić taksówkę?
chyh <u>moh</u>-zheh pahn/<u>pah</u>-n'ee zah-<u>muh</u>-veech' tahk-<u>suhf</u>-keh

I'd like a taxi now (in an hour).
Chciałbym/Chciałabym zamówić taksówkę na jak najszybciej (za godzinę).
hch'<u>yahw</u>-byhm/hch'yah-<u>wah</u>-byhm zah-<u>muh</u>-veech' tahk-<u>suhf</u>-keh nah yahk nahy-<u>shyhp</u>-ch'yehy (zah goh-<u>dj'ee</u>-neh)

Pick me up at …
Proszę po mnie przyjechać na …
proh-sheh poh mn'yeh pshyh-yeh-hahch'nah …

Take me …
Proszę mnie zawieźć …
proh-sheh mn'yeh zah-vyehsh'ch' …

to this address
pod ten adres
poht tehn ahd-rehs

to the airport
na lotnisko
nah loht-n'ee-skoh

to the train station
na dworzec kolejowy
nah dvoh-zhehts koh-leh-yoh-vyh

to the bus station
na dworzec autobusowy
nah dvoh-zhehts ahw-toh-buh-soh-vyh

Can you take a different route?
Czy może pan pojechać inną trasą?
chyh moh-zheh pahn poh-yeh-hahch' een-nohm trah-sohm

Can you drive faster/slower?
Mógłby pan jechać szybciej/wolniej?
muhgw-byh pahn yeh-hahch' shyhp-ch'yehy/ vohl-n'yehy

Stop here. / Wait here.
Proszę się tu zatrzymać. / Proszę tu poczekać.
<u>proh</u>-sheh sh'yeh tuh zah-<u>tshyh</u>-mahch' /
<u>proh</u>-sheh tuh poh-<u>cheh</u>-kahch'

How much will it cost?
Ile to będzie kosztowało?
<u>ee</u>-leh toh <u>behn</u>-dj'yeh kohsh-toh-<u>vah</u>-woh

You said it would cost ...
Mówił pan, że to będzie kosztowało ...
<u>muh</u>-veew pahn zheh toh <u>behn</u>-dj'yeh
kohsh-toh-<u>vah</u>-woh ...

Keep the change.
Reszty nie trzeba.
<u>rehsh</u>-tyh n'yeh <u>tsheh</u>-bah

Driving

Renting a Car

Where is the car rental?
Gdzie jest wypożyczalnia samochodów?
gdj'yeh yehst vyh-poh-zhyh-<u>chahl</u>-n'yah
sah-moh-<u>hoh</u>-duhf

I'd like ...
Chciałbym/Chciałabym ...
hch'<u>yahw</u>-byhm/hch'yah-<u>wah</u>-byhm ...

a cheap car
tani samochód
tah-n'ee sah-moh-huht

a compact car
niewielki samochód
n'yeh-vyehl-kee sah-moh-huht

a van
furgonetkę
fuhr-goh-neht-keh

an SUV
samochód sportowo-rekreacyjny
sah-moh-huht spohr-toh-voh
reh-kreh-ah-tsyhy-nyh

an automatic transmission
**samochód z automatyczną skrzynią
biegów**
sah-moh-huht sahw-toh-mah-tyhch-
nohm skshyh-n'yohm byeh-guhf

a manual transmission
samochód z ręczną skrzynią biegów
sah-moh-huht zrehnch-nohm skshyh-
n'yohm byeh-guhf

a scooter
skuter
skuh-tehr

a motorcycle
motocykl
moh-toh-tsyhkl

---

air conditioning
samochód z klimatyzacją
sah-<u>moh</u>-huht sklee-mah-tyh-<u>zah</u>-
tsyohm

a child seat
fotelik dziecięcy
foh-<u>teh</u>-leek dj'yeh-<u>ch'yehn</u>-tsyh

How much does it cost ...?
Jaki jest koszt ...?
<u>yah</u>-kee yehst kohsht ...

per day
za dzień
zah dj'yehn'

per week
za tydzień
zah <u>tyh</u>-dj'yehn'

per kilometer
za kilometr
zah kee-<u>loh</u>-mehtr

for unlimited mileage
bez limitu kilometrów
behz lee-<u>mee</u>-tuh kee-loh-<u>meht</u>-ruhf

with full insurance
z pełnym ubezpieczeniem
<u>spehw</u>-nyhm uh-behz-pyeh-<u>cheh</u>-n'yehm

What kind of fuel does it use?
Na jakim jeździ paliwie?
nah <u>yah</u>-keem <u>yehzh</u>'-dj'yee pah-<u>lee</u>-vyeh

Are there any discounts?
Czy są zniżki?
chyh sohm <u>zn'ee</u>-shkee?

I (don't) have an international driver's license.
Mam międzynarodowe prawo jazdy.
mahm myehn-dzyh-nah-roh-<u>doh</u>-veh <u>prah</u>-voh <u>yahz</u>-dyh
Nie mam międzynarodowego prawa jazdy.
n'yeh mahm myehn-dzyh-nah-roh-doh-<u>veh</u>-goh <u>prah</u>-vah <u>yahz</u>-dyh

I don't need it until …
Nie będzie mi potrzebny do …
n'yeh <u>behn</u>-dj'yeh mee poh-<u>tshehb</u>-nyh doh …

> Monday
> **poniedziałku**
> poh-n'yeh-<u>dj'yahw</u>-kuh

> Tuesday
> **wtorku**
> <u>ftohr</u>-kuh

> Wednesday
> **środy**
> <u>sh'roh</u>-dyh

> Thursday
> **czwartku**
> <u>chfahr</u>-tkuh

> Friday
> **piątku**
> <u>pyohn</u>-tkuh

Saturday
soboty
soh-<u>boh</u>-tyh

Sunday
niedzieli
n'yeh-<u>dj'yeh</u>-lee

Fuel and Repairs

Where's the gas station?
Gdzie jest stacja benzynowa?
gdj'yeh yehst <u>stah</u>-tsyah behn-zyh-<u>noh</u>-vah

Fill it up.
Do pełna proszę.
doh <u>pehw</u>-nah <u>proh</u>-sheh

You Might Hear

Musi pan/pani zapłacić zadatek.
<u>muh</u>-sh'yee pahn/<u>pah</u>-n'ee zah-<u>pwah</u>-ch'eech' zah-<u>dah</u>-tehk
I'll need a deposit.

Proszę tu podpisać.
<u>proh</u>-sheh tuh poht-<u>pee</u>-sahch'
Sign here.

I need …
Potrzebna mi jest …
poh-<u>tsheh</u>-bnah mee yehst …

gas
benzyna
behn-<u>zyh</u>-nah

leaded
ołowiowa
oh-woh-<u>vyoh</u>-vah

unleaded
bezołowiowa
behz-oh-woh-<u>vyoh</u>-vah

regular
zwykła (Pb 95)
<u>zvyh</u>-kwah (peh beh dj'eh-vyen'-<u>dj'yeh</u>-
sh'yohnt pyehn'ch')

super
wysokooktanowa (Pb 98)
vyh-soh-koh-ohk-tan-<u>noh</u>-vah (peh
beh dj'eh-vyen'-<u>dj'yeh</u>-sh'yohnt <u>oh</u>-
sh'yehm)

premium
wysokooktanowa (Pb 98)
vyh-soh-koh-ohk-tan-<u>noh</u>-vah (peh
beh dj'eh-vyen'-<u>dj'yeh</u>-sh'yohnt <u>oh</u>-
sh'yehm)

diesel
olej napędowy (ON)
<u>oh</u>-lehy nah-pehn-<u>doh</u>-vyh

> ### You Might See
>
> **samoobsługa**
> self-service
>
> **pełna obsługa**
> full-service

Check the …
Proszę sprawdzić …
<u>proh</u>-sheh <u>sprahf</u>-dj'eech' …

> battery
> **akumulator**
> ah-kuh-muh-<u>lah</u>-tohr
>
> brakes
> **hamulce**
> hah-<u>muhl</u>-tseh
>
> headlights
> **światła przednie**
> <u>sh'fyah</u>-twah <u>pshehd</u>-n'yeh
>
> oil
> **olej**
> <u>oh</u>-lehy
>
> radiator
> **chłodnicę**
> hwoh-<u>dn'ee</u>-tseh
>
> tail lights
> **światła tylne**
> <u>sh'fyah</u>-twah <u>tyhl</u>-neh

tires
opony
oh-<u>poh</u>-nyh

transmission
skrzynię biegów
<u>skshyh</u>-n'yeh <u>byeh</u>-guhf

The car broke down.
Zepsuł mi się samochód.
<u>zehp</u>-suhw mee sh'yeh sah-<u>moh</u>-huht

The car won't start.
Samochód nie chce zapalić.
sah-<u>moh</u>-huht n'yeh htseh zah-<u>pah</u>-leech'

I ran out of gas.
Skończyła mi się benzyna.
skohn'-<u>chyh</u>-wah mee sh'yeh behn-<u>zyh</u>-nah

I have a flat tire.
Przebiłem/Przebiłam oponę.
psheh-<u>bee</u>-wehm/psheh-<u>bee</u>-wahm
oh-<u>poh</u>-neh

I need a …
Potrzebny/Potrzebna mi jest …
poh-<u>tsheh</u>-bnyh/poh-<u>tsheh</u>-bnah mee yehst …

jumper cable
kabel rozruchowy
<u>kah</u>-behl rohz-ruh-<u>hoh</u>-vyh

mechanic
mechanik
meh-<u>hah</u>-n'eek

tow truck
pomoc drogowa
<u>poh</u>-mohts droh-<u>goh</u>-vah

Can you fix the car?
Czy może pan naprawić mój samochód?
chyh <u>moh</u>-zheh pahn nah-<u>prah</u>-veech'
muhy sah-<u>moh</u>-huht

When will it be ready?
Na kiedy będzie gotowy?
nah <u>kyeh</u>-dyh <u>behn</u>-dj'yeh goh-<u>toh</u>-vyh

Driving Around

Can I park here?
Czy mogę tu zaparkować?
chyh <u>moh</u>-geh tuh zah-pahr-<u>koh</u>-vahch'

Where's the parking lot/garage?
Gdzie jest parking?
gdj'yeh yehst <u>pahr</u>-keeng

How much does it cost?
Ile kosztuje?
<u>ee</u>-leh toh kohsh-<u>tuh</u>-yeh

Is parking free?
Czy parking jest bezpłatny?
chyh <u>pahr</u>-keeng yehst behz-<u>pwah</u>-tnyh

What's the speed limit?
Jakie jest ograniczenie prędkości?
<u>yah</u>-kyeh yehst oh-grah-n'ee-<u>cheh</u>-n'yeh
prehnt-<u>kohsh'</u>-ch'yee

How much is the toll?
Ile płaci się za przejazd autostradą?
<u>ee</u>-leh <u>pwah</u>-ch'yee sh'yeh zah <u>psheh</u>-yahst
ahw-toh-<u>strah</u>-dohm

Can I turn here?
Czy mogę tu skręcać?
chyh <u>moh</u>-geh tuh <u>skrehn</u>-tsahch'

Problems with a Car

There's been an accident.
Zdarzył się wypadek.
<u>zdah</u>-zhyhw sh'yeh vyh-<u>pah</u>-dehk

Call the police/an ambulance.
Proszę wezwać policję/karetkę.
<u>proh</u>-sheh <u>vehz</u>-vahch' poh-<u>lee</u>-tsyeh/
kah-<u>reht</u>-keh

My car has been stolen.
Ukradziono mi samochód.
uh-krah-<u>dj'yoh</u>-noh mee sah-<u>moh</u>-huht

My license plate number is …
**Numer moich tablic rejestracyjnych
to …**
<u>nuh</u>-mehr <u>moh</u>-yeeh <u>tah</u>-bleets reh-yeh-
strah-<u>tsyhy</u>-nyhh toh …

Can I have your insurance information?
Czy mogę prosić o pana/pani ubezpieczenie?
chyh <u>moh</u>-geh <u>proh</u>-sh'eech' oh <u>pah</u>-nah/
<u>pah</u>-n'ee uh-behz-pyeh-<u>cheh</u>-n'yeh

Getting Directions

Excuse me, please!
Przepraszam!
psheh-<u>prah</u>-shahm!

Can you help me?
Czy może mi pan/pani pomóc?
chyh <u>moh</u>-zheh mee pahn/<u>pah</u>-n'ee
<u>poh</u>-muhts

Is this the way to …?
Czy to droga do …?
chyh toh <u>droh</u>-gah doh …

How far is it to …?
Jak daleko jest stąd do …?
yahk dah-<u>leh</u>-koh yehst stohnd doh …

Is this the right road to …?
Czy to właściwa droga do …?
chyh toh vwahsh'-<u>ch'ee</u>-vah <u>droh</u>-gah doh …

How much longer until we get to …?
Za ile dojedziemy do …?
zah <u>ee</u>-leh doh-yeh-<u>dj'yeh</u>-myh doh …

You Might See

Stop
Stop

Ustąp pierwszeństwa przejazdu
Yield

Droga jednokierunkowa
One way

Zakaz wjazdu
Do not enter

Ograniczenie prędkości
Speed limit

Where's …?
Gdzie jest …?
gdj'yeh yehst …

> … Street
> **ulica …**
> uh-<u>lee</u>-tsah …

> this address
> **to miejsce**
> toh <u>myehy</u>-stseh

> the highway
> **autostrada**
> ahw-toh-<u>strah</u>-dah

> the downtown area
> **centrum miasta**
> <u>tsehn</u>-truhm <u>myah</u>-stah

Where am I?
Gdzie ja jestem?
gdj'yeh yah <u>yehs</u>-tehm

Can you show me on the map?
Czy może mi pan/pani pokazać na mapie?
chyh <u>moh</u>-zheh mee pahn/<u>pah</u>-n'ee poh-<u>kah</u>-zahch' nah <u>mah</u>-pyeh

Do you have a road map?
Ma pan/pani mapę drogową?
mah pahn/<u>pah</u>-n'ee <u>mah</u>-peh droh-<u>goh</u>-vohm

How do I get to …?
Jak mam się dostać do …?
yahk mahm sh'yeh <u>dohs</u>-tahch' doh …

How long does it take …?
Ile to zajmie …?
<u>ee</u>-leh toh <u>zahy</u>-myeh …

> on foot
> **piechotą**
> pyeh-<u>hoh</u>-tohm

> by car
> **samochodem**
> sah-moh-<u>hoh</u>-dehm

> using public transportation
> **komunikacją publiczną**
> koh-muh-n'ee-<u>kahts</u>-yohm puh-<u>bleech</u>-nohm

I'm lost.
Zgubiłem/Zgubiłam się.
zguh-<u>bee</u>-wehm/zguh-<u>bee</u>-wahm sh'yeh

You Might Hear

Proszę iść (*on foot*)/**jechać** (*by car*) **prosto.**
<u>proh</u>-sheh eesh'ch'/<u>yeh</u>-hahch' <u>proh</u>-stoh
Go straight ahead.

Proszę skręcić w prawo.
<u>proh</u>-sheh <u>skrehn</u>-ch'eech' <u>fprah</u>-voh
Turn right.

Proszę skręcić w lewo.
<u>proh</u>-sheh <u>skrehn</u>-ch'eech' <u>vleh</u>-voh
Turn left.

po drugiej stronie ulicy
poh <u>druh</u>-gyehy <u>stroh</u>-n'yeh uh-<u>lee</u>-tsyh
across the street

za rogiem
zah <u>roh</u>-gyehm
around the corner

do przodu	**do tyłu**
doh <u>pshoh</u>-duh	doh <u>tyh</u>-wuh
forward	backward
za	**przed**
zah	psheht
behind	in front (of)

---

na następnym skrzyżowaniu
nah nahs-tehm-pnyhm skshyh-zhoh-vah-n'yuh
at the next intersection

na następnych światłach
nah nahs-tehm-pnyhh sh'fyaht-wahh
at the next traffic light

przy	**przed**	**za**
pshyh	psheht	zah
next to	before	after

w pobliżu
fpoh-blee-zhuh
near

daleko
dah-leh-koh
far

na północ
nah puhw-nohts
north

na południe
nah poh-wuh-dn'yeh
south

na wschód
nah fs-huht
east

na zachód
nah zah-huht
west

Proszę ...
proh-sheh ...
Take ...

  przejechać wiadukt
  psheh-yeh-hahch' vyah-duhkt
  the bridge

  zjechać z autostrady
  zyeh-hahch' zahw-toh-strah-dyh
  the exit

pojechać autostradą
poh-<u>yeh</u>-hahch' ahw-toh-<u>strah</u>-dohm
the highway

pojechać ulicą/aleją …
poh-<u>yeh</u>-hahch' uh-<u>lee</u>-tsohm/ah-<u>leh</u>-yohm
… Street/Avenue

pojechać rondem
poh-<u>yeh</u>-hahch' <u>rohn</u>-dehm
the traffic circle

przejechać tunelem
psheh-<u>yeh</u>-hahch' tuh-<u>neh</u>-lehm
the tunnel

ACCOMMODATIONS

Can you recommend ...?
Czy może pan/pani polecić ...?
chyh <u>moh</u>-zheh pahn/<u>pah</u>-n'ee poh-<u>leh</u>-
ch'eech' ...

> a hotel
> **jakiś hotel**
> <u>yah</u>-keesh' <u>hoh</u>-tehl

> an inn
> **jakąś gospodę**
> <u>yah</u>-kohnsh' gohs-<u>poh</u>-deh

> a motel
> **jakiś motel**
> <u>yah</u>-keesh' <u>moh</u>-tehl

> a guesthouse
> **jakiś pensjonat**
> <u>yah</u>-keesh' pehn-<u>syoh</u>-naht

> a (youth) hostel
> **jakieś schronisko młodzieżowe**
> <u>yah</u>-kyehsh' shroh-<u>n'ee</u>-skoh
> mwoh-dj'yeh-<u>zhoh</u>-veh

Where is the nearest ...?
Gdzie jest najbliższy/najbliższa ...?
gdj'yeh yehst nahy-<u>bleesh</u>-shyh/nahy-
<u>bleesh</u>-shah ...

I'm looking for ... accommodations.
Szukam ... zakwaterowania.
<u>shuh</u>-kahm ... zah-kfah-teh-roh-<u>vah</u>-n'yah

inexpensive
niedrogiego
n'yeh-droh-<u>gyeh</u>-goh

luxurious
luksusowego
luhk-suh-soh-<u>veh</u>-goh

traditional
tradycyjnego
trah-dyh-tsyhy-<u>neh</u>-goh

clean
czystego
chyhs-<u>teh</u>-goh

conveniently located
dogodnie położonego
doh-<u>goh</u>-dn'yeh poh-woh-zhoh-<u>neh</u>-goh

Is there English-speaking staff?
Czy obsługa mówi po angielsku?
chyh ohp-<u>swuh</u>-gah <u>muh</u>-vee poh
ahn-<u>gyehl</u>-skuh

Booking a Room and Checking In

Do you have any rooms available?
Czy są wolne pokoje?
chyh sohm <u>vohl</u>-neh poh-<u>koh</u>-yeh

vacancy
wolny pokój
<u>vohl</u>-nyh <u>poh</u>-kuhy

no vacancy
brak wolnych pokoi
brahk <u>vohl</u>-nyhh poh-<u>koh</u>-yee

I'd like a room for tonight.
**Chciałbym/Chciałabym wynająć pokój
na tę noc.**
hch'yahw-byhm/hch'yah-<u>wah</u>-byhm vyh-
<u>nah</u>-yohnch' <u>poh</u>-kuhy nah teh nohts

Can I make a reservation?
Czy mogę zrobić rezerwację?
chyh <u>moh</u>-geh <u>zroh</u>-beech' reh-zehr-<u>vah</u>-
tsyeh

I'd like to reserve a room ...
**Chciałbym/Chciałabym zarezerwować
pokój ...**
hch'yahw-byhm/hch'yah-<u>wah</u>-byhm zah-
reh-zehr-<u>voh</u>-vahch' <u>poh</u>-kuhy ...

> for XX nights
> **na XX nocy**
> nah XX <u>noh</u>-tsyh

> for one person
> **dla jednej osoby**
> dlah <u>yehd</u>-nehy oh-<u>soh</u>-byh

> for two people
> **dla dwóch osób**
> dlah dvuhh <u>oh</u>-suhp

> with a queen-size bed
> **z podwójnym łóżkiem**
> z pohd-<u>vuhy</u>-nyhm <u>wuhsh</u>-kyehm

with two beds
z dwoma łóżkami
z <u>dvoh</u>-mah wuhsh-<u>kah</u>-mee

How much is it?
Ile to kosztuje?
<u>ee</u>-leh toh kohsh-<u>tuh</u>-yeh

How much is it per night/person?
Jaka jest cena za dobę/osobę?
<u>yah</u>-kah yehst <u>tseh</u>-nah zah <u>doh</u>-beh/
oh-<u>soh</u>-beh

Can I pay by credit card?
Czy mogę zapłacić kartą kredytową?
chyh <u>moh</u>-geh zah-<u>pwah</u>-ch'eech' <u>kahr</u>-tohm
kreh-dyh-<u>toh</u>-vohm

Is breakfast included?
Czy śniadanie jest wliczone?
chyh sh'n'yah-<u>dah</u>-n'yeh yehst vlee-<u>choh</u>-neh

My credit card number is …
Numer mojej karty kredytowej to …
<u>nuh</u>-mehr <u>moh</u>-yehy <u>kahr</u>-tyh kreh-dyh-
<u>toh</u>-vehy toh …

Do you have …?
Czy mają państwo …?
chyh <u>mah</u>-yohm <u>pahn'</u>-stfoh …

private bathrooms
łazienki w pokojach
wah-<u>zh'yehn</u>-kee fpoh-<u>koh</u>-yahh

cots
składane łóżka
skwah-<u>dah</u>-neh <u>wuhsh</u>-kah

a crib
łóżeczko dziecięce
wuh-<u>zhehch</u>-koh dj'yeh-<u>ch'yehn</u>-tseh

linens
pościel
<u>pohsh'</u>-ch'yehl

towels
ręczniki
rehn-<u>chn'ee</u>-kee

a restaurant
restaurację
rehs-tahw-<u>rahts</u>-yeh

a kitchen
kuchnię
<u>kuhh</u>-n'yeh

a microwave
kuchenkę mikrofalową
kuh-<u>hehn</u>-keh mee-kroh-fah-<u>loh</u>-vohm

room service
obsługę pokoi
ohp-<u>swuh</u>-geh poh-<u>koh</u>-yee

non-smoking rooms
pokoje dla niepalących
poh-<u>koh</u>-yeh dlah n'yeh-pah-<u>lohn</u>-tsyhh

an elevator
windę
veen-deh

laundry service
pralnię
prahl-n'yeh

a safe
sejf
sehyf

phones
telefony
teh-leh-foh-nyh

air conditioning
klimatyzację
klee-mah-tyh-zah-tsyeh

wireless internet
bezprzewodowy internet
behs-psheh-voh-doh-vyh een-tehr-neht

a business center
centrum biznesowe
tsehn-truhm beez-neh-soh-veh

television
telewizję
teh-leh-veez-yeh

a gym
siłownię
sh'ee-wohv-n'yeh

a pool
basen
bah-sehn

Is there a curfew?
Czy jest cisza nocna?
chyh yehst <u>ch'ee</u>-shah <u>nohts</u>-nah

When is check-in?
Kiedy można się zameldować?
<u>kyeh</u>-dyh <u>mohzh</u>-nah sh'yeh zah-mehl-<u>doh</u>-vahch'

May I see the room?
Czy mogę obejrzeć pokój?
chyh <u>moh</u>-geh oh-<u>behy</u>-zhehch' <u>poh</u>-kuhy

How can somebody call my room?
Jak można dodzwonić się do mojego pokoju?
yahk <u>mohzh</u>-nah doh-<u>dzvoh</u>-n'eech' sh'yeh doh moh-<u>yeh</u>-goh poh-<u>koh</u>-yuh

Do you have anything …?
Czy mają państwo coś …?
chyh <u>mah</u>-yohm <u>pahn'</u>-stfoh tsohsh' …

   bigger
   większego
   vyehn-<u>ksheh</u>-goh

   cleaner
   czystszego
   chyhs-<u>tsheh</u>-goh

   quieter
   cichszego
   ch'eeh-<u>sheh</u>-goh

less expensive
tańszego
tahn'-<u>sheh</u>-goh

Does that include sales tax (VAT)?
Czy cena obejmuje VAT?
chyh <u>tseh</u>-nah oh-behy-<u>muh</u>-yeh vaht

I'll take it.
Wezmę go.
<u>vehz</u>-meh goh

I don't have a reservation.
Nie mam rezerwacji.
n'yeh mahm reh-zehr-<u>vah</u>-tsyee

I have a reservation under ...
Mam rezerwację na nazwisko ...
mahm reh-zehr-<u>vah</u>-tsyeh nah nahz-<u>vee</u>-skoh ...

Is the room ready?
Czy pokój jest gotowy?
chyh <u>poh</u>-kuhy yehst goh-<u>toh</u>-vyh

When will the room be ready?
Kiedy pokój będzie gotowy?
<u>kyeh</u>-dyh <u>poh</u>-kuhy <u>behn</u>-dj'yeh goh-<u>toh</u>-vyh

room number
numer pokoju
<u>nuh</u>-mehr poh-<u>koh</u>-yuh

floor
piętro
<u>pyehn</u>-troh

room key
klucz do pokoju
kluhch doh poh-<u>koh</u>-yuh

At the Hotel

Where is the …?
Gdzie jest …?
gdj'yeh yehst …

> bar
> **bar**
> bahr

> bathroom
> **łazienka**
> wah-<u>zh'yehn</u>-kah

> convenience store
> **sklepik całodobowy**
> <u>skleh</u>-peek tsah-woh-doh-<u>boh</u>-vyh

> dining room
> **jadalnia**
> yah-<u>dahl</u>-n'yah

> elevator
> **winda**
> <u>veen</u>-dah

> information desk
> **informacja**
> een-fohr-<u>mah</u>-tsyah

lobby
hol
hohl

pool
basen
<u>bah</u>-sehn

restaurant
restauracja
rehs-tahw-<u>rah</u>-tsyah

shower
prysznic
<u>pryhsh</u>-n'eets

Can I have ...?
Czy mogę prosić o ...?
chyh <u>moh</u>-geh <u>proh</u>-sh'eech' oh ...

a blanket
koc
kohts

a new room key
inny klucz do pokoju
<u>een</u>-nyh kluhch doh poh-<u>koh</u>-yuh

a pillow
poduszkę
poh-<u>duhsh</u>-keh

a plug for the bath
korek do wanny
<u>koh</u>-rehk doh <u>vahn</u>-nyh

soap
mydło
myh-dwoh

clean sheets
czystą pościel
chyhs-tohm pohsh'-ch'yehl

towels
ręczniki
rehn-chn'ee-kee

toilet paper
papier toaletowy
pah-pyehr toh-ah-leh-toh-vyh

a wake-up call at …
budzenie o godzinie …
buh-dzeh-n'yeh oh goh-dj'yee-n'yeh …

I would like to place these items in the safe.
**Chciałbym/Chciałabym złożyć te
rzeczy w sejfie.**
hch'yahw-byhm/hch'yah-wah-byhm zwoh-
zhyhch' teh zheh-chyh fsehy-fyeh

I would like to retrieve my items from the
safe.
**Chciałbym/Chciałabym wyjąć moje
rzeczy z sejfu.**
hch'yahw-byhm/hch'yah-wah-byhm vyh-
yohnch' moh-yeh zheh-chyh s sehy-fuh

Can I stay an extra night?
Czy mogę zostać na jeszcze jedną noc?
chyh <u>moh</u>-geh <u>zohs</u>-tahch' nah <u>yehsh</u>-cheh
<u>yehd</u>-nohm nohts

Problems at the Hotel

There's a problem with the room.
Mam problem.
mahm <u>proh</u>-blehm

The ... doesn't work.
... nie działa.
... n'yeh <u>dj'yah</u>-wah

> air conditioning
> **klimatyzacja**
> klee-mah-tyh-<u>zah</u>-tsyah

> door lock
> **zamek u drzwi**
> <u>zah</u>-mehk uh djvee

> hot water
> **gorąca woda**
> goh-<u>rohn</u>-tsah <u>voh</u>-dah

> shower
> **prysznic**
> <u>pryhsh</u>-n'eets

> sink
> **umywalka**
> uh-myh-<u>vahl</u>-kah

toilet
toaleta
toh-ah-<u>leh</u>-tah

The lights won't turn on.
Nie mogę zapalić światła.
n'yeh <u>moh</u>-geh zah-<u>pah</u>-leech' <u>sh'fyah</u>-twah

The ... aren't clean.
... nie są czyste.
... n'yeh sohm <u>chyhs</u>-teh

pillows
poduszki
poh-<u>duhsh</u>-kee

sheets
pościel
<u>pohsh'</u>-ch'yehl

towels
ręczniki
rehn-<u>chn'ee</u>-kee

The room has bugs/mice.
W pokoju są robaki/myszy.
fpoh-<u>koh</u>-yuh sohm roh-<u>bah</u>-kee/<u>myh</u>-shyh

The room is too noisy.
W pokoju jest za głośno.
fpoh-<u>koh</u>-yuh yehst zah <u>gwohsh'</u>-noh

I've lost my key.
Zgubiłem/Zgubiłam klucz.
zguh-<u>bee</u>-wehm/zguh-<u>bee</u>-wahm kluhch

I've locked myself out.
Zatrzasnąłem/Zatrzasnęłam klucz w pokoju.
zah-tshah-<u>snoh</u>-wehm/zah-tshah-<u>sneh</u>-wahm kluhch fpoh-<u>koh</u>-yuh

Checking Out

When is check-out?
O której mam się wymeldować?
oh <u>ktuh</u>-rehy mahm sh'yeh vyh-mehl-<u>doh</u>-vahch'

When is the earliest/latest I can check out?
O której najwcześniej/najpóźniej mogę się wymeldować?
oh <u>ktuh</u>-rehy nahy-<u>fchehsh'</u>-n'yehy/nahy-<u>puhzh'</u>-n'yehy <u>moh</u>-geh sh'yeh vyh-mehl-<u>doh</u>-vahch'

I would like to check out.
Chciałbym/Chciałabym się wymeldować.
<u>hch'yahw</u>-byhm/hch'yah-<u>wah</u>-byhm sh'yeh vyh-mehl-<u>doh</u>-vahch'

I would like a receipt/an itemized bill.
Proszę o pokwitowanie/szczegółowy rachunek.
<u>proh</u>-sheh oh poh-kfee-toh-<u>vah</u>-n'yeh/ shcheh-guh-<u>woh</u>-vyh rah-<u>huh</u>-nehk

There's a mistake on this bill.
Na tym rachunku jest błąd.
nah tyhm rah-<u>huhn</u>-kuh yehst bwohnt

Please take this off the bill.
Proszę usunąć tę pozycję z rachunku.
proh-sheh uh-<u>suh</u>-nohnch' teh poh-<u>zyh</u>-
tsyeh zrah-<u>huhn</u>-kuh

The total is incorrect.
Całkowita suma nie zgadza się.
tsahw-koh-<u>vee</u>-tah <u>suh</u>-mah n'yeh <u>zgah</u>-
dzah sh'yeh

I would like to pay ...
Chciałbym/Chciałabym zapłacić ...
hch'<u>yahw</u>-byhm/hch'yah-<u>wah</u>-byhm zah-
<u>pwah</u>-ch'eech' ...

by credit card
kartą kredytową
<u>kahr</u>-tohm kreh-dyh-<u>toh</u>-vohm

by (traveler's) check
czekiem (podróżnym)
<u>cheh</u>-kyehm (poh-<u>druhzh</u>-nyhm)

in cash
gotówką
goh-<u>tuhf</u>-kohm

Can I leave my bags here until ...?
Czy mogę zostawić tutaj bagaż do ...?
chyh <u>moh</u>-geh zoh-<u>stah</u>-veech' <u>tuh</u>-tahy
<u>bah</u>-gahzh doh ...

Renting

I'd like to rent …
Chciałbym/Chciałabym wynająć …
hch'yahw-byhm/hch'yah-wah-byhm
vyh-nah-yohnch' …

> an apartment
> **mieszkanie**
> myeh-shkah-n'yeh

> a room
> **pokój**
> poh-kuhy

> a house
> **dom**
> dohm

How much is it per week?
Ile to będzie tygodniowo?
ee-leh toh behn-dj'yeh tyh-goh-dn'yoh-voh

I intend to stay for XX months.
Zamierzam się zatrzymać na XX miesięcy.
zah-myeh-zhahm sh'yeh zah-tshyh-mahch'
nah XX myeh-sh'yehn-tsyh

Is it furnished?
Czy są tam meble?
chyh sohm tahm meh-bleh

ACCOMMODATIONS

Does it have …?
Czy jest tam …?
chyh yehst tahm …

> a kitchen
> **kuchnia**
> kuhh-n'yah

> dishes
> **naczynia**
> nah-chyh-n'yah

> cooking utensils
> **sprzęt kuchenny**
> spshehnt kuh-hehn-nyh

> a washing machine
> **pralka**
> prahl-kah

> a dryer
> **suszarka**
> suh-shahr-kah

> linens
> **pościel**
> pohsh'-ch'yehl

> towels
> **ręczniki**
> rehn-chn'ee-kee

Do you require a deposit?
Czy pobierają państwo kaucję?
chyh poh-byeh-rah-yohm pahn'-stfoh
kahw-tsyeh

When is the rent due?
Kiedy płaci się czynsz?
kyeh-dyh pwah-ch'ee sh'yeh chyhnsh

Who is the superintendent?
Kto jest dozorcą?
ktoh yehst doh-zohr-tsohm

Who should I contact for repairs?
**Z kim mam się kontaktować w
sprawie napraw?**
skeem mahm sh'yeh kohn-tahk-toh-vahch'
fsprah-vyeh nah-prahf

Camping

campsite
kemping
kehm-peeng

Can I camp here?
Czy mogę tu rozbić namiot?
chyh moh-geh tuh rohz-beech' nah-myoht

Do you have ... for rent?
Czy wypożyczacie ...?
chyh vyh-poh-zhyh-chah-ch'yeh ...

tents
namioty
nah-myoh-tyh

sleeping bags
śpiwory
sh'pee-<u>voh</u>-ryh

cooking equipment
sprzęt kuchenny
spshehnt kuh-<u>hehn</u>-nyh

Do you have …?
Czy mają państwo …?
chyh <u>mah</u>-yohm <u>pahn'</u>-stfoh …

a shower block
prysznice
pryh-<u>shn'ee</u>-tseh

laundry facilities
pralnię
<u>prahl</u>-n'yeh

electricity
prąd
prohnt

How much is it per …?
Jaka jest cena za …?
<u>yah</u>-kah yehst <u>tseh</u>-nah zah …

lot
miejsce (namiotowe)
<u>myehy</u>-stseh (nah-myoh-<u>toh</u>-veh)

person
osobę
oh-<u>soh</u>-beh

night
noc
nohts

Are there ... that I should be careful of?
**Czy powinienem/powinnam uważać
na jakieś ...?**
chyh poh-vee-<u>n'yeh</u>-nehm/poh-<u>veen</u>-
nahm uh-<u>vah</u>-zhahch' nah <u>yah</u>-kyehsh' ...

animals
zwierzęta
zvyeh-<u>zhehn</u>-tah

plants
rośliny
roh-<u>sh'lee</u>-nyh

insects
owady
oh-<u>vah</u>-dyh

Where should I park?
Gdzie mam zaparkować?
gdj'yeh mahm zah-pahr-<u>koh</u>-vahch'

DINING OUT

Meals

breakfast	lunch
śniadanie	**obiad**
sh'n'yah-<u>dah</u>-n'yeh	<u>oh</u>-byaht

dinner	dessert
kolacja	**deser**
koh-<u>lah</u>-tsyah	<u>deh</u>-sehr

a snack
przekąska
psheh-<u>kohn</u>-skah

Finding a Place to Eat

Can you recommend …?
Czy może mi pan/pani polecić …?
chyh <u>moh</u>-zheh mee pahn/<u>pah</u>-n'ee poh-<u>leh</u>-ch'eech' …

   a good restaurant
   dobrą restaurację
   <u>doh</u>-brohm rehs-tahw-<u>rah</u>-tsyeh

   a restaurant with local dishes
   restaurację z polską kuchnią
   rehs-tahw-<u>rah</u>-tsyeh <u>spohl</u>-skohm <u>kuhh</u>-n'yohm

an inexpensive restaurant
niedrogą restaurację
n'yeh-<u>droh</u>-gohm rehs-tahw-<u>rah</u>-tsyeh

a popular bar
popularny bar
poh-puh-<u>lahr</u>-nyh bahr

I'm hungry/thirsty.
Chce mi się jeść/pić.
htseh mee sh'yeh yehsh'ch'/peech'

Types of Restaurants

café
kawiarnia
kah-<u>vyahr</u>-n'yah

restaurant
restauracja
rehs-tahw-<u>rah</u>-tsyah

fast food
fast food
fahst fuht

snack bar
bar zakąskowy, snack bar
bahr zah-kohn-<u>skoh</u>-vyh, snahk bahr

teahouse
herbaciarnia
hehr-bah-<u>ch'yahr</u>-n'yah

bistro
bistro
<u>bee</u>-stroh

steak house
restauracja specjalizująca się w stekach
rehs-tahw-<u>rah</u>-tsyah speh-tsyah-lee-zuh-
<u>yohn</u>-tsah sh'yeh <u>fsteh</u>-kahh

buffet
bufet
<u>buh</u>-feht

bar
bar
bahr

kosher restaurant
restauracja koszerna
rehs-tahw-<u>rah</u>-tsyah koh-<u>shehr</u>-nah

vegan restaurant
restauracja wegańska
rehs-tahw-<u>rah</u>-tsyah veh-<u>gahn'</u>-skah

vegetarian restaurant
restauracja wegetariańska
rehs-tahw-<u>rah</u>-tsyah veh-geh-tah-<u>ryahn'</u>-
skah

pizzeria
pizzeria
pee-<u>tsehr</u>-yah

Reservations and Getting a Table

I have a reservation for …
Mam rezerwację na …
mahm reh-zehr-<u>vah</u>-tsyeh nah …

The reservation is under …
Rezerwacja jest na nazwisko …
reh-zehr-<u>vah</u>-tsyah yehst nah nahz-<u>vee</u>-skoh
…

I'd like to reserve a table for …
**Chciałbym/Chciałabym zarezerwować
stolik na …**
<u>hch'yahw</u>-byhm/hch'yah-<u>wah</u>-byhm
zah-reh-zehr-<u>voh</u>-vahch' <u>stoh</u>-leek nah …

Can we sit …?
Czy możemy usiąść …?
chyh moh-<u>zheh</u>-myh <u>uh</u>-sh'yohn'sh'ch' …

> over here
> **tutaj**
> <u>tuh</u>-tahy

> over there
> **tam**
> tahm

> by a window
> **przy oknie**
> pshyh <u>ohk</u>-n'yeh

> outside
> **na zewnątrz**
> nah <u>zehv</u>-nohnch

in a non-smoking area
w części dla niepalących
<u>fchehn'</u>-sh'ch'yee dlah n'yeh-pah-<u>lohn</u>-
tsyhh

How long is the wait?
Jak długo musimy czekać?
yahk <u>dwuh</u>-goh muh-<u>sh'ee</u>-myh <u>cheh</u>-kahch'

It's for here. / It's to go.
Na miejscu. / Na wynos.
nah <u>myehy</u>-stsuh / nah <u>vyh</u>-nohs

Ordering

Excuse me!
Przepraszam!
psheh-<u>prah</u>-shahm

I'd like to order.
Chciałbym/Chciałabym zamówić.
<u>hch'yahw</u>-byhm/hch'yah-<u>wah</u>-byhm
zah-<u>muh</u>-veech'

Can I have a ... please?
Czy mogę prosić o ...?
chyh <u>moh</u>-geh <u>proh</u>-sh'eech' oh ...

menu
menu
meh-<u>n'ee</u>

wine list
kartę win
<u>kahr</u>-teh veen

drink menu
kartę napojów
<u>kahr</u>-teh nah-<u>poh</u>-yuhf

children's menu
menu dla dzieci
meh-<u>n'ee</u> dlah <u>dj'yeh</u>-ch'yee

Do you have a menu in English?
Czy mają państwo menu po angielsku?
chyh <u>mah</u>-yohm <u>pahn'</u>-stfoh meh-<u>n'ee</u> poh
ahn-<u>gyehl</u>-skuh

Do you have a set/fixed price menu?
Czy mają państwo zestawy?
chyh <u>mah</u>-yohm <u>pahn'</u>-stfoh zeh-<u>stah</u>-vyh

What are the specials?
Jakie są dania dnia?
<u>yah</u>-kyeh sohm <u>dah</u>-n'yah dn'yah

Do you have …?
Czy mają państwo …?
chyh <u>mah</u>-yohm <u>pahn'</u>-stfoh …

Can you recommend some local dishes?
**Czy może pan/pani polecić jakieś
dania kuchni polskiej?**
chyh <u>moh</u>-zheh pahn/<u>pah</u>-n'ee poh-leh-
ch'eech' <u>yah</u>-kyehsh' <u>dah</u>-n'yah <u>kuh</u>-hn'yee
<u>pohl</u>-skyehy

What do you recommend?
Co może pan/pani polecić?
tsoh <u>moh</u>-zheh pahn/<u>pah</u>-n'ee poh-<u>leh</u>-ch'eech'

I'll have …
Poproszę …
poh-<u>proh</u>-sheh …

Can I have …?
Czy mogę prosić …?
chyh <u>moh</u>-geh <u>proh</u>-sh'eech' …?

> a glass of …
> **szklankę …** (*for water*)
> <u>shklahn</u>-keh …
> **kieliszek …** (*for alcohol*)
> kyeh-<u>lee</u>-shehk…

> a bottle of …
> **butelkę …**
> buh-<u>tehl</u>-keh …

> a pitcher of …
> **dzbanek …**
> <u>dzbah</u>-nehk …

What's this?
Co to jest?
tsoh toh yehst?

What's in this?
Z czego to jest zrobione?
<u>scheh</u>-goh toh yehst zroh-<u>byoh</u>-neh

Is it …?
Czy to jest …?
chyh toh yehst …?

> spicy
> **ostre**
> <u>ohs</u>-treh

> bitter
> **gorzkie**
> <u>gohsh</u>-kyeh

> sweet
> **słodkie**
> <u>swoht</u>-kyeh

> hot
> **gorące**
> goh-<u>rohn</u>-tseh

> cold
> **zimne**
> <u>zh'eem</u>-neh

Do you have any vegetarian dishes?
Czy mają państwo jakieś dania wegetariańskie?
chyh <u>mah</u>-yohm <u>pahn'</u>-stfoh <u>yah</u>-kyehsh' <u>dah</u>-n'yah veh-geh-tah-<u>ryahn'</u>-skyeh

I'd like it with/without …
Poproszę to z/bez …
poh-<u>proh</u>-sheh toh z/behz …

> ### You Might Hear
>
> Enjoy your meal!
> **Smacznego!**
> smah-<u>chneh</u>-goh

Are there any drink specials?
Czy polecają państwo jakieś drinki?
chyh poh-leh-<u>tsah</u>-yohm <u>pahn'</u>-stfoh <u>yah</u>-kyehsh' <u>dreen</u>-kee

Can I see the drink menu?
Czy mogę prosić listę drinków?
chyh <u>moh</u>-geh <u>proh</u>-sh'eech' <u>lee</u>-steh <u>dreen</u>-kuhf

Can I see the wine list?
Czy mogę prosić kartę win?
chyh <u>moh</u>-geh <u>proh</u>-sh'eech' <u>kahr</u>-teh veen

I'd like a bottle of …
Poproszę butelkę …
poh-<u>proh</u>-sheh buh-<u>tehl</u>-keh …

> red wine
> **czerwonego wina**
> chehr-voh-<u>neh</u>-goh <u>vee</u>-nah

> white wine
> **białego wina**
> byah-<u>weh</u>-goh <u>vee</u>-nah

> rosé wine
> **różowego wina**
> ruh-zhoh-<u>veh</u>-goh <u>vee</u>-nah

the house wine
wina stołowego
vee-nah stoh-woh-veh-goh

dessert wine
wina deserowego
vee-nah deh-seh-roh-veh-goh

dry wine
wytrawnego wina
vyh-trahv-neh-goh vee-nah

champagne
szampana
shahm-pah-nah

A light/dark beer, please.
Poproszę jasne/ciemne piwo.
poh-proh-sheh yahs-neh/ch'yehm-neh
pee-voh

Special Dietary Needs

Is this dish free of animal product?
**Czy w tej potrawie nie ma produktów
zwierzęcych?**
chyh ftehy poh-trah-vyeh n'yeh mah proh-
duhk-tuhf zvyeh-zhehn-tsyhh

I'm allergic to …
Jestem uczulony/uczulona na …
yehs-tehm uh-chuh-loh-nyh/uh-chuh-loh-
nah nah …

I can't eat …
Nie mogę jeść …
n'yeh <u>moh</u>-geh yehsh'ch' …

dairy
produktów mlecznych
proh-<u>duhk</u>-tuhf <u>mleh</u>-chnyhh

egg
jajek
<u>yah</u>-yehk

gelatin
żelatyny
zheh-lah-<u>tyh</u>-nyh

gluten
glutenu
gluh-<u>teh</u>-nuh

meat
mięsa
<u>myehn</u>-sah

MSG
glutaminianu sodu
gluh-tah-mee-<u>n'yah</u>-nuh <u>soh</u>-duh

nuts
orzechów
oh-<u>zheh</u>-huhf

peanuts
orzeszków ziemnych
oh-<u>zhehsh</u>-kuhf <u>zh'yehm</u>-nyhh

seafood
owoców morza
oh-<u>voh</u>-tsuhf <u>moh</u>-zhah

spicy foods
pikantnych potraw
pee-<u>kahnt</u>-nyhh <u>poh</u>-trahf

wheat
pszenicy
psheh-<u>n'yee</u>-tsyh

I'm diabetic.
Mam cukrzycę.
mahm tsuh-<u>kshyh</u>-tseh

Do you have any sugar-free products?
Czy mają państwo produkty bezcukrowe?
chyh <u>mah</u>-yohm <u>pahn'</u>-stfoh proh-<u>duh</u>-ktyh
behs-tsuh-<u>kroh</u>-veh

Do you have any artificial sweeteners?
Czy mają państwo słodziki?
chyh <u>mah</u>-yohm <u>pahn'</u>-stfoh swoh-<u>dj'yee</u>-kee

I'm vegan/vegetarian.
Jestem weganinem/wegetarianinem. (*masc.*)
<u>yehs</u>-tehm veh-gah-<u>n'yee</u>-nehm/veh-geh-tah-
ryah-<u>n'yee</u>-nehm

Jestem weganką/wegetarianką. (*fem.*)
<u>yehs</u>-tehm veh-<u>gahn</u>-kohm/veh-geh-tah-
<u>ryahn</u>-kohm

decaffeinated
bezkofeinowa
behs-koh-feh-ee-<u>noh</u>-vah

free-range
hodowane w naturalnych warunkach
hoh-doh-<u>vah</u>-neh vnah-tuh-<u>rahl</u>-nyhh vah-<u>ruhn</u>-kahh

genetically modified
modyfikowana genetycznie
moh-dyh-fee-koh-<u>vah</u>-nah geh-neh-<u>tyhch</u>-n'yeh

gluten-free
bezglutenowa
behs-gluh-teh-<u>noh</u>-vah

low fat
z małą zawartością tłuszczu
<u>zmah</u>-wohm zah-vahr-<u>tosh'</u>-ch'yohm <u>twuh</u>-shchuh

low in sugar/cholesterol
z małą zawartością cukru/cholesterolu
<u>zmah</u>-wohm zah-vahr-<u>tosh'</u>-ch'yohm <u>tsuh</u>-kruh/hoh-leh-steh-<u>roh</u>-luh

salt-free
bez soli
behs <u>soh</u>-lee

organic
organiczna
ohr-gah-<u>n'yee</u>-chnah

I'm on a special diet.
Jestem na specjalnej diecie.
yehs-tehm nah speh-tsyahl-nehy dyeh-ch'yeh

Complaints at a Restaurant

This isn't what I ordered.
Nie zamawiałem/zamawiałam tego.
n'yeh zah-mah-vyah-wehm/zah-mah-vyah-
wahm teh-goh

I ordered …
Zamawiałem/Zamawiałam …
zah-mah-vyah-wehm/zah-mah-vyah-wahm …

This is …
To jest …
toh yehst …

> cold
> **zimne**
> zh'eem-neh

> undercooked
> **niedogotowane**
> n'yeh-doh-goh-toh-vah-neh

> overcooked
> **rozgotowane**
> rohz-goh-toh-vah-neh

> spoiled
> **zepsute**
> zehp-suh-teh

not fresh
nieświeże
n'yeh-<u>sh'fyeh</u>-zheh

too spicy
za ostre
zah <u>ohs</u>-treh

too tough
za twarde
zah <u>tfahr</u>-deh

not vegetarian
niewegetariańskie
n'yeh-veh-geh-tah-<u>ryahn'</u>-skyeh

Can you take it back, please?
Czy może to pan/pani zabrać z powrotem?
chyh <u>moh</u>-zheh toh pahn/<u>pah</u>-n'ee <u>zah</u>-brahch' spoh-<u>vroh</u>-tehm

I cannot eat this.
Nie mogę tego jeść.
n'yeh <u>moh</u>-geh <u>teh</u>-goh yehsh'ch'

We're leaving.
Wychodzimy.
vyh-hoh-<u>dj'yee</u>-myh

How much longer until we get our food?
Jak długo jeszcze musimy czekać na nasze zamówienie?
yahk <u>dwuh</u>-goh <u>yehsh</u>-cheh muh-<u>sh'yee</u>-myh <u>cheh</u>-kahch' nah <u>nah</u>-sheh zah-muh-<u>vyeh</u>-n'yeh

We cannot wait any longer.
Nie możemy już dłużej czekać.
n'yeh moh-<u>zheh</u>-myh yuhsh <u>dwuh</u>-zhehy
<u>cheh</u>-kahch'

Paying at a Restaurant

Check, please!
Poproszę rachunek.
poh-<u>proh</u>-sheh rah-<u>huh</u>-nehk

We'd like to pay separately.
Chcielibyśmy zapłacić osobno.
hch'yeh-lee-<u>byhsh</u>'-myh zah-<u>pwah</u>-ch'eech'
oh-<u>soh</u>-bnoh

Can we have separate checks?
**Czy możemy prosić o oddzielne
rachunki?**
chyh moh-<u>zheh</u>-myh <u>proh</u>-sh'eech' oh ohd-
<u>dj'yehl</u>-neh rah-<u>huhn</u>-kee

We're paying together.
Zapłacimy razem.
zah-<u>pwah</u>-ch'ee-myh <u>rah</u>-zehm

Is service included?
Czy obsługa jest wliczona w cenę?
chyh ohp-<u>swuh</u>-gah yehst vlee-<u>choh</u>-nah
vrah-<u>huh</u>-nehk

What is this charge for?
Za co jest ta opłata?
zah tsoh yehst tah oh-<u>pwah</u>-tah

There is a mistake in this bill.
Na tym rachunku jest błąd.
nah tyhm rah-<u>huhn</u>-kuh yehst bwohnt

I didn't order that. I ordered …
Nie zamawiałem/zamawiałam tego.
Zamawiałem/Zamawiałam …
n'yeh zah-mah-<u>vyah</u>-wehm/zah-mah-<u>vyah</u>-
wahm <u>teh</u>-goh. zah-mah-<u>vyah</u>-wehm/zah-
mah-<u>vyah</u>-wahm …

Can I have a receipt/itemized bill, please?
Czy mogę prosić o pokwitowanie/
szczegółowy rachunek?
chyh <u>moh</u>-geh <u>proh</u>-sh'eech' oh poh-kfee-
toh-<u>vah</u>-n'yeh/shcheh-guh-<u>woh</u>-vyh rah-
<u>huh</u>-nehk

It was delicious!
To było wyśmienite!
toh <u>byh</u>-woh vyhsh'-myeh-<u>n'yee</u>-teh

FOOD & DRINK

Cooking Methods

baked
pieczony
pyeh-<u>choh</u>-nyh

boiled
gotowany
goh-toh-<u>vah</u>-nyh

braised
duszony
duh-<u>shoh</u>-nyh

breaded
panierowany
pah-n'yeh-roh-<u>vah</u>-nyh

creamed
ucierany
uh-ch'yeh-<u>rah</u>-nyh

diced
pokrojony w kostkę
poh-kroh-<u>yoh</u>-nyh
<u>fkoh</u>-stkeh

filleted
filetowany
fee-leh-toh-<u>vah</u>-nyh

grilled
z grilla
<u>zgree</u>-lah

microwaved
z kuchenki mikro-falowej
skuh-<u>hehn</u>-kee mee-kroh-fah-<u>loh</u>-vehy

mixed
zmiksowany
zmee-ksoh-<u>vah</u>-nyh

poached
z wody
<u>zvoh</u>-dyh

re-heated
odgrzewany
oht-gzheh-<u>vah</u>-nyh

roasted
pieczony
pyeh-<u>choh</u>-nyh

sautéed
sauté
soh-<u>teh</u>

smoked
wędzony
vehn-<u>dzoh</u>-nyh

rare
krwisty
<u>krfee</u>-styh

steamed
gotowany na parze
goh-toh-<u>vah</u>-nyh nah
<u>pah</u>-zheh

medium rare
średnio wysmażony
<u>sh'reh</u>-dn'yoh vyh-
smah-<u>zhoh</u>-nyh

stewed
duszony
duh-<u>shoh</u>-nyh

well-done
dobrze wysmażony
<u>doh</u>-bzheh vyh-smah-
<u>zhoh</u>-nyh

stuffed
faszerowany
fah-sheh-roh-<u>vah</u>-nyh

on the side
jako przystawka
<u>yah</u>-koh pshyh-<u>stahf</u>-
kah

toasted
opiekany
oh-pyeh-<u>kah</u>-nyh

Tastes

bitter
gorzki
<u>goh</u>-shkee

spicy
ostry
<u>oh</u>-stryh

sour
kwaśny
<u>kfah</u>-sh'nyh

salty
słony
<u>swoh</u>-nyh

sweet
słodki
<u>swoh</u>-tkee

bland
mdły
mdwyh

Breakfast Foods

bacon **boczek** <u>boh</u>-chehk	granola **muesli** <u>muh</u>-slee
bread **chleb** hlehp	honey **miód** myuht
butter **masło** <u>mah</u>-swoh	jam/jelly **dżem** djehm
cereal **płatki śniadaniowe** <u>pwah</u>-tkee sh'n'yah-dah-<u>n'yoh</u>-veh	omelet **omlet** <u>ohm</u>-leht
cheese **ser** sehr	sausage **kiełbasa** kyehw-<u>bah</u>-sah
eggs **jajka** <u>yahy</u>-kah	yogurt **jogurt** <u>yoh</u>-guhrt

Vegetables

asparagus **szparagi** shpah-<u>rah</u>-gee	avocado **awokado** ah-voh-<u>kah</u>-doh

beans
fasola
fah-<u>soh</u>-lah

broccoli
brokuły
broh-<u>kuh</u>-wyh

cabbage
kapusta
kah-<u>puh</u>-stah

carrot
marchew
<u>mahr</u>-hehf

cauliflower
kalafior
kah-<u>lah</u>-fyohr

celery
seler naciowy
<u>seh</u>-lehr nah-<u>ch'yoh</u>-vyh

chickpeas
ciecierzyca
ch'yeh-ch'yeh-<u>zhyh</u>-tsah

corn
kukurydza
kuh-kuh-<u>ryh</u>-dzah

cucumber
ogórek
oh-<u>guh</u>-rehk

eggplant
bakłażan
bah-<u>kwah</u>-zhahn

garlic
czosnek
<u>chohs</u>-nehk

lentils
soczewica
soh-cheh-<u>vee</u>-tsah

lettuce
sałata
sah-<u>wah</u>-tah

mushroom
grzyb/pieczarka
gzhyhp/pyeh-<u>chahr</u>-kah

okra
okra
<u>oh</u>-krah

olives
oliwki
oh-<u>lee</u>-fkee

onion
cebula
tseh-<u>buh</u>-lah

peas
groszek
<u>groh</u>-shehk

pepper
papryka
pah-<u>pryh</u>-kah

potato
ziemniak
<u>zh'yehm</u>-n'yahk

radish
rzodkiewka
zhoht-<u>kyehf</u>-kah

spinach
szpinak
<u>shpee</u>-nahk

sweet potato
słodki ziemniak
<u>swoht</u>-kee <u>zh'yehm</u>-n'yahk

tomato
pomidor
poh-<u>mee</u>-dohr

Fruits and Nuts

apricot
morela
moh-<u>reh</u>-lah

apple
jabłko
<u>yahp</u>-koh

banana
banan
<u>bah</u>-nahn

blueberry
borówka/jagoda
boh-<u>ruhf</u>-kah/yah-<u>goh</u>-dah

cashew
orzech nerkowca
<u>oh</u>-zhehh nehr-<u>kohf</u>-tsah

cherry
czereśnia
cheh-<u>rehsh'</u>-n'yah

Clementine
klementynka
kleh-mehn-<u>tyhn</u>-kah

mandarin
mandarynka
mahn-dah-<u>ryhn</u>-kah

coconut
orzech kokosowy
<u>oh</u>-zhehh koh-koh-<u>soh</u>-vyh

melon
melon
<u>meh</u>-lohn

date
daktyl
<u>dahk</u>-tyhl

orange
pomarańcza
poh-mah-<u>rahn'</u>-chah

fig
figa
<u>fee</u>-gah

peanut
orzeszek ziemny
oh-<u>zheh</u>-shehk <u>zh'yehm</u>-nyh

grape
winogrono
vee-noh-<u>groh</u>-noh

peach
brzoskwinia
bzhoh-<u>skfee</u>-n'yah

grapefruit
grejpfrut
<u>grehyp</u>-fruht

pear
gruszka
<u>gruh</u>-shkah

lemon
cytryna
tsyh-<u>tryh</u>-nah

pineapple
ananas
ah-<u>nah</u>-nahs

lime
limonka
lee-<u>mohn</u>-kah

plum
śliwka
<u>sh'lee</u>-fkah

pomegranate
granat
<u>grah</u>-naht

raspberry
malina
mah-<u>lee</u>-nah

strawberry
truskawka
truh-<u>skahf</u>-kah

tangerine
mandarynka
mahn-dah-<u>ryhn</u>-kah

walnut
orzech włoski
<u>oh</u>-zhehh <u>vwoh</u>-skee

watermelon
arbuz
<u>ahr</u>-buhs

Meat

beef
wołowina
voh-woh-<u>vee</u>-nah

burger
hamburger
hahm-<u>buhr</u>-gehr

chicken
kurczak
<u>kuhr</u>-chahk

duck
kaczka
<u>kah</u>-chkah

goat
koźle
mięso/koźlina
<u>koh</u>-zh'leh <u>myehn</u>-soh/koh-<u>zh'lee</u>-nah

ham
szynka
<u>shyhn</u>-kah

lamb
jagnię
<u>yahg</u>-n'yeh

pork
wieprzowina
vyeh-pshoh-<u>vee</u>-nah

turkey
indyk
<u>een</u>-dyhk

rabbit
królik
<u>kruh</u>-leek

veal
cielęcina
ch'yeh-lehn-<u>ch'ee</u>-nah

steak
stek
stehk

Seafood

calamari
kałamarnica
kah-wah-mahr-<u>n'yee</u>-tsah

octopus
ośmiornica
osh'-myohr-<u>n'yee</u>-tsah

crab
krab
krahp

salmon
łosoś
<u>woh</u>-sohsh'

fish
ryba
<u>ryh</u>-bah

shrimp
krewetka
kreh-<u>veh</u>-tkah

lobster
homar
<u>hoh</u>-mahr

Dessert

cake	ice cream
ciasto	**lody**
<u>ch'yah</u>-stoh	<u>loh</u>-dyh

cookie
kruche ciasteczko
<u>kruh</u>-heh ch'yah-
<u>steh</u>-chkoh

Drinks

Non-alcoholic drinks

apple juice
sok jabłkowy
sohk yahp-<u>koh</u>-vyh

coffee (black)
kawa (czarna)
<u>kah</u>-vah (<u>chahr</u>-nah)

coffee with milk
kawa z mlekiem
<u>kah</u>-vah <u>zmleh</u>-kyehm

hot chocolate
gorąca czekolada
goh-<u>rohn</u>-tsah cheh-koh-<u>lah</u>-dah

juice
sok
sohk

lemonade
lemoniada
leh-moh-<u>n'yah</u>-dah

milk
mleko
<u>mleh</u>-koh

mineral water
woda mineralna
<u>voh</u>-dah mee-neh-<u>rahl</u>-nah

orange juice
sok pomarańczowy
sohk poh-mah-rahn'-<u>choh</u>-vyh

sparkling water
woda gazowana
<u>voh</u>-dah gah-zoh-<u>vah</u>-nah

soft drink
napój bezalkoholowy
<u>nah</u>-puhy behz-ahl-koh-hoh-<u>loh</u>-vyh

soymilk
mleko sojowe
<u>mleh</u>-koh soh-<u>yoh</u>-veh

tea
herbata
hehr-<u>bah</u>-tah

Alcoholic drinks

beer ...
piwo ...
<u>pee</u>-voh ...

   bottled
   butelkowe
   buh-tehl-<u>koh</u>-veh

   draft
   beczkowe
   beh-<u>chkoh</u>-veh

   canned
   w puszce
   <u>fpuhsh</u>-tseh

brandy
brandy/koniak
<u>brehn</u>-dyh/<u>koh</u>-n'yahk

champagne
szampan
<u>shahm</u>-pahn

cocktail
koktajl
<u>kohk</u>-tahyl

gin
gin
djeen

liqueur
likier
<u>lee</u>-kyehr

margarita
margarita
mahr-gah-<u>ree</u>-tah

martini
martini
mahr-<u>tee</u>-n'yee

vodka
wódka
<u>vuht</u>-kah

rum
rum
ruhm

scotch
szkocka (whisky)
<u>shkoh</u>-tskah (<u>wees</u>- kee)

tequila
tequila
teh-<u>kee</u>-lah

vermouth
wermut
<u>vehr</u>-muht

whisky
whisky
<u>wees</u>-kee

wine
wina
<u>vee</u>-nah

> red wine
> **czerwonego wina**
> chehr-voh-<u>neh</u>-goh <u>vee</u>-nah

> white wine
> **białego wina**
> byah-<u>weh</u>-goh <u>vee</u>-nah

> rosé wine
> **różowego wina**
> ruh-zhoh-<u>veh</u>-goh <u>vee</u>-nah

> dessert wine
> **wina deserowego**
> <u>vee</u>-nah deh-seh-roh-<u>veh</u>-goh

> dry wine
> **wytrawnego wina**
> vyh-trahv-<u>neh</u>-goh <u>vee</u>-nah

> champagne
> **szampana**
> shahm-<u>pah</u>-nah

Grocery Shopping

Where is the nearest market/supermarket?
Gdzie jest najbliższy targ/supermarket?
gdj'yeh yehst nahy-<u>bleesh</u>-shyh tahrg/suh-
pehr-<u>mahr</u>-keht

Where are the baskets/carts?
Gdzie są koszyki/wózki?
gdj'yeh sohm koh-<u>shyh</u>-kee/<u>vuhs</u>-kee

I'd like some of this/that.
Poproszę trochę tego/tamtego.
poh-<u>proh</u>-sheh <u>troh</u>-heh <u>teh</u>-goh/tahm-
<u>teh</u>-goh

Can I have …?
Poproszę …
poh-<u>proh</u>-sheh …

A (half) kilo of …
(pół) kilo …
(puhw) <u>kee</u>-loh …

A liter of …
litr …
leetr …

A piece of …
kawałek …
kah-<u>vah</u>-wehk …

A little more/less.
Trochę więcej/mniej.
<u>troh</u>-heh <u>vyehn</u>-tsehy/mn'yehy

Where can I find …?
Gdzie znajdę …?
gdj'yeh <u>znahy</u>-deh …

cleaning products
środki czystości
sh'<u>roh</u>-tkee chyh-<u>stoh</u>-sh'ch'yee

dairy products
nabiał
<u>nah</u>-byahw

the deli section
delikatesy
deh-lee-kah-<u>teh</u>-syh

fresh produce
świeże produkty rolne
sh'<u>fyeh</u>-zheh proh-<u>duh</u>-ktyh <u>rohl</u>-neh

fresh fish
świeże ryby
sh'<u>fyeh</u>-zheh <u>ryh</u>-byh

frozen foods
mrożonki
mroh-<u>zhohn</u>-kee

household goods
artykuły gospodarstwa domowego
ahr-tyh-<u>kuh</u>-wyh gohs-poh-<u>dahr</u>-stfah
doh-moh-<u>veh</u>-goh

meats
mięso
<u>myehn</u>-soh

poultry
drób
druhp

I need to go to …
Muszę iść …
<u>muh</u>-sheh eesh'ch '…

the bakery
do piekarni
doh pyeh-<u>kahr</u>-n'yee

the butcher shop
do sklepu mięsnego
doh <u>skleh</u>-puh myehn-<u>sneh</u>-goh

convenience store
sklepik ca³odobowy
<u>skleh</u>-peek tsah-woh-doh-<u>boh</u>-vyh

the fish market
na targ rybny
nah tahrg <u>ryh</u>-bnyh

the produce market
na targ
nah tahrg

the supermarket
do supermarketu
doh suh-pehr-mahr-<u>keh</u>-tuh

gram(s)
gram(y)
grahm(<u>grah</u>-myh)

kilo(s)
kilo
<u>kee</u>-loh

a piece of ...
kawałek ...
kah-<u>vah</u>-wehk ...

two pieces of ...
dwa kawałki ...
dvah kah-<u>vahw</u>-kee ...

Can I have a little/lot of ... please?
Poproszę troszkę/dużo ...
poh-<u>proh</u>-sheh <u>troh</u>-shkeh/<u>duh</u>-zhoh ...

That's enough, thanks.
Dziękuję, wystarczy.
dj'yehn-<u>kuh</u>-yeh, vyh-<u>stahr</u>-chyh

a bottle
butelka
buh-<u>tehl</u>-kah

a jar
słoik
<u>swoh</u>-yeek

You Might See

Termin przydatności do spożycia ...
or
Data ważności ...
Sell by ...

Przechowywać w lodówce.
Keep refrigerated.

Spożyć w ciągu ... dni po otwarciu.
Eat within ... days of opening.

Przed spożyciem podgrzać.
Reheat before consuming.

koszerne
kosher

organiczne
organic

może być spożywane przez wegetarian
Suitable for vegetarians.

można podgrzewać w kuchence
mikrofalowej
microwaveable

a packet
paczka,torebka
<u>pahch</u>-kah/toh-<u>rehp</u>-kah

a box
pudełko
puh-<u>dehw</u>-koh

Paying for Groceries

Where is the checkout?
Gdzie jest kasa?
gdj'yeh yehst <u>kah</u>-sah

Do I pay here?
Czy mogę tu zapłacić?
chyh <u>moh</u>-geh tuh zah-<u>pwah</u>-ch'eech'

Do you accept credit cards?
Czy mogę zapłacić kartą kredytową?
chyh <u>moh</u>-geh zah-<u>pwah</u>-ch'eech' <u>kahr</u>-
tohm kreh-dyh-<u>toh</u>-vohm

I'll pay in cash / by credit card.
Zapłacę gotówką / kartą kredytową.
zah-<u>pwah</u>-tseh goh-<u>tuhf</u>-kohm / <u>kahr</u>-
tohm kreh-dyh-<u>toh</u>-vohm

Paper/Plastic, please.
Poproszę papierową/plastikową.
poh-<u>proh</u>-sheh pah-pyeh-<u>roh</u>-vohm/plah-
stee-<u>koh</u>-vohm

I don't need a bag.
Nie potrzebuję torby.
n'yeh poh-tsheh-<u>buh</u>-yeh <u>tohr</u>-byh

I have my own bag.
Mam własną torbę.
mahm <u>vwah</u>-snohm <u>tohr</u>-beh

MONEY

Currency and Conversion

Where can I exchange money?
Gdzie mogę wymienić pieniądze?
gdj'yeh <u>moh</u>-geh vyh-<u>myeh</u>-n'eech' pyeh-
<u>n'yohn</u>-dzeh

Is there a currency exchange office nearby?
Czy w pobliżu jest kantor?
chyh fpoh-<u>blee</u>-zhuh yehst <u>kahn</u>-tohr

I'd like to exchange … for …
**Chciałbym/Chciałabym wymienić …
na …**
<u>hch'yahw</u>-byhm/hch'yah-<u>wah</u>-byhm vyh-
<u>myeh</u>-n'eech' … nah …

    U.S. dollars
    dolary amerykańskie
    do-<u>lah</u>-ryh ah-meh-ryh-<u>kahn'</u>-skyeh

    pounds
    funty
    <u>fuhn</u>-tyh

    Canadian dollars
    dolary kanadyjskie
    do-<u>lah</u>-ryh kah-nah-<u>dyhy</u>-skyeh

    Euros
    euro
    <u>ehw</u>-roh

traveler's checks
czeki podróżne
<u>cheh</u>-kee pohd-<u>ruhzh</u>-neh

What is the exchange rate?
Jaki jest kurs wymiany?
<u>yah</u>-kee yehst kuhrs vyh-<u>myah</u>-nyh

What is the commission charge?
Jaka jest prowizja?
<u>yah</u>-kah yehst proh-<u>veez</u>-yah

Can you write that down for me?
Czy może mi to pan/pani zapisać?
czyh <u>moh</u>-zheh mee toh <u>pahn</u>/<u>pah</u>-nee
zah-<u>pee</u>-sahch'

Banking

Is there a bank nearby?
Czy jest tu w pobliżu bank?
chyh yehst tuh fpoh-<u>blee</u>-zhuh bahnk

Where is the nearest ATM?
Gdzie jest najbliższy bankomat?
gdj'yeh yehst nahy-<u>blee</u>-zhshyh bahn-<u>koh</u>-maht

What time does the bank open/close?
O której otwierają/zamykają bank?
oh <u>ktuh</u>-rehy oht-fyeh-<u>rah</u>-yohm/zah-myh-<u>kah</u>-yohm bahnk

You Might See

włóż kartę insert card	**rachunek bieżący** checking
numer PIN PIN number	**rachunek oszczędnościowy** savings
wprowadź enter	
	wypłata withdrawal
popraw clear	
	wpłata deposit
anuluj cancel	
potwierdzenie receipt	

Can I cash this check here?
Czy mogę zrealizować tu ten czek?
chyh <u>moh</u>-geh zreh-ah-lee-<u>zoh</u>-vahch' tuh
tehn chehk

I would like to get a cash advance.
Chciałbym/Chciałabym dostać zaliczkę w gotówce.
hch'<u>yahw</u>-byhm/hch'yah-<u>wah</u>-byhm <u>doh</u>-
stahch' zah-<u>lee</u>-chkeh fgoh-<u>tuhf</u>-tseh

I would like to cash some traveler's checks.

Chciałbym/Chciałabym zrealizować czeki podróżne.

<u>hch'yahw</u>-byhm/hch'yah-<u>wah</u>-byhm zreh-ah-lee-<u>zoh</u>-vahch' <u>cheh</u>-kee pohd-<u>ruhzh</u>-neh

I've lost my traveler's checks.

Zgubiłem/Zgubiłam czeki podróżne.

zguh-<u>bee</u>-wehm/zguh-<u>bee</u>-wahm <u>cheh</u>-kee pohd-<u>ruhzh</u>-neh

The ATM ate my card.

Bankomat połknął moją kartę.

bahn-<u>koh</u>-maht <u>pohw</u>-knohw <u>moh</u>-yohm <u>kahr</u>-teh

SHOPPING & SERVICES

Shopping

Where's the …?
Gdzie jest …
gdj'yeh yehst …

> antiques store
> **sklep z antykami**
> sklehp zahn-tyh-<u>kah</u>-mee

> bakery
> **piekarnia**
> pyeh-<u>kahr</u>-n'yah

> bank
> **bank**
> bahnk

> bookstore
> **księgarnia**
> ksh'yehn-<u>gahr</u>-n'yah

> camera store
> **sklep fotograficzny**
> sklehp foh-toh-grah-<u>feech</u>-nyh

> clothing store
> **sklep odzieżowy**
> sklehp oh-dj'yeh-<u>zhoh</u>-vyh

> convenience store
> **sklepik całodobowy**
> <u>skleh</u>-peek tsah-woh-doh-<u>boh</u>-vyh

delicatessen
delikatesy
deh-lee-kah-<u>teh</u>-syh

department store
dom towarowy
dohm toh-vah-<u>roh</u>-vyh

electronics store
sklep z elektroniką
sklehp zeh-lehk-troh-<u>n'ee</u>-kohm

gift shop
sklep z upominkami
sklehp zuh-poh-meen-<u>kah</u>-mee

health food store
sklep ze zdrową żywnością
sklehp zeh <u>zdroh</u>-vohm zhyhv-<u>nohsh'</u>-
ch'yohm

jeweler
jubiler
yuh-<u>bee</u>-lehr

liquor store
sklep monopolowy
sklehp moh-noh-poh-<u>loh</u>-vyh

mall
centrum handlowe
<u>tsehn</u>-truhm hahn-<u>dloh</u>-veh

market
targ
tahrg

music store
sklep muzyczny
sklehp muh-<u>zyh</u>-chnyh

pastry shop
cukiernia
tsuh-<u>kyehr</u>-n'yah

pharmacy
apteka
ahp-<u>teh</u>-kah

shoe store
sklep obuwniczy
sklehp oh-buhv-<u>n'ee</u>-chyh

souvenir store
sklep z pamiątkami
sklehp spahm-yohnt-<u>kah</u>-mee

supermarket
supermarket
suh-pehr-<u>mahr</u>-keht
(*see Grocery shopping, page 99-104*)

toy store
sklep z zabawkami
sklehp z zah-bahf-<u>kah</u>-mee

Getting help

Where's the ...?
Gdzie jest ...?
gdj'yeh yehst ...

> cashier
> **kasa**
> <u>kah</u>-sah

> escalator
> **schody ruchome**
> <u>s hoh</u>-dyh ruh-<u>hoh</u>-meh

> elevator
> **winda**
> <u>veen</u>-dah

> fitting room
> **przymierzalnia**
> pshyh-myeh-<u>zhahl</u>-n'yah

> store map
> **tablica informacyjna**
> tah-<u>blee</u>-tsah een-fohr-mah-<u>tsyhy</u>-nah

Can you help me?
Czy może mi pan/pani pomóc?
chyh <u>moh</u>-zheh mee pahn/<u>pah</u>-nee <u>poh</u>-muhts

I'm looking for ...
Szukam ...
<u>shuh</u>-kahm ...

Where can I find …?
Gdzie znajdę …?
gdj'yeh <u>znahy</u>-deh …

I would like …
Chciałbym/Chciałabym …
hch'yahw-byhm/<u>hch'yah</u>-<u>wah</u>-byhm …

I'm just looking.
Tylko się rozglądam.
<u>tyhl</u>-koh sh'yeh rohz-glohn-dahm

Preferences

I want something …
Chciałbym/Chciałabym coś …
<u>hch'yahw</u>-byhm/<u>hch'yah</u>-wah-byhm tsohsh' …

big	small
dużego	**małego**
duh-<u>zheh</u>-goh	mah-<u>weh</u>-goh
cheap	expensive
taniego	**drogiego**
tah-<u>n'yeh</u>-goh	droh-<u>gyeh</u>-goh
local	
miejscowego	
myehy-stsoh-<u>veh</u>-goh	
nice	
ładnego	
wahd-<u>neh</u>-goh	

I can only pay …
Mogę tylko zapłacić …
<u>moh</u>-geh tyhl-koh zah-<u>pwah</u>-ch'eech'…

Is it authentic?
Czy to jest oryginalne?
chyh toh yehst oh-ryh-gee-<u>nahl</u>-neh

Can you show me that?
Może mi pan/pani to pokazać?
chyh <u>moh</u>-zheh mee pahn/<u>pah</u>-nee toh
poh-<u>kah</u>-zahch'

Can I see it?
Czy mogę to zobaczyć?
chyh <u>moh</u>-geh toh zoh-<u>bah</u>-chyhch'

Do you have any others?
Czy mają państwo jakieś inne?
chyh <u>mah</u>-yohm <u>pahn'</u>-stfoh <u>yah</u>-kyehsh'
<u>een</u>-neh

Can you ship/wrap this?
**Czy może pan/pani to wysłać/zapako-
wać?**
chyh <u>moh</u>-zheh pahn/<u>pah</u>-n'ee toh <u>vyh</u>-
swahch'/zah-pah-<u>koh</u>-vahch'

Do you have this in …?
Czy mają państwo to w kolorze …?
chyh mah-yohm pahn'-stfoh toh fkoh-<u>loh</u>-
zheh …

> black
> **czarnym**
> <u>chahr</u>-nyhm
>
> blue
> **niebieskim**
> n'yeh-<u>byehs</u>-keem
>
> brown
> **brązowym**
> brohn-<u>zoh</u>-vyhm
>
> gray
> **szarym**
> <u>shah</u>-ryhm
>
> green
> **zielonym**
> zh'yeh-<u>loh</u>-nyhm
>
> orange
> **pomarańczowym**
> poh-mah-rahn'-<u>choh</u>-vyhm
>
> pink
> **różowym**
> ruh-<u>zhoh</u>-vyhm
>
> purple
> **fioletowym**
> fyoh-leh-<u>toh</u>-vyhm

red
czerwonym
chehr-<u>voh</u>-nyhm

white
białym
<u>byah</u>-wyhm

yellow
żółtym
<u>zhuhw</u>-tyhm

Do you have anything lighter/darker?
**Czy mają państwo coś jaśniejszego/
ciemniejszego?**
chyh <u>mah</u>-yohm <u>pahn'</u>-stfoh tsohsh' yahsh'-
nyehy-<u>sheh</u>-goh/ch'yehm-nyehy-<u>sheh</u>-goh

Haggling

That's too expensive.
To za drogo.
toh zah <u>droh</u>-goh

Do you have anything cheaper?
Czy mają państwo coś tańszego?
chyh <u>mah</u>-yohm <u>pahn'</u>-stfoh tsohsh' tahn'-
<u>sheh</u>-goh

I'll give you …
Zapłacę panu/pani …
zah-<u>pwah</u>-tseh <u>pah</u>-nuh/<u>pah</u>-n'ee …

I'll have to think about it.
Muszę się nad tym zastanowić.
muh-sheh sh'yeh naht tyhm zahs-tah-noh-veech'

Is that your best price?
To najniższa cena?
toh nahy-n'eezh-shah tseh-nah

Can you give me a discount?
Da mi pan/pani zniżkę?
dah mee pahn/pah-n'ee zn'eezh-keh

Deciding

That's not quite what I want.
To nie to, czego szukam.
toh n'yeh toh cheh-goh shuh-kahm

I don't like it.
To mi się nie podoba.
toh mee sh'yeh n'yeh poh-doh-bah

It's too expensive.
To jest za drogie.
toh yehst zah droh-gyeh

I'll take it.
Wezmę to.
vehz-meh toh

Paying

Where can I pay?
Gdzie mogę zapłacić?
gdj'yeh <u>moh</u>-geh zah-<u>pwah</u>-ch'eech'

How much?
Ile to kosztuje?
<u>ee</u>-leh toh kohsh-<u>tuh</u>-yeh

Does the price include tax?
Czy podatek jest wliczony?
chyh poh-<u>dah</u>-tehk yehst vlee-<u>choh</u>-nyh

I'll pay in cash / by credit card.
Zapłacę gotówką / kartą kredytową.
zah-<u>pwah</u>-tseh goh-<u>tuhf</u>-kohm / <u>kahr</u>-tohm kreh-dyh-<u>toh</u>-vohm

Do you accept traveler's checks?
Czy przyjmują państwo czeki podróżne?
chyh pshyhy-<u>muh</u>-yohm <u>pahn'</u>-stfoh <u>cheh</u>-kee poh-<u>druhzh</u>-neh

Can I have a receipt?
Czy mogę prosić o paragon?
chyh <u>moh</u>-geh <u>proh</u>-sh'eech' oh pah-<u>rah</u>-gohn

Complaining

This is broken.
To jest zepsute.
toh yehst zeh-<u>psuh</u>-teh

It doesn't work.
To nie działa.
toh n'yeh <u>dj'yah</u>-wah

I'd like ...
Chciałbym/Chciałabym ...
<u>hch'yahw</u>-byhm/hch'yah-<u>wah</u>-byhm ...

> to exchange this
> **to wymienić**
> toh vyh-<u>myeh</u>-n'eech'

> to return this
> **to oddać**
> toh <u>ohd</u>-dahch'

> a refund
> **zwrot pieniędzy**
> zvroht pyeh-<u>n'ehn</u>-dzyh

> to speak to the manager
> **porozmawiać z kierownikiem**
> poh-rohz-<u>mah</u>-vyahch' skyeh-rohv-
> <u>n'ee</u>-kyehm

Services

barber
fryzjer męski
<u>fryh</u>-zyehr <u>mehn</u>-skee

dry cleaner
pralnia chemiczna
<u>prahl</u>-n'yah heh-<u>meech</u>-nah

hair salon
salon fryzjerski
<u>sah</u>-lohn fryh-<u>zyehr</u>-skee

laundromat
pralnia samoobsługowa
<u>prahl</u>-n'yah sah-moh-ohp-swuh-<u>goh</u>-vah

nail salon
zakład manicure
<u>zahk</u>-wahd mah-<u>n'ee</u>-kyuhr

spa
spa
spah

travel agency
biuro podróży
<u>byuh</u>-roh pohd-<u>ruh</u>-zhyh

Hair Salon / Barber

I'd like a …
Chciałbym/Chciałabym prosić o …
hch'yahw-byhm/hch'yah-<u>wah</u>-byhm <u>proh</u>-sh'eech' oh …

> color
> **ufarbowanie**
> uh-fahr-boh-<u>vah</u>-n'yeh

> cut
> **ostrzyżenie**
> ohs-tshyh-<u>zheh</u>-n'yeh

> perm
> **trwałą**
> <u>trfah</u>-wohm

> shave
> **golenie**
> goh-<u>leh</u>-n'yeh

> trim
> **podcięcie włosów**
> poht-<u>ch'yen'</u>-ch'yeh <u>vwoh</u>-suhf

Cut about this much off.
Proszę obciąć mniej więcej tyle.
<u>proh</u>-sheh <u>ohp</u>-ch'yohnch' mnyehy <u>vyehn</u>-tsehy <u>tyh</u>-leh

Can I have a shampoo?
Czy mogę prosić o umycie głowy?
chyh <u>moh</u>-geh <u>proh</u>-sh'eech' oh uh-<u>myh</u>-ch'yeh <u>gwoh</u>-vyh

Cut it shorter here.
Tu proszę krócej obciąć.
tuh <u>proh</u>-sheh <u>kruh</u>-tsehy <u>ohp</u>-ch'yohnch'

Leave it longer here.
Tu proszę zostawić dłuższe.
tuh <u>proh</u>-sheh zoh-<u>stah</u>-veech' <u>dwuhsh</u>-sheh

Spa

I'd like a …
Proszę …
<u>proh</u>-sheh …

> facial
> **zabieg na twarz**
> <u>zah</u>-byehk nah tfahsh

> manicure
> **manicure**
> mah-<u>n'ee</u>-kyuhr

> massage
> **masaż**
> <u>mah</u>-sahsh

> pedicure
> **pedicure**
> peh-<u>dee</u>-kyuhr

> wax
> **depilację woskiem**
> deh-pee-<u>lahts</u>-yeh <u>vohs</u>-kyehm

aromatherapy
aromaterapia
ah-roh-mah-teh-<u>rah</u>-pyah

acupuncture
akupunktura
ah-kuh-puhn-<u>ktuh</u>-rahas above

sauna
sauna
<u>sahw</u>-nah

Laundry

Is there …?
Czy mają państwo …?
chyh mah-yohm <u>pahn'</u>-stfoh …

> full-service
> **pełną obsługę**
> <u>pehw</u>-nohm ohp-<u>swuh</u>-geh

> self-service
> **samoobsługę**
> sah-moh-ohp-<u>swuh</u>-geh

> same-day service
> **pranie w ciągu jednego dnia**
> <u>prah</u>-n'yeh <u>fch'yohn</u>-guh yehd-<u>neh</u>-goh dn'yah

Do you have …?
Czy mają państwo …
chyh <u>mah</u>-yohm <u>pahn'</u>-stfoh …

bleach
wybielacz
vyh-<u>byeh</u>-lahch

change
bilon
<u>bee</u>-lohn

detergent
detergent
deh-<u>tehr</u>-gehnt

dryer sheets
chusteczki do suszarki
huh-<u>stehch</u>-kee doh suh-<u>shahr</u>-kee

fabric softener
środek do zmiękczania tkanin
<u>sh'roh</u>-dehk doh zmyehn<u>k-chah</u>-n'yah
<u>tkah</u>-n'een

This machine is broken.
Ta maszyna jest zepsuta.
tah mah-<u>shyh</u>-nah yehst zeh-<u>psuh</u>-tah

How does this work?
Jak się ją obsługuje?
yahk sh'yeh yohm ohp-swuh-<u>guh</u>-yeh

When will my clothes be ready?
Kiedy będą gotowe moje ubrania?
kyeh-dyh <u>behn</u>-dohm goh-<u>toh</u>-veh
<u>moh</u>-yeh uh-<u>brah</u>-n'yah

whites
białe
<u>byah</u>-weh

colors
kolory
koh-<u>loh</u>-ryh

delicates
delikatne
deh-lee-<u>kaht</u>-neh

hand wash
prać ręcznie
prahch' <u>rehnch</u>-n'yeh

gentle cycle
delikatny cykl
deh-lee-<u>kaht</u>-nyh tsyhkl

dry clean only
czyścić chemicznie
<u>chyhsh'</u>-ch'eech' heh-<u>mee</u>ch-n'yeh

cold water
zimna woda
<u>zh'eem</u>-nah <u>voh</u>-dah

warm water
ciepła woda
<u>ch'yeh</u>-pwah <u>voh</u>-dah

hot water
gorąca woda
goh-<u>rohn</u>-tsah <u>voh</u>-dah

SOCIAL INTERACTION

Introductions

Hello.	Hi!
Dzień dobry.	**Cześć!**
dj'yehn' <u>dohb</u>-ryh	chehsh'ch

Sir	Madam
Proszę pana	**Proszę pani**
<u>proh</u>-sheh <u>pah</u>-nah	<u>proh</u>-sheh <u>pah</u>-nee

Mr.	Ms./Mrs.
panie	**pani**
<u>pah</u>-n'yeh	<u>pah</u>-nee

Dr. (*medical*)
panie doktorze / pani doktor
<u>pah</u>-n'yeh dohk-<u>toh</u>-zheh / <u>pah</u>-nee <u>dohk</u>-tohr

Dr. (*academic*)
panie doktorze / pani doktor
<u>pah</u>-n'yeh dohk-<u>toh</u>-zheh / <u>pah</u>-nee <u>dohk</u>-tohr

What's your name?
Jak się pan/pani nazywa?
yahk sh'yeh pahn/<u>pah</u>-nee nah-<u>zyh</u>-vah

My name is ...
Nazywam się ...
nah-<u>zyh</u>-vahm sh'yeh ...

Pleased to meet you.
Miło mi pana/panią poznać.
<u>mee</u>-woh mee <u>pah</u>-nah/<u>pah</u>-n'yohm <u>pohz</u>-nahch'

Nationality

Where are you from?
Skąd pan/pani jest?
skohnt pahn/<u>pah</u>-nee yehst

I'm from …
Jestem z …
<u>yehs</u>-tehm z …

>the USA
>**USA**
>uh-ehs-ah

>Great Britain
>**Wielkiej Brytanii**
><u>vyehl</u>-kyehy bryh-<u>tah</u>-n'ee

>Canada
>**Kanady**
>kah-<u>nah</u>-dyh

>Ireland
>**Irlandii**
>eer-<u>lahn</u>-dee

>Australia
>**Australii**
>ahw-<u>strah</u>-lee

New Zealand
Nowej Zelandii
<u>noh</u>-vehy zeh-<u>lahn</u>-dee

I'm ...
Jestem ...
<u>yehs</u>-tehm ...

American
Amerykaninem / Amerykanką
ah-meh-ryh-kah-<u>n'ee</u>-nehm /
ah-meh-ryh-<u>kahn</u>-kohm

English
Anglikiem / Angielką
ahn-<u>glee</u>-kyehm / ahn-<u>gyehl</u>-kohm

Welsh
Walijczykiem / Walijką
vah-leey-<u>chyh</u>-kyehm / vah-<u>leey</u>-kohm

Scottish
Szkotem / Szkotką
<u>shkoh</u>-tehm / <u>shkoht</u>-kohm

Irish
Irlandczykiem / Irlandką
eer-lahnt-<u>chyh</u>-kyehm / eer-<u>lahnt</u>-kohm

Canadian
Kanadyjczykiem / Kanadyjką
kah-nah-dyhy-<u>chyh</u>-kyehm / kah-nah-
<u>dyhy</u>-kohm

Australian
Australijczykiem / Australijką
ahw-strah-leey-<u>chyh</u>-kyehm / ahw-
strah-<u>leey</u>-kohm

a New Zealander
Nowozelandczykiem/
Nowozelandką
noh-voh-zeh-lahnt-<u>chyh</u>-kyehm /
noh-voh-zeh-<u>lahnt</u>-kohm

Where were you born?
Gdzie się pan(i) urodził/urodziła?
gdj'yeh sh'yeh pahn(pah-nee) uh-<u>roh</u>-dj'eew/
uh-roh-<u>dj'ee</u>-wah

I was born in …
Urodziłem/Urodziłam się w …
uh-roh-<u>dj'ee</u>-wehm/uh-roh-<u>dj'ee</u>-wahm
sh'yeh v …

Family

This is …
To jest …
toh yehst …

> my husband
> **mój mąż**
> muhy mohnsh

> my wife
> **moja żona**
> <u>moh</u>-yah <u>zhoh</u>-nah

> my partner
> **mój partner / moja partnerka**
> muhy <u>pahrt</u>-nehr / <u>moh</u>-yah pahrt-
> <u>nehr</u>-kah

my mother
moja matka
<u>moh</u>-yah <u>maht</u>-kah

my father
mój ojciec
muhy <u>ohy</u>-ch'yehts

my older brother
mój starszy brat
muhy <u>stahr</u>-shyh braht

my younger brother
mój młodszy brat
muhy <u>mwoht</u>-shyh braht

my older sister
moja starsza siostra
<u>moh</u>-yah <u>stahr</u>-shah <u>sh'yoh</u>-strah

my younger sister
moja młodsza siostra
<u>moh</u>-yah <u>mwoht</u>-shah <u>sh'yoh</u>-strah

my cousin
mój kuzyn (*masc.*)
muhy <u>kuh</u>-zyhn
moja kuzynka (*fem.*)
<u>moh</u>-yah kuh-<u>zyhn</u>-kah

my aunt
moja ciocia
<u>moh</u>-yah <u>ch'yoh</u>-ch'yah

my uncle
mój wujek
muhy <u>vuh</u>-yehk

my grandmother
moja babcia
moh-yah bahp-ch'yah

my grandfather
mój dziadek
muhy dj'yah-dehk

my mother-in-law
moja teściowa
moh-yah tehsh'-ch'yoh-vah

my father-in-law
mój teść
muhy tehsh'ch'

my brother-in-law
mój szwagier
muhy shfah-gyehr

my sister-in-law
moja szwagierka (*sister of wife or
husband*)
moh-yah shfah-gyehr-kah
moja bratowa (*wife of brother*)

my step-mother
moja macocha
moh-yah mah-tsoh-hah

my step-father
mój ojczym
muhy ohy-chyhm

my step-sister
moja przyrodnia siostra
moh-yah pshyh-rohd-n'yah sh'yoh-strah

my step-brother
mój przyrodni brat
muhy pshyh-<u>rohd</u>-n'ee braht

Work and School

What do you do?
Czym się pan/pani zajmuje?
chyhm sh'yeh pahn/<u>pah</u>-nee zahy-<u>muh</u>-yeh

I'm a student.
Studiuję.
stuhd-<u>yuh</u>-yeh

I work for …
Pracuję w …
prah-<u>tsuh</u>-yeh v …

I'm retired.
Jestem na emeryturze.
<u>yehs</u>-tehm nah eh-meh-ryh-<u>tuh</u>-zheh

Age

How old are you?
Ile ma pan/pani lat?
<u>ee</u>-leh mah pahn/<u>pah</u>-nee laht

I am … years old.
Mam … lat.
mahm … laht

Religion

What religion are you?
Jakiego jest pan/pani wyznania?
yah-<u>kyeh</u>-goh yehst pahn/<u>pah</u>-nee vyhz-<u>nah</u>-n'yah

I am …
Jestem …
<u>yehs</u>-tehm …

agnostic
agnostykiem / agnostyczką
ah-gnoh-<u>styh</u>-kyehm / ah-gnoh-<u>styhch</u>-kohm

atheist
ateistą / ateistką
ah-teh-<u>ees</u>-tohm / ah-teh-<u>eest</u>-kohm

Buddhist
buddystą / buddystką
buhd-<u>dyhs</u>-tohm / buhd-<u>dyhst</u>-kohm

Catholic
katolikiem / katoliczką
kah-toh-<u>lee</u>-kyehm / kah-toh-<u>leech</u>-kohm

Christian
chrześcijaninem / chrześcijanką
hsheh-sh'ch'ee-yah-<u>nee</u>-nehm /
hsheh-sh'ch'ee-<u>yahn</u>-kohm

Hindu
hinduistą / hinduistką
heen-duh-<u>ees</u>-tohm / heen-duh-<u>eest</u>-kohm

Jewish
żydem / żydówką
zhyh-dehm / zyh-duhf-kohm

Muslim
muzułmaninem / muzułmanką
muh-zuhw-mah-nee-nehm /
muh-zuhw-mahn-kohm

Etiquette

How are you?
Jak się pan/pani ma?
yahk sh'yeh pahn/pah-nee mah

Fine, thanks.
Dziękuję, dobrze.
dj'yehn-kuh-yeh, dohb-zheh

And you?
A pan/pani?
ah pahn/pah-nee

Good morning.
Dzień dobry.
dj'yehn' dohb-ryh

Good afternoon.
Dzień dobry.
dj'yehn' dohb-ryh

Good evening.
Dobry wieczór.
dohb-ryh vyeh-chuhr

Good night.
Dobranoc.
doh-brah-nohts

See you later.
Na razie.
nah rah-zh'yeh

See you (soon).
Do zobaczenia (wkrótce).
doh zoh-bah-cheh-n'yah (fkruht-tseh)

See you tomorrow.
Do jutra.
doh yuh-trah

Goodbye.
Do widzenia.
doh vee-dzeh-n'yah

Welcome!
Witaj! (*sing*) / **Witajcie!** (*plural*)
vee-tahy / vee-tahy-ch'yeh

Please.
Proszę.
proh-sheh

Thank you.
Dziękuję.
dj'yehn-kuh-yeh

You're welcome.
Proszę bardzo.
<u>proh</u>-sheh <u>bahr</u>-dzoh

I'm sorry.
Przepraszam.
psheh-<u>prah</u>-shahm

Excuse me.
Przepraszam.
psheh-<u>prah</u>-shahm

Interests

Do you like …?
Czy lubi pan/pani …?
chyh <u>luh</u>-bee pahn/<u>pah</u>-nee …

> art
> **sztukę**
> <u>shtuh</u>-keh
>
> cinema
> **kino**
> <u>kee</u>-noh
>
> music
> **muzykę**
> muh-<u>zyh</u>-keh
>
> sports
> **sport**
> spohrt

theater
teatr
<u>teh</u>-ahtr

Yes, very much.
Tak, bardzo.
tahk, <u>bahr</u>-dzoh

Not really.
Niespecjalnie.
n'yeh-speh-<u>tsyahl</u>-n'yeh

A little.
Trochę.
<u>troh</u>-heh

I like …
Lubię …
<u>luh</u>-byeh …

I don't like …
Nie lubię …
n'yeh <u>luh</u>-byeh …

Leisure

Can you recommend …?
Czy może pan/pani polecić …
chyh <u>moh</u>-zheh pahn/<u>pah</u>-nee poh-<u>leh</u>-ch'eech' …

a book
jakąś książkę
<u>yah</u>-kohnsh' <u>ksh'yohn</u>-shkeh

a CD
jakąś płytę kompaktową / jakieś CD
<u>yah</u>-kohnsh' <u>pwyh</u>-teh kohm-pahk-<u>toh</u>-vohm / <u>yah</u>-kyehsh' see dee

an exhibit
jakąś wystawę
<u>yah</u>-kohnsh' vyh-<u>stah</u>-veh

a museum
jakieś muzeum
<u>yah</u>-kyehsh' muh-<u>zeh</u>-uhm

a film
jakiś film
<u>yah</u>-keesh' feelm

a play
jakąś sztukę
<u>yah</u>-kohnsh' <u>shtuh</u>-keh

What's playing tonight?
Co grają dziś wieczorem?
tsoh <u>grah</u>-yohm dj'eesh' vyeh-<u>choh</u>-rehm

I like … films.
Lubię …
<u>luh</u>-byeh …

action
filmy akcji
<u>feel</u>-myh <u>ahk</u>-tsyee

art
kino artystyczne
<u>kee</u>-noh ahr-tyh-<u>styh</u>-chneh

comedy
komedie
koh-<u>meh</u>-dyeh

drama
dramaty
drah-<u>mah</u>-tyh

foreign
filmy zagraniczne
<u>feel</u>-myh zah-grah-<u>nee</u>-chneh

horror
horrory
hohr-<u>roh</u>-ryh

indie
kino niezależne
<u>kee</u>-noh n'yeh-zah-<u>leh</u>-zhneh

musical
musicale
muh-zee-<u>kah</u>-leh

mystery
filmy kryminalne
<u>feel</u>-myh kryh-mee-<u>nahl</u>-neh

romance
romanse
roh-<u>mahn</u>-seh

suspense
filmy suspens
<u>feel</u>-myh <u>sahs</u>-pehns

What are the movie times?
O której są seanse?
oh <u>ktuh</u>-rehy sohm seh-<u>ahn</u>-seh

Sports

I like ...
Lubię ...
<u>luh</u>-byeh ...

hiking
piesze wycieczki
<u>pyeh</u>-sheh vyh-<u>ch'yeh</u>-chkee

bicycling
jazdę na rowerze
<u>yah</u>-zdeh nah roh-<u>veh</u>-zheh

boxing
boks
bohks

soccer
piłkę nożną
<u>peew</u>-keh <u>nohzh</u>-nohm

baseball
baseball
<u>behyz</u>-bohl

basketball
koszykówkę
koh-shyh-<u>kuhf</u>-keh

diving
nurkowanie
nuhr-koh-<u>vah</u>-n'yeh

football (American)
futbol amerykański
<u>fuht</u>-bohl ah-meh-ryh-<u>kahn</u>'-skee

golf
grę w golfa
greh v <u>gohl</u>-fah

martial arts
sztuki walki
<u>shtuh</u>-kee <u>vahl</u>-kee

swimming
pływanie
pwyh-<u>vah</u>-n'yeh

surfing
surfing
<u>sehr</u>-feeng

skiing
jazdę na nartach
<u>yah</u>-zdeh nah <u>nahr</u>-tahh

tennis
grę w tenisa
greh fteh-<u>nee</u>-sah

volleyball
grę w siatkówkę
greh fsh'yaht-<u>kuhf</u>-keh

When's the game?
Kiedy jest mecz?
<u>kyeh</u>-dyh yehst mehch

What's the score?
Jaki jest wynik?
<u>yah</u>-kee yehst <u>vyh</u>-n'eek

Who's winning?
Kto wygrywa?
ktoh vyh-<u>gryh</u>-vah

Do you want to play?
Chciałby pan/Chciałaby pani zagrać?
hch'<u>yahw</u>-byh pahn/hch'yah-<u>wah</u>-byh pah-
nee <u>zah</u>-grahch'

Can I join in?
Czy mogę się przyłączyć?
chyh <u>moh</u>-geh sh'yeh <u>pshyh</u>-wohn-chyhch'

Friends and Romance

What are your plans for …?
Czy ma pan/pani plany na …?
chyh mah pahn/<u>pah</u>-nee <u>plah</u>-nyh nah …

> tonight
> **wieczór**
> <u>vyeh</u>-chuhr

> tomorrow
> **jutro**
> <u>yuht</u>-roh

> the weekend
> **weekend**
> <u>wee</u>-kehnt

Would you like to get a drink?
Może pójdziemy na drinka?
<u>moh</u>-zheh puhy-<u>dj'yeh</u>-myh nah <u>dreen</u>-kah

Where would you like to go?
Gdzie ma pan/pani ochotę pójść?
gdj'yeh mah pahn/<u>pah</u>-nee oh-<u>hoh</u>-teh
puhysh'ch'

Would you like to go dancing?
Może pójdziemy potańczyć?
<u>moh</u>-zheh puhy-<u>dj'yeh</u>-myh poh-tahn'-
chyhch'

I'm busy.
Jestem zajęty/zajęta.
<u>yehs</u>-tehm zah-<u>yehn</u>-tyh/zah-<u>yehn</u>-tah

No, thank you.
Nie, dziękuję.
n'yeh, dj'yehn-<u>kuh</u>-yeh

I'd like that.
Chętnie.
<u>hehnt</u>-n'yeh

That sounds great!
Świetnie!
sh'<u>vyeht</u>-n'yeh

Go away!
Idź sobie!
eedj' <u>soh</u>-byeh

Stop it!
Przestań!
pshehs-tahn'

I'm here with …
Jestem tu z …
yehs-tehm tuh z …

> my boyfriend
> **moim chłopakiem**
> moh-eem hwoh-pah-kyehm

> my girlfriend
> **moją dziewczyną**
> moh-yohm dj'yehf-chyh-nohm

> my husband
> **moim mężem**
> moh-eem mehn-zhehm

> my wife
> **moją żoną**
> moh-yohm zhoh-nohm

I'm …
Jestem …
yehs-tehm …

> single
> **wolny / wolna**
> vohl-nyh / vohl-nah

> married
> **żonaty / mężatką**
> zhoh-nah-tyh / mehn-zhaht-kohm

separated
w separacji
fseh-pah-<u>rah</u>-tsee

divorced
rozwiedziony / rozwiedziona
rohz-vyeh-<u>dj'yoh</u>-nyh /
rohz-vyeh-<u>dj'yoh</u>-nah

I'm seeing someone.
Spotykam się z kimś.
spoh-<u>tyh</u>-kahm sh'yeh skeemsh'

Do you like men or women?
Wolisz mężczyzn czy kobiety?
<u>voh</u>-leesh <u>mehnzh</u>-chyhzn czyh koh-<u>byeh</u>-tyh

I'm …
Jestem …
<u>yehs</u>-tehm …

bisexual
biseksualny / biseksualna
bee-sehk-suh-<u>ahl</u>-nyh/
bee-sehk-suh-<u>ahl</u>-nah

heterosexual
heteroseksualny / heteroseksualna
heh-teh-roh-sehk-suh-<u>ahl</u>-nyh/
heh-teh-roh-sehk-suh-<u>ahl</u>-nah

homosexual
gejem / lesbijką
<u>geh</u>-yehm / lehs-<u>beey</u>-kohm

Can I kiss you?
Mogę cię pocałować?
<u>moh</u>-geh ch'yeh poh-tsah-<u>woh</u>-vahch'

I like you.
Podobasz mi się.
poh-<u>doh</u>-bahsh mee sh'yeh

I love you.
Kocham cię.
<u>koh</u>-hahm ch'yeh

COMMUNICATIONS

Mail

Where is the post office?
Gdzie jest poczta?
gdj'yeh yehst <u>pohch</u>-tah

Is there a mailbox nearby?
Czy w pobliżu jest skrzynka pocztowa?
chyh fpoh-<u>blee</u>-zhuh yehst <u>skshyhn</u>-kah
pohch-<u>toh</u>-vah

Can I buy stamps?
Czy mogę kupić znaczki?
chyh <u>moh</u>-geh <u>kuh</u>-peech' <u>znah</u>-chkee

I would like to send a ...
Chciałbym/Chciałabym wysłać ...
<u>hch'yahw</u>-byhm/<u>hch'yah</u>-wah-byhm <u>vyh</u>-
swahch' ...

> letter
> **list**
> leest

> package/parcel
> **paczkę**
> <u>pahch</u>-keh

> postcard
> **kartkę pocztową**
> <u>kahr</u>-tkeh pohch-<u>toh</u>-vohm

Please send this via …
Proszę to wysłać …
<u>proh</u>-sheh toh <u>vyh</u>-swahch' …

air mail
pocztą lotniczą
<u>pohch</u>-tohm loht-<u>nee</u>-chohm

registered mail
listem poleconym
<u>lees</u>-tehm poh-leh-<u>tsoh</u>-nyhm

priority mail
priorytetem
preeyoh-ryh-<u>teh</u>-tehm

regular mail
zwykłym listem
<u>zvyh</u>-kwyhm <u>lees</u>-tehm

It's going to …
Chciałbym/Chciałabym wysłać to do …
<u>hch'yahw</u>-byhm/<u>hch'yah</u>-wah-byhm <u>vyh</u>-swahch' toh doh …

the United States
Stanów Zjednoczonych
<u>stah</u>-nuhf zyeh-dnoh-<u>choh</u>-nyhh

Canada
Kanady
kah-<u>nah</u>-dyh

Great Britain
Wielkiej Brytanii
<u>vyehl</u>-kyehy bryh-<u>tah</u>-nee

How much does it cost?
Ile to kosztuje?
ee-leh toh kohsh-tuh-yeh

When will it arrive?
Kiedy dojdzie na miejsce?
kyeh-dyh dohy-dj'yeh nah meeyehy-stseh

It contains …
To zawiera …
toh zah-vyeh-rah …

What is …?
Jaki jest …?
yah-kee yehst …

> your address
> **pani/pana adres**
> pah-nee/pah-nah ah-drehs

> the address for the hotel
> **adres hotelu**
> ah-drehs hoh-teh-luh

> the address I should have my mail
> sent to
> **adres, na który można wysyłać mi**
> **korespondencję?**
> ah-drehs nah ktuh-ryh mohzh-nah
> vyh-syh-wahch' mee koh-rehs-pohn-
> dehn-tsyeh

Can you write down the address for me?
Czy może mi pan/pani zapisać adres?
czyh <u>moh</u>-zheh mee <u>pahn</u>/<u>pah</u>-nee zah-
<u>pee</u>-sahch' <u>ah</u>-drehs

Is there any mail for me?
Czy jest dla mnie jakaś poczta?
czyh yehst dlah mn'yeh <u>yah</u>-kahsh' <u>pohch</u>-tah

international
międzynarodowy
myehn-dzyh-nah-roh-<u>doh</u>-vyh

domestic
krajowy
krah-<u>yoh</u>-vyh

postage
koszty przesyłki
<u>koh</u>-shtyh psheh-<u>syhw</u>-kee

stamp
znaczek
<u>znah</u>-chehk

envelope
koperta
koh-<u>pehr</u>-tah

postal code
kod pocztowy
kohd pohch-<u>toh</u>-vyh

customs office
urząd celny
<u>uh</u>-zhohnt <u>tsehl</u>-nyh

postal insurance
ubezpieczenie przesyłki
uh-behs-pyeh-<u>cheh</u>-n'yeh psheh-<u>syhw</u>-kee

Telecommunications

Telephones, Faxing and Mobile Phones

Where is a pay phone?
Gdzie jest automat telefoniczny?
gdj'yeh yehst ahw-<u>toh</u>-maht teh-leh-foh-<u>nee</u>-chnyh

Can I use your phone?
Czy mogę skorzystać z pana/pani telefonu?
chyh <u>moh</u>-geh skoh-<u>zhyh</u>-stahch' s <u>pah</u>-nah/<u>pah</u>-nee teh-leh-<u>foh</u>-nuh

I would like to …
Chciałbym/Chciałabym …
<u>hch'yahw</u>-byhm/<u>hch'yah</u>-wah-byhm …

   make an overseas phone call
   zadzwonić za granicę
   zah-<u>dzvoh</u>-neech' zah grah-<u>nee</u>-tseh

make a local call
uzyskać połączenie lokalne
uh-<u>zyh</u>-skahch' poh-wohn-<u>cheh</u>-n'yeh
loh-<u>kahl</u>-neh

send a fax
wysłać faks
<u>vyh</u>-swahch' fahks

What number do I dial for …?
Jaki jest numer …?
<u>yah</u>-kee yehst <u>nuh</u>-mehr …

infomation
na informację
nah een-fohr-<u>mah</u>-tsyeh

an outside line
zewnętrzny
zeh-<u>vnehn</u>-tshnyh

an operator
do operatora
doh oh-peh-rah-<u>toh</u>-rah

What is the phone number for the …?
Jaki jest numer do …?
<u>yah</u>-kee yehst <u>nuh</u>-mehr doh …

hotel
hotelu
hoh-<u>teh</u>-luh

office
biura
<u>beeuh</u>-rah

restaurant
restauracji
rehs-tahw-<u>rah</u>-tsyee

embassy
ambasady
ahm-bah-<u>sah</u>-dyh

What is your ...?
Jaki jest pana/pani ...?
<u>yah</u>-kee yehst <u>pah</u>-nah/<u>pah</u>-nee ...

phone number
numer telefonu
<u>nuh</u>-mehr teh-leh-<u>foh</u>-nuh

home phone number
numer domowy
<u>nuh</u>-mehr doh-<u>moh</u>-vyh

work number
numer do pracy
<u>nuh</u>-mehr doh <u>prah</u>-tsyh

fax number
numer faksu
<u>nuh</u>-mehr <u>fah</u>-ksuh

mobile phone number
numer telefonu komórkowego
<u>nuh</u>-mehr teh-leh-<u>foh</u>-nuh koh-muhr-
koh-<u>veh</u>-goh

Can you write down your number for me?
Czy może mi pan/pani zapisać swój numer?
czyh <u>moh</u>-zheh mee pahn/<u>pah</u>-nee zah-<u>pee</u>-sahch' sfuhy <u>nuh</u>-mehr

My number is …
Mój numer to …
Muhy <u>nuh</u>-mehr toh …

What is the country code for …?
Jaki jest numer kierunkowy do …?
<u>yah</u>-kee yehst <u>nuh</u>-mehr kyeh-ruhn-<u>koh</u>-vyh doh …

I would like to buy …
Chciałbym/Chciałabym kupić …
<u>hch'yahw</u>-byhm/<u>hch'yah</u>-wah-byhm <u>kuh</u>-peech' …

> a domestic phone card
> **krajową kartę telefoniczną**
> krah-<u>yoh</u>-vohm <u>kahr</u>-teh teh-leh-foh-<u>nee</u>-chnohm

> an international phone card
> **międzynarodową kartę telefoniczną**
> myehn-dzyh-nah-roh-<u>doh</u>-vohm <u>kahr</u>-teh teh-leh-foh-<u>nee</u>-chnohm

> a disposable cell phone
> **telefon komórkowy jednorazowego użytku**
> teh-<u>leh</u>-fohn koh-muhr-<u>koh</u>-vyh yeh-dnoh-rah-zoh-<u>veh</u>-goh uh-<u>zhyh</u>-tkuh

a SIM card
kartę SIM
kahr-teh seem

a mobile phone recharge card
kartę doładowania
kahr-teh doh-wah-doh-vah-n'yah

What is the cost per minute?
Ile kosztuje minuta?
ee-leh koh-shtuh-yeh mee-nuh-tah

I need a phone with XX minutes.
Potrzebuję telefon z XX minutami.
poh-tsheh-buh-yeh teh-leh-fohn s XX mee-nuh-tah-mee

How do I make calls?
Jak się (z tego) dzwoni?
yahk sh'yeh (steh-goh) dzvoh-nee

collect call
rozmowa na koszt rozmówcy
roh-zmoh-vah nah kohsht rohz-muh-ftsyh

toll-free
bezpłatna / za darmo
behs-pwah-tnah / zah dahr-moh

pre-paid cell phone
karta pre-paid
kahr-tah pree-pehyd

phone number
numer telefonu
<u>nuh</u>-mehr teh-leh-<u>foh</u>-nuh

extention (number)
numer wewnętrzny
<u>nuh</u>-mehr vehv-<u>nehn</u>-tshnyh

phone book
książka telefoniczna
<u>ksh'yohn</u>-shkah teh-leh-foh-<u>nee</u>-chnah

voicemail
poczta głosowa
<u>pohch</u>-tah gwoh-<u>soh</u>-vah

On the phone

Hello?
Halo?
<u>hah</u>-loh

Hello. This is …
Dzień dobry. Mówi …
dj'yehn' <u>dohb</u>-ryh. <u>Muh</u>-vee …

May I speak to …?
**Czy mógłbym/mogłabym rozmawiać z
…?**
czyh <u>muhgw</u>-byhm/<u>mohg</u>-wah-byhm
rohz-<u>mah</u>-vyahch's …

... isn't here. May I take a message?
... nie ma w tej chwili. Czy mam przekazać wiadomość?
... n'yeh mah f tehy <u>hfee</u>-lee. Chyh mahm psheh-<u>kah</u>-zahch' vyah-<u>doh</u>-mohsh'ch'

I would like to leave a message for ...
Chciałbym/Chciałabym zostawić wiadomość dla ...
hch'<u>yahw</u>-byhm/hch'<u>yah</u>-wah-byhm zoh-<u>stah</u>-veech' vyah-<u>doh</u>-mohsh'ch' dlah ...

Sorry, wrong number.
Przepraszam, pomyłka.
psheh-<u>prah</u>-shahm, poh-<u>myhw</u>-kah

Please call back later.
Proszę zadzwonić później.
<u>proh</u>-sheh zah-<u>dzvoh</u>-neech' <u>puhzh'</u>-n'yehy

I'll call back later.
Zadzwonię później.
zah-<u>dzvoh</u>-n'yeh <u>puhzh'</u>-n'yehy

Bye.
Do widzenia.
doh vee-<u>dzeh</u>-n'yah

Computers and the Internet

Where is the nearest …?
Gdzie jest najbliższy/najbliższa …?
gdj'yeh yehst nahy-<u>blee</u>-zhshyh/nahy-<u>blee</u>-zhshah …

Internet café
kafejka internetowa
kah-<u>fehy</u>-kah een-tehr-neh-<u>toh</u>-vah

computer repair shop
punkt naprawy komputerów
puhnkt nah-<u>prah</u>-vyh kohm-puh-<u>teh</u>-ruhf

Do you have …?
Czy mają państwo …?
chyh <u>mah</u>-yohm <u>pahn'</u>-stfoh …

available computers
wolne komputery
<u>vohl</u>-neh kohm-puh-<u>teh</u>-ryh

(wireless) Internet
(bezprzewodowy) internet
(behs-psheh-voh-<u>doh</u>-vyh) een-<u>tehr</u>-n eht

a printer
drukarkę
druh-<u>kahr</u>-keh

a scanner
skaner
<u>skah</u>-nehr

How do you …?
Jak się …?
yahk sh'yeh …

> turn on this computer
> **włącza ten komputer**
> vwohn-chah tehn kohm-puh-tehr

> log in
> **zalogować**
> zah-loh-goh-vahch'

> connect to the wi-fi
> **podłączyć do bezprzewodowej sieci**
> pohd-wohn-chyhch' doh behs-psheh-
> voh-doh-vehy sh'yeh-ch'yee

> type in English
> **włącza znaki angielskie**
> vwohn-chah znah-kee ahn-gyehl-skyeh

How much does it cost for …?
Ile kosztuje …?
ee-leh kohsh-tuh-yeh …

> 15 minutes
> **15 minut**
> pyeht-nahsh'-ch'yeh mee-nuht

> 30 minutes
> **30 minut**
> tshyh-dj'yehsh'-ch'ee mee-nuht

> one hour
> **godzina**
> goh-dj'ee-nah

What is the password?
Jakie jest hasło?
yah-kyeh yehst hah-swoh

My computer …
Mój komputer …
muhy kohm-puh-tehr …

    doesn't work
    nie działa
    n'yeh dj'yah-wah

    is frozen
    zawiesił się
    zah-vyeh-seew sh'yeh

    won't turn on
    nie chce się włączyć
    n'yeh htseh sh'yeh vwohn-chyhch'

    crashed
    zepsuł się
    zehp-suhw sh'yeh

    doesn't have an Internet connection
    nie ma połączenia z internetem
    n'yeh mah poh-wohn-cheh-n'yah
    zeen-tehr-neh-tehm

Windows
Windows
ween-dowz

Macintosh
Macintosh
mah-keen-tohsh

Linux
Linux
lee-nuhks

computer
komputer
kohm-<u>puh</u>-tehr

laptop
laptop
lahp-tohp

USB port
port USB
pohrt <u>uh</u>-<u>ehs</u>-<u>beh</u>

ethernet cable
kabel sieciowy
<u>kah</u>-behl sh'yeh-<u>ch'yoh</u>-vyh

CD
CD
<u>see</u>-<u>dee</u>

DVD
DVD
<u>dee</u>-<u>vee</u>-<u>dee</u>

e-mail
e-mail
<u>ee</u>-mehyl

BUSINESS

Professions and Specializations

What do you do?
Czym się pan/pani zajmuje?
chyhm sh'yeh pahn/<u>pah</u>-n'ee zahy-<u>muh</u>-yeh

I'm ...
Jestem ...
<u>yehs</u>-tehm ...

an aid worker
pracownikiem pomocy społecznej
prah-tsoh-<u>vn'ee</u>-kyehm poh-<u>moh</u>-tsyh
spoh-<u>wehch</u>-nehy

an accountant
księgowym / księgową
ksh'yehn-<u>goh</u>-vyhm / ksh'yehn-<u>goh</u>-vohm

an administrative assistant
asystentem / asystentką
ah-syhs-<u>tehn</u>-tehm / ah-syhs-<u>tehnt</u>-kohm

an architect
architektem
ahr-hee-<u>tehk</u>-tehm

an assistant
asystentem / asystentką
ah-syhs-<u>tehn</u>-tehm / ah-syhs-<u>tehnt</u>-kohm

an artist
artystą / artystką
ahr-<u>tyhs</u>-tohm / ahr-<u>tyhst</u>-kohm

a banker
bankierem
bahn-<u>kyeh</u>-rehm

a businessman / businesswoman
biznesmenem / biznesmenką
beez-nehs-<u>meh</u>-nehm /
beez-nehs-<u>mehn</u>-kohm

a carpenter
stolarzem
stoh-<u>lah</u>-zhehm

a CEO
dyrektorem naczelnym
dyh-rehk-<u>toh</u>-rehm nah-<u>chehl</u>-nyhm

a clerk
urzędnikiem / urzędniczką
uh-zhehn-<u>dn'ee</u>-kyehm /
uh-zhehn-<u>dn'eech</u>-kohm

a consultant
konsultantem / konsultantką
kohn-suhl-<u>tahn</u>-tehm /
kohn-suhl-<u>tahnt</u>-kohm

a contractor
**przedsiębiorcą budowlanym /
wykonawcą**
psheht-sh'yehm-<u>byohr</u>-tsohm buh-
doh-<u>vlah</u>-nyhm / vyh-koh-<u>nahf</u>-tsohm

a construction worker
robotnikiem budowlanym
roh-boh-<u>tn'ee</u>-kyehm buh-doh-<u>vlah</u>-
nyhm

a coordinator
koordynatorem / koordynatorką
koh-ohr-dyh-nah-<u>toh</u>-rehm /
koh-ohr-dyh-nah-<u>tohr</u>-kohm

a dentist
stomatologiem
stoh-mah-toh-<u>loh</u>-gyehm

a director
dyrektorem
dyh-rehk-<u>toh</u>-rehm

a doctor
lekarzem
leh-<u>kah</u>-zhehm

an editor
redaktorem / redaktorką
reh-dahk-<u>toh</u>-rehm /
reh-dahk-<u>tohr</u>-kohm

an electrician
elektrykiem
eh-lehk-<u>tryh</u>-kyehm

an engineer
inżynierem
een-zhyh-<u>n'yeh</u>-rehm

an intern
stażystą / stażystką
stah-<u>zhyhs</u>-tohm / stah-<u>zhyhst</u>-kohm

a journalist
dziennikarzem / dziennikarką
dj'yehn-n'ee-<u>kah</u>-zhehm /
dj'yehn-n'ee-<u>kahr</u>-kohm

a lawyer
prawnikiem / prawniczką
prahv-<u>n'ee</u>-kyehm / prahv-<u>n'eech</u>-kohm

a librarian
bibliotekarzem / bibliotekarką
beeb-lyoh-teh-<u>kah</u>-zhehm /
beeb-lyoh-teh-<u>kahr</u>-kohm

a manager
kierownikiem / kierowniczką
kyeh-rohv-<u>n'ee</u>-kyehm /
kyeh-rohv-<u>n'eech</u>-kohm

a nurse
pielęgniarzem / pielęgniarką
pyeh-lehn-<u>gn'yah</u>-zhehm /
pyeh-lehn-<u>gn'yahr</u>-kohm

a politician
politykiem
poh-lee-<u>tyh</u>-kyehm

a secretary
sekretarzem / sekretarką
seh-kreh-<u>tah</u>-zhehm /
seh-kreh-<u>tahr</u>-kohm

a student
studentem / studentką
stuh-<u>dehn</u>-tehm / stuh-<u>dehnt</u>-kohm

a supervisor
kierownikiem / kierowniczką
kyeh-rohv-<u>n'ee</u>-kyehm /
kyeh-rohv-<u>n'eech</u>-kohm

a teacher
nauczycielem / nauczycielką
nah-uh-chyh-<u>ch'yeh</u>-lehm /
nah-uh-chyh-<u>ch'yehl</u>-kohm

a writer
pisarzem / pisarką
pee-<u>sah</u>-zhehm / pee-<u>sahr</u>-kohm

I work in …
Pracuję w …
prah-<u>tsuh</u>-yeh v …

academia
środowisku akademickim
sh'roh-doh-<u>vees</u>-kuh ah-kah-deh-<u>meets</u>-keem

accounting
księgowości
ksh'yehn-goh-<u>vohsh'</u>-ch'ee

advertising
reklamie
reh-<u>klah</u>-myeh

banking
bankowości
bahn-koh-<u>vohsh'</u>-ch'ee

education
szkolnictwie
shkohl-<u>neets</u>-tfyeh

engineering
przemyśle inżynieryjnym
psheh-<u>myhsh'</u>-leh een-zhyh-n'yeh-
<u>ryhy</u>-nyhm

finance
finansach
fee-<u>nahn</u>-sahh

law
wymiarze sprawiedliwości
vyh-<u>myah</u>-zheh sprah-vyeh-dlee-
<u>vohsh'</u>-ch'ee

manufacturing
przemyśle wytwórczym
psheh-<u>myhsh'</u>-leh vyht-<u>fuhr</u>-chyhm

the medical field
służbie zdrowia
<u>swuhzh</u>-byeh <u>zdroh</u>-vyah

public relations
public relations
<u>pahb</u>-leek ree-<u>lehy</u>-shyhns

publishing
przemyśle wydawniczym
psheh-<u>myhsh'</u>-leh vyh-dahv-<u>n'ee</u>-chyhm

a restaurant
restauracji
rehs-tahw-<u>rah</u>-tsyee

a store
sklepie
<u>skleh</u>-pyeh

social services
opiece społecznej
oh-<u>pyeh</u>-tseh spoh-<u>wehch</u>-nehy

the travel industry
przemyśle turystycznym
psheh-<u>myhsh'</u>-leh tuh-ryhs-<u>tyhch</u>-nyhm

I work in the arts.
Zajmuję się sztuką. / Jestem artystą.
zahy-<u>muh</u>-yeh sh'yeh <u>shtuh</u>-kohm /
<u>yehs</u>-tehm ahr-<u>tyhs</u>-tohm

I work in business.
Zajmuję się biznesem.
zahy-<u>muh</u>-yeh sh'yeh beez-<u>neh</u>-sehm

I work in government.
Pracuję dla rządu.
prah-<u>tsuh</u>-yeh dlah <u>zhohn</u>-duh

I work in journalism.
Zajmuję się dziennikarstwem.
zahy-<u>muh</u>-yeh sh'yeh dj'yehn-n'ee-<u>kahr</u>-
stfehm

I work in marketing.
Zajmuję się marketingiem.
zahy-<u>muh</u>-yeh sh'yeh mahr-keh-<u>teen</u>-gyehm

I work in politics.
Zajmuję się polityką.
zahy-<u>muh</u>-yeh sh'yeh poh-lee-<u>tyh</u>-kohm

BUSINESS

Business Communication and Interaction

I have a meeting/appointment with …
Mam spotkanie z …
mahm spoht-<u>kah</u>-n'yeh z …

Where's the …?
Gdzie jest …?
gdj'yeh yehst …

> business center
> **centrum biznesowe**
> <u>tsehn</u>-truhm beez-neh-<u>soh</u>-veh

> convention hall
> **sala konferencyjna**
> <u>sah</u>-lah kohn-feh-rehn-<u>tsyhy</u>-nah

> meeting room
> **sala spotkań**
> <u>sah</u>-lah <u>spoht</u>-kahn'

Can I have your business card?
Czy mogę prosić o pana/pani wizytówkę?
chyh <u>moh</u>-geh <u>proh</u>-sh'eech' oh <u>pah</u>-nah/ <u>pah</u>-n'ee vee-zyh-<u>tuhf</u>-keh

Here's my business card.
To moja wizytówka.
toh <u>moh</u>-yah vee-zyh-<u>tuhf</u>-kah

I'm here for a ...
Przyjechałem/Przyjechałam na ...
pshyh-yeh-<u>hah</u>-wehm/pshyh-yeh-<u>hah</u>-
wahm nah ...

> conference
> **konferencję**
> kohn-feh-<u>rehn</u>-tsyeh

> meeting
> **spotkanie**
> spoht-<u>kah</u>-n'yeh

> seminar
> **seminarium**
> seh-mee-<u>nah</u>-ryuhm

My name is ...
Nazywam się ...
nah-<u>zyh</u>-vahm sh'yeh ...

May I introduce my colleague ...
**Proszę pozwolić mi przedstawić
kolegę/koleżankę ...**
<u>proh</u>-sheh pohz-<u>voh</u>-leech' mee psheht-<u>stah</u>-
veech' koh-<u>leh</u>-geh/koh-leh-<u>zhahn</u>-keh ...

Pleased to meet you.
Miło mi pana/panią poznać.
<u>mee</u>-woh mee <u>pah</u>-nah/<u>pah</u>-n'yohm
<u>pohz</u>-nahch'

I'm sorry I'm late.
Przepraszam za spóźnienie.
psheh-<u>prah</u>-shahm zah spuhzh'-<u>n'yeh</u>-n'yeh

You can reach me at …
Można się ze mną kontaktować …
<u>mohzh</u>-nah sh'yeh zeh mnohm kohn-tahk-<u>toh</u>-vahch' …

I'm here until …
Zostanę tu do …
zohs-<u>tah</u>-neh tuh doh …

I need to …
Muszę …
<u>muh</u>-sheh …

   make a photocopy
   zrobić kserokopię
   <u>zroh</u>-beech' kseh-roh-<u>koh</u>-pyeh

   make a telephone call
   zatelefonować
   zah-teh-leh-foh-<u>noh</u>-vahch'

   send a fax
   wysłać faks
   <u>vyh</u>-swahch' fahks

   send a package (overnight)
   wysłać paczkę (pocztą kurierską)
   <u>vyh</u>-swahch' <u>pahch</u>-keh

   use the Internet
   skorzystać z internetu
   skoh-<u>zhyhs</u>-tahch' zeen-tehr-<u>neh</u>-tuh

It was a pleasure meeting you.
Miło było pana/panią poznać.
<u>mee</u>-woh <u>byh</u>-woh <u>pah</u>-nah/<u>pah</u>-n'yohm <u>pohz</u>-nahch'

I look forward to meeting with you again.
**Z niecierpliwością czekam na nasze
następne spotkanie.**
zn'yeh-ch'yehr-plee-<u>vohsh</u>'-ch'yohm <u>cheh</u>-
kahm nah <u>nah</u>-sheh nahs-<u>tehmp</u>-neh
spoht-<u>kah</u>-n'yeh

You Might Hear

Dziękuję za przybycie.
dj'yehn-<u>kuh</u>-yeh zah pshyh-<u>byh</u>-ch'yeh
Thank you for coming.

Proszę chwileczkę poczekać.
<u>proh</u>-sheh hfee-<u>lehch</u>-keh poh-<u>cheh</u>-kahch'
One moment, please.

**Czy jest pan umówiony/pani umówiona
na spotkanie?**
chyh yehst pahn uh-muh-<u>vyoh</u>-nyh/<u>pah</u>-n'ee
uh-muh-<u>vyoh</u>-nah nah spoht-<u>kah</u>-n'yeh
Do you have an appointment?

Z kim?
skeem
With whom?

Zaraz się z panem/panią spotka.
<u>zah</u>-rahz sh'yeh <u>spah</u>-nehm/<u>spah</u>-n'yohm
<u>spoht</u>-kah
He will be right with you.

Proszę usiąść.
<u>proh</u>-sheh <u>uh</u>-sh'yohn'sh'ch'
Please have a seat.

Business Vocabulary

advertisement
ogłoszenie / reklama
oh-gwoh-<u>sheh</u>-n'yeh / reh-<u>klah</u>-mah

advertising
reklama
reh-<u>klah</u>-mah

bonus
premia
<u>preh</u>-myah

boss
szef
shehf

briefcase
teczka
<u>tehch</u>-kah

business
biznes / interesy / działalność handlowa
<u>beez</u>-nehs / een-teh-<u>reh</u>-syh /
dj'yah-<u>wahl</u>-nohsh'ch' hahn-<u>dloh</u>-vah

business card
wizytówka
vee-zyh-<u>tuhf</u>-kah

business casual (dress)
pół-oficjalny (strój)
puhw oh-fee-<u>tsyahl</u>-nyh (struhy)

business plan
biznesplan
<u>beez</u>-nehs-plahn

casual (dress)
nieoficjalny (strój)
n'yeh-oh-fee-<u>tsyahl</u>-nyh (struhy)

cell phone number
numer telefonu komórkowego
<u>nuh</u>-mehr teh-leh-<u>foh</u>-nuh koh-muhr-koh-<u>veh</u>-goh

certification
certyfikat / zaświadczenie
tsehr-tyh-<u>fee</u>-kaht / zah-sh'fyaht-<u>cheh</u>-n'yeh

colleague
kolega/koleżanka z pracy
koh-<u>leh</u>-gah/koh-leh-<u>zhahn</u>-kah <u>sprah</u>-tsyh

company
firma / spółka / przedsiębiorstwo
<u>feer</u>-mah / <u>spuhw</u>-kah / psheht-sh'yehm-<u>byohr</u>-stfoh

competition
konkurencja
kohn-kuh-<u>rehn</u>-tsyah

competitor
konkurent
kohn-<u>kuh</u>-rehnt

computer
komputer
kohm-<u>puh</u>-tehr

conference
konferencja
kohn-feh-<u>rehn</u>-tsyah

contract
umowa / kontrakt
uh-<u>moh</u>-vah / <u>kohn</u>-trahkt

course
kurs
kuhrs

cubicle
kabina
kah-<u>bee</u>-nah

CV
życiorys / CV
zhyh-<u>ch'yoh</u>-ryhs / see vee

deduction
potrącenie
poh-trohn-<u>tseh</u>-n'yeh

degree
stopień naukowy
<u>stoh</u>-pyehn' nah-uh-<u>koh</u>-vyh

desk
biurko
<u>byuhr</u>-koh

e-mail address
adres email
<u>ah</u>-drehs <u>ee</u>-mehyl

employee
pracownik
prah-<u>tsohv</u>-neek

employer
pracodawca
prah-tsoh-<u>dahf</u>-tsah

equal opportunity
równouprawnienie
ruhv-noh-uh-prahv-<u>n'yeh</u>-n'yeh

expenses
wydatki
vyh-<u>daht</u>-kee

experience
doświadczenie
dohsh'-fyaht-<u>cheh</u>-n'yeh

fax number
numer faksu
<u>nuh</u>-mehr <u>fahk</u>-suh

field
dziedzina
dj'yeh-<u>dj'ee</u>-nah

formal (dress)
oficjalny (strój)
oh-fee-<u>tsyahl</u>-nyh (struhy)

full-time
na pełnym etacie
nah <u>pehw</u>-nyhm eh-<u>tah</u>-ch'yeh

global
globalny / ogólnoświatowy
gloh-<u>bahl</u>-nyh / oh-guhl-noh-sh'fyah-<u>toh</u>-vyh

income
dochód
<u>doh</u>-huht

income tax
podatek dochodowy
poh-<u>dah</u>-tehk doh-hoh-<u>doh</u>-vyh

insurance
ubezpieczenie
uh-behz-pyeh-<u>cheh</u>-n'yeh

job
praca
<u>prah</u>-tsah

joint venture
joint venture / wspólne przedsięwzięcie
djohynt <u>vehn</u>-chehr / <u>fspuhl</u>-neh psheht-
sh'yehn-<u>vzh'yehn</u>-ch'yeh

license
licencja / zezwolenie
lee-<u>tsehn</u>-tsyah / zehz-voh-<u>leh</u>-n'yeh

mailing
**przesyłanie pocztą materiałów
reklamowych**
psheh-syh-<u>wah</u>-n'yeh <u>pohch</u>-tohm mah-
teh-<u>ryah</u>-wuhf reh-klah-<u>moh</u>-vyhh

marketing
marketing
mahr-<u>keh</u>-teeng

meeting
spotkanie
spoht-<u>kah</u>-n'yeh

minimum wage
płaca minimalna
<u>pwah</u>-tsah mee-n'ee-<u>mahl</u>-nah

multinational
przedsiębiorstwo międzynarodowe
psheht-sh'yehm-<u>byohr</u>-stfoh myehn-dzyh-
nah-roh-<u>doh</u>-veh

office
biuro
byuh-roh

office phone number
numer telefonu do biura
nuh-mehr teh-leh-foh-nuh doh byuh-rah

paperwork
praca papierkowa / dokumenty
prah-tsah pah-pyehr-koh-vah / doh-kuh-
mehn-tyh

part-time
na niepełnym etacie
nah n'yeh-pehw-nyhm eh-tah-ch'yeh

printer
drukarka
druh-kahr-kah

profession
zawód
zah-vuht

professional
profesjonalista (*noun*)
proh-feh-syoh-nah-lees-tah
profesjonalny / zawodowy (*adj*)
proh-feh-syoh-nahl-nyh / zah-voh-doh-vyh

project
projekt / przedsięwzięcie
<u>proh</u>-yehkt / psheht-sh'yehn-<u>vzh'yehn</u>-
ch'yeh

promotion
awans
<u>ah</u>-vahns

raise
podwyżka
pohd-<u>vyhsh</u>-kah

reimbursement
zwrot
zvroht

resume
życiorys
zhyh-<u>ch'yoh</u>-ryhs

salary
pensja
<u>pehn</u>-syah

scanner
skaner
<u>skah</u>-nehr

seminar
seminarium
seh-mee-<u>nah</u>-ryuhm

suit
garnitur (*for men*) / **kostium** (*for women*)
gahr-<u>n'ee</u>-tuhr / <u>kohs</u>-tyuhm

supervisor
kierownik
kyeh-<u>rohv</u>-neek

tax ID
numer identyfikacji podatkowej
<u>nuh</u>-mehr ee-dehn-tyh-fee-<u>kah</u>-tsyee poh-
daht-<u>koh</u>-vehy

tie
krawat
<u>krah</u>-vaht

trade fair
targi handlowe
<u>tahr</u>-gee hahn-<u>dloh</u>-veh

uniform
uniform
uh-<u>n'ee</u>-fohrm

union
związek zawodowy
<u>zvyohn</u>-zehk zah-voh-<u>doh</u>-vyh

wages
zarobki / płaca
zah-<u>rohp</u>-kee / <u>pwah</u>-tsah

work number
numer telefonu do pracy
<u>nuh</u>-mehr teh-leh-<u>foh</u>-nuh doh <u>prah</u>-tsyh

work permit
pozwolenie na pracę
pohz-voh-<u>leh</u>-n'yeh nah <u>prah</u>-tseh

HEALTH

At the Doctor

Making an Appointment

Can you recommend a good doctor?
Czy może pan/pani polecić dobrego lekarza?
chyh <u>moh</u>-zheh pahn/<u>pah</u>-n'ee poh-<u>leh</u>-ch'eech' doh-<u>breh</u>-goh leh-<u>kah</u>-zhah

I'd to make an appointment for ...
Chciałbym/Chciałabym zamówić wizytę na ...
hch'<u>yahw</u>-byhm/hch'yah-<u>wah</u>-byhm zah-<u>muh</u>-veech' vee-<u>zyh</u>-teh nah ...

today
dzisiaj
<u>dj'ee</u>-sh'yahy

tomorrow
jutro
<u>yuh</u>-troh

next week
przyszły tydzień
<u>pshyh</u>-shwyh <u>tyh</u>-dj'yehn'

as soon as possible
jak najbliższy termin
yahk nahy-<u>bleesh</u>-shyh <u>tehr</u>-meen

You Might Hear

Czy jest pan/pani na coś uczulony/ uczulona?
chyh yehst pahn/<u>pah</u>-n'ee nah tsohsh'
uh-chuh-<u>loh</u>-nyh/uh-chuh-<u>loh</u>-nah
Do you have any allergies?

Czy zażywa pan/pani jakieś leki?
chyh zah-zhyh-vah pahn/<u>pah</u>-n'ee <u>yah</u>-
kyehsh'<u>leh</u>-kee
Are you on any medications?

Proszę tutaj podpisać.
<u>proh</u>-sheh <u>tuh</u>-tahy pohd-<u>pee</u>-sahch'
Sign here.

Can the doctor come here?
Czy lekarz może przyjść i zbadać mnie tutaj?
chyh <u>leh</u>-kahzh <u>moh</u>-zheh pshyhysh'ch' ee
<u>zbah</u>-dahch' mn'yeh <u>tuh</u>-tahy

What are the office hours?
Jakie są godziny przyjęć?
<u>yah</u>-kyeh sohm goh-<u>dj'ee</u>-nyh <u>pshyh</u>-yehnch'

It's urgent.
To pilna sprawa.
toh <u>peel</u>-nah <u>sprah</u>-vah

I need a doctor who speaks English.
Potrzebny mi jest lekarz mówiący po angielsku.
poh-<u>tsheh</u>-bnyh mee yehst <u>leh</u>-kahzh muh-<u>vyohn</u>-tsyh poh ahn-<u>gyehl</u>-skuh

How long is the wait?
Ile trzeba będzie czekać?
<u>ee</u>-leh <u>tsheh</u>-bah <u>behn</u>-dj'yeh <u>cheh</u>-kahch'

Ailments

I have …
Mam …
mahm …

allergies
uczulenie
uh-chuh-<u>leh</u>-n'yeh

an allergic reaction
reakcję alergiczną
reh-<u>ahk</u>-tsyeh ah-lehr-<u>gee</u>-chnohm

arthritis
artretyzm
ahr-<u>treh</u>-tyhzm

asthma
astmę
<u>ahst</u>-meh

a backache
bóle w plecach
<u>buh</u>-leh <u>fpleh</u>-tsahh

bug bites
ślady po ukąszeniu insektów
sh'lah-dyh poh uh-kohn-sheh-n'yuh
een-sehk-tuhf

chest pain
bóle w klatce piersiowej
buh-leh fklaht-tseh pyehr-sh'yoh-vehy

cramps
skurcze
skuhr-cheh

diabetes
cukrzycę
tsuh-kshyh-tseh

diarrhea
biegunkę
byeh-guhn-keh

a fever
gorączkę
goh-rohn-chkeh

the flu
grypę
gryh-peh

a fracture
złamanie
zwah-mah-n'yeh

high blood pressure
wysokie ciśnienie
vyh-soh-kyeh ch'eesh'-n'yeh-n'yeh

an infection
infekcję
een-<u>fehk</u>-tsyeh

indigestion
niestrawność
n'yeh-<u>strahv</u>-nohsh'ch'

low blood pressure
niskie ciśnienie
<u>n'ees</u>-kyeh ch'eesh'-<u>n'yeh</u>-n'yeh

pain
bóle
<u>buh</u>-leh

a rash
wysypkę
vyh-<u>syhp</u>-keh

swelling
opuchliznę
oh-puh-<u>hlee</u>-zneh

a sprain
zwichnięcie
zvee-<u>hn'yehn</u>-ch'yeh

sunburn
oparzenie słoneczne
oh-pah-<u>zheh</u>-n'yeh swoh-<u>neh</u>-chneh

sunstroke
udar słoneczny
<u>uh</u>-dahr swoh-<u>neh</u>-chnyh

a urinary tract infection
infekcję dróg moczowych
een-<u>fehk</u>-tsyeh druhg moh-<u>choh</u>-vyhh

a venereal disease
chorobę weneryczną
hoh-<u>roh</u>-beh veh-neh-<u>ryh</u>-chnohm

I have a cold.
Jestem przeziębiony/przeziębiona.
<u>yehs</u>-tehm pzheh-zh'yehm-<u>byoh</u>-nyh/
pzheh-zh'yehm-<u>byoh</u>-nah

I have an earache.
Boli mnie ucho.
<u>boh</u>-lee mn'yeh <u>uh</u>-hoh

I have a heart condition.
Choruję na serce.
hoh-<u>ruh</u>-yeh nah <u>sehr</u>-tseh

I have a stomachache.
Boli mnie brzuch.
<u>boh</u>-lee mn'yeh bzhuhh

I have a toothache.
Boli mnie ząb.
<u>boh</u>-lee mn'yeh zohmb

I need medication for …
Potrzebuję lekarstwa na …
poh-tsheh-<u>buh</u>-yeh leh-<u>kahr</u>-stfah nah …

I'm ...
Mam ...
mahm ...

anemic
anemię
ah-<u>neh</u>-myeh

bleeding
krwotok
<u>krfoh</u>-tohk

consitpated
zaparcie
zah-<u>pahr</u>-ch'yeh

dizzy
zawroty głowy
zah-<u>vroh</u>-tyh <u>gwoh</u>-vyh

having trouble breathing
problem z oddychaniem
<u>proh</u>-blehm zohd-dyh-<u>hah</u>-n'yehm

nauseous
mdłości
<u>mdwoh</u>-sh'ch'yee

My period is late.
Spóźnia mi się miesiączka.
<u>spuh</u>-zh'n'yah mee sh'yeh myeh-<u>sh'yohn</u>-chkah

I'm pregnant.
Jestem w ciąży.
<u>yehs</u>-tehm <u>fch'yohn</u>-zhyh

You Might Hear

To jest ...
toh yehst ...
It's ...

złamane	**zakażone**
zwah-<u>mah</u>-neh	zah-kah-<u>zhoh</u>-neh
broken	infected
zakaźne	**skręcone**
zah-<u>kahzh'</u>-neh	skrehn-<u>tsoh</u>-neh
contagious	sprained

I'm vomiting.
Wymiotuję.
vyh-myoh-<u>tuh</u>-yeh

I've been sick for ... days.
Źle się czuję od ... dni.
zh'leh sh'yeh <u>chuh</u>-yeh ohd ... dn'yee

I'm taking ...
Zażywam ...
zah-<u>zhyh</u>-vahm ...

It hurts here.
Boli mnie tutaj.
<u>boh</u>-lee mn'yeh <u>tuh</u>-tahy

It's gotten worse/better.
Jest gorzej/lepiej.
yehst <u>goh</u>-zhehy/<u>leh</u>-pyehy

You Might Hear

Proszę głęboko oddychać.
proh-sheh gwehm-boh-koh ohd-dyh-hahch'
Breathe deeply.

Proszę zakasłać.
proh-sheh zah-kah-swahch'
Cough please.

Proszę się rozebrać.
proh-sheh sh'yeh roh-zeh-brahch'
Undress, please.

Czy boli tutaj?
chyh boh-lee tuh-tahy
Does it hurt here?

Proszę otworzyć usta.
proh-sheh oh-tfoh-zhyhch' uhs-tah
Open your mouth.

Powinien pan/Powinna pani pójść do specjalisty.
poh-vee-n'yehn pahn/poh-veen-nah pah-n'ee puhysh'ch' doh speh-tsyah-lee-styh
You should see a specialist.

Pójdzie pan/pani do szpitala.
puhy-dj'yeh pahn/pah-n'ee doh shpee-tah-lah
You must go to the hospital.

Potrzebna będzie wizyta kontrolna.
poh-tsheh-bnah behn-dj'yeh vee-zyh-tah kohn-trohl-nah
You need a follow-up.

Proszę wrócić za dwa tygodnie.
proh-sheh vruh-ch'eech' zah dvah tyh-gohd-n'yeh
Come back in two weeks.

Treatments and Instructions

Do I need a prescription medicine?
Czy dostanę lekarstwo na receptę?
chyh doh-stah-neh leh-kahr-stfoh nah reh-tsehp-teh

Can you prescribe a generic drug?
Czy mogę dostać lek generyczny?
chyh moh-geh doh-stahch' lehk geh-neh-ryh-chnyh

Is this over the counter?
Czy to lekarstwo jest dostępne bez recepty?
chyh toh leh-kahr-stfoh yehst doh-stehm-pneh behz reh-tsehp-tyh

How much do I take?
Jaką dawkę mam przyjmować?
yah-kohm dahf-keh mahm pshyhy-moh-vahch'

How often do I take this?
Jak często mam to zażywać?
yahk chehn-stoh mahm toh zah-zhyh-vahch'

You Might Hear

Musimy panu/pani ...
muh-sh'ee-myh pah-nuh/pah-n'ee ...
You need ...

zrobić badanie krwi
zroh-beech' bah-dah-n'yeh krvee
a blood test

zrobić zastrzyk
zroh-beech' zahs-tzhyhk
an injection

podać kroplówkę dożylną
poh-dahch' kroh-pluhf-keh doh-zhyhl-nohm
an IV

zrobić badanie na paciorkowcowe zapalenie gardła
zroh-beech' bah-dah-n'yeh nah pah-ch'yohr-kohf-tsoh-veh zah-pah-leh-n'yeh gahr-dwah
a strep test

zrobić badanie moczu
zroh-beech' bah-dah-n'yeh moh-chuh
a urine test

You Might Hear

Przepiszę panu/pani ...
psheh-<u>pee</u>-sheh <u>pah</u>-nuh/<u>pah</u>-n'ee ...
I'm prescribing you ...

antybiotyki
ahn-tyh-byoh-<u>tyh</u>-kee
antibiotics

leki przeciwwirusowe
<u>leh</u>-kee psheh-ch'eev-vee-ruh-<u>soh</u>-veh
anti-virals

maść
mahsh'ch'
an ointment

środki przeciwbólowe
<u>sh'roh</u>-tkee psheh-ch'eev-buh-<u>loh</u>-veh
painkillers

Are there side effects?
Czy są efekty uboczne?
chyh sohm eh-<u>feh</u>-ktyh uh-<u>bohch</u>-neh

Is this safe for children?
Czy mogą je zażywać dzieci?
chyh <u>moh</u>-gohm yeh zah-<u>zhyh</u>-vahch'
<u>dj'yeh</u>-ch'yee

You Might Hear

Proszę to brać ...
proh-sheh toh brahch' ...
Take ...

> **po jedzeniu**
> poh yeh-dzeh-n'yuh
> after eating

> **przed pójściem spać**
> psheht puhysh'-ch'yehm spahch'
> before bed

> **przed posiłkiem**
> psheht poh-sh'eew-kyehm
> before meals

> **rano**
> rah-noh
> in the morning

> **na czczo**
> nah chchoh
> on an empty stomach

> **doustnie**
> doh-uhst-n'yeh
> orally

> **dwa razy dziennie**
> dvah rah-zyh dj'yehn-n'yeh
> twice daily

> **z dużą ilością wody**
> zduh-zhohm ee-lohsh'-ch'yohm voh-dyh
> with plenty of water

You Might See

tylko do użytku zewnętrznego
for external use only

połykać w całości
swallow whole

może powodować senność
may cause drowsiness

nie przyjmować z alkoholem
do not mix with alcohol

I'm allergic to …
Mam uczulenie na …
mahm uh-chuh-<u>leh</u>-n'yeh nah …

anti-inflammatories
leki przeciwzapalne
<u>leh</u>-kee psheh-ch'eev-zah-<u>pahl</u>-neh

aspirin
aspirynę
ah-spee-<u>ryh</u>-neh

codeine
kodeinę
koh-deh-<u>ee</u>-neh

penicillin
penicylinę
peh-n'ee-tsyh-<u>lee</u>-neh

Payment and Insurance

I have insurance.
Jestem ubezpieczony/ubezpieczona.
yehs-tehm uh-behz-pyeh-choh-nyh/
uh-behz-pyeh-choh-nah

Do you accept …?
Czy przyjmują państwo …?
chyh pshyhy-muh-yohm pahn'-stfoh …

How much does it cost?
Ile to kosztuje?
ee-leh toh kohsh-tuh-yeh

Can I have an itemized receipt for my
insurance please?
**Czy mogę dostać pokwitowanie dla
mojego ubezpieczenia z wyszczegól-
nieniem wszystkich opłat?**
chyh moh-geh doh-stahch' poh-kfee-toh-
vah-n'yeh dlah moh-yeh-goh uh-behz-
pyeh-cheh-n'yah zvyh-shcheh-guhl-n'yeh-
n'yehm fshyh-stkeeh oh-pwaht

Can I pay by credit card?
Czy mogę zapłacić kartą kredytową?
chyh moh-geh zah-pwah-ch'eech' kahr-
tohm kreh-dyh-toh-vohm

Will my insurance cover this?
Czy moje ubezpieczenie to pokryje?
chyh moh-yeh uh-behz-pyeh-cheh-n'yeh
toh poh-kryh-yeh

Parts of the Body

abdomen
brzuch
bzhuhh

anus
odbyt
ohd-byht

appendix
wyrostek
robaczkowy
vyh-roh-stehk roh-
bahch-koh-vyh

arm
ramię / ręka
rah-myeh / rehn-kah

back
plecy
pleh-tsyh

belly button
pępek
pehm-pehk

bladder
pęcherz
pehn-hehzh

bone
kość
kohsh'ch'

buttocks
pośladki
poh-sh'laht-kee

breast
pierś
pyehrsh'

chest
klatka piersiowa
klah-tkah pyehr-
sh'yoh-vah

ear
ucho
uh-hoh

elbow
łokieć
woh-kyehch'

eye
oko
oh-koh

face
twarz
tfahsh

finger
palec (u ręki)
pah-lehts (uh rehn-
kee)

foot	joint
stopa	**staw**
<u>stoh</u>-pah	stahv
gland	kidney
gruczoł	**nerka**
<u>gruh</u>-chohw	<u>nehr</u>-kah
hair	knee
włosy	**kolano**
<u>vwoh</u>-syh	koh-<u>lah</u>-noh
hand	knuckles
dłoń	**stawy palców**
dwohn'	<u>stah</u>-vyh <u>pahl</u>-tsuhf
heart	leg
serce	**noga**
<u>sehr</u>-tseh	<u>noh</u>-gah
hip	lip
biodro	**warga**
<u>byoh</u>-droh	<u>vahr</u>-gah
intestines	liver
jelita	**wątroba**
yeh-<u>lee</u>-tah	vohn-<u>troh</u>-bah
jaw	lung
szczęka	**płuco**
<u>shchehn</u>-kah	<u>pwuh</u>-tsoh

mouth
usta
<u>uhs</u>-tah

skin
skóra
<u>skuh</u>-rah

muscle
mięsień
<u>myehn</u>-sh'yehn'

stomach
żołądek
zhoh-<u>wohn</u>-dehk

neck
szyja / kark
<u>shyh</u>-yah / kahrk

testicles
jądra
<u>yohn</u>-drah

nose
nos
nohs

thigh
udo
<u>uh</u>-doh

penis
penis
<u>peh</u>-n'ees

throat
gardło
<u>gahr</u>-dwoh

rectum
odbytnica
ohd-byht-<u>n'ee</u>-tsah

thumb
kciuk
kch'yuhk

rib
żebro
<u>zheh</u>-broh

toe
palec u nogi
<u>pah</u>-lehts uh <u>noh</u>-gee

shoulder
bark / ramię
bahrk / <u>rah</u>-myeh

tooth / teeth
ząb / zęby
zohmb / <u>zehm</u>-byh

tongue	vagina
język	**pochwa**
yehn-zyhk	pohh-fah
tonsils	vein
migdałki	**żyła**
meeg-dahw-kee	zhyh-wah
urethra	waist
cewka moczowa	**talia**
tsehf-kah moh-choh-vah	tah-lyah
	wrist
uterus	**nadgarstek**
macica	nahd-gahr-stehk
mah-ch'ee-tsah	

Other Medical Facilities

Optometrist

I need an eye exam.
Chciałbym/Chciałabym zbadać wzrok.
hch'yahw-byhm/hch'yah-wah-byhm zbah-dahch' vzrohk

I've lost …
Zgubiłem/Zgubiłam …
zguh-bee-wehm/zguh-bee-wahm …

    a lens
    szkło
    shkwoh

my contacts
moje szkła/soczewki kontaktowe
<u>moh</u>-yeh shkwah/soh-<u>chehf</u>-kee
kohn-tahk-<u>toh</u>-veh

my glasses
moje okulary
<u>moh</u>-yeh oh-kuh-<u>lah</u>-ryh

Should I continue to wear these?
Czy mam nadal nosić te?
chyh mahm <u>nah</u>-dahl <u>noh</u>-sh'eech' teh

Can I select new frames?
Czy mogę wybrać nowe oprawki?
chyh <u>moh</u>-geh <u>vyh</u>-brahch' <u>noh</u>-veh oh-<u>prahf</u>-kee

How long will it take?
Ile to potrwa?
<u>ee</u>-leh toh <u>poh</u>-trvah

I'm nearsighted/farsighted.
Jestem krótkowidzem/dalekowidzem.
<u>yehs</u>-tehm kruh-tkoh-<u>vee</u>-dzehm/
dah-leh-koh-<u>vee</u>-dzehm

Dentist

This tooth hurts.
Boli mnie ten ząb.
<u>boh</u>-lee mn'yeh tehn zohmb

I have a toothache.
Boli mnie ząb.
boh-lee mn'yeh zohmb

I have a cavity.
Mam ubytek w zębie.
mahm uh-byh-tehk vzehm-byeh

I've lost a filling.
Wypadła mi plomba.
vyh-pah-dwah mee plohm-bah

My tooth is broken.
Ząb mi się złamał.
zohmb mee sh'yeh zwah-mahw

Can you fix these dentures?
Czy da się naprawić tę protezę?
chyh dah sh'yeh nah-prah-veech' teh
proh-teh-zeh

My teeth are sensitive.
Moje zęby są nadwrażliwe.
moh-yeh zehm-byh sohm nahd-vrah-zhlee-veh

Gynecologist

I have cramps.
Mam bóle miesiączkowe.
mahm buh-leh myeh-sh'yohn-chkoh-veh

My period is late.
Spóźnia mi się okres.
spuh-zh'n'yah mee sh'yeh oh-krehs

You Might Hear

Musimy zrobić plombę.
muh-<u>sh'ee</u>-myh <u>zroh</u>-beech' <u>plohm</u>-beh
You need a filling.

Dam panu/pani zastrzyk/znieczulenie miejscowe.
dahm <u>pah</u>-nuh/<u>pah</u>-n'ee <u>zahs</u>-tzhyhk/zn'yeh-chuh-<u>leh</u>-n'yeh myehy-<u>stsoh</u>-veh
I'm giving you an injection/a local anesthetic.

Muszę usunąć tego zęba.
<u>muh</u>-sheh uh-<u>suh</u>-nohnch' <u>teh</u>-goh <u>zehm</u>-bah
I have to extract this tooth.

Proszę nic nie jeść przez ... godzin.
<u>proh</u>-sheh n'eets n'yeh yehsh'ch' pzhehz ...
<u>goh</u>-dj'een
Don't eat anything for ... hours.

I have an infection.
Mam infekcję.
mahm een-<u>fehk</u>-tsyeh

I'm on the Pill.
Biorę pigułki antykoncepcyjne.
<u>byoh</u>-reh pee-<u>guhw</u>-kee ahn-tyh-kohn-tsehp-<u>tsyhy</u>-neh

I'm not pregnant.
Nie jestem w ciąży.
n'yeh <u>yehs</u>-tehm <u>fch'yohn</u>-zhyh

I'm ... months pregnant.
Jestem w ... miesiącu ciąży.
<u>yehs</u>-tehm v ... myeh-<u>sh'yohn</u>-tsuh <u>ch'yohn</u>-zhyh

My last period was ...
Ostatnią miesiączkę miałam ...
ohs-<u>taht</u>-n'yohm myeh-<u>sh'yohn</u>-chkeh <u>myah</u>-wahm ...

I need ...
Chciałabym ...
hch'yah-<u>wah</u>-byhm ...

> a contraceptive
> **jakiś środek antykoncepcyjny**
> <u>yah</u>-keesh' <u>sh'roh</u>-dehk ahn-tyh-kohn-tsehp-<u>tsyhy</u>-nyh

> the morning-after pill
> **pigułkę wczesnoporonną**
> pee-<u>guhw</u>-keh fcheh-snoh-poh-<u>rohn</u>-nohm

> a pregnancy test
> **test ciążowy**
> tehst ch'yohn-<u>zhoh</u>-vyh

> an STD test
> **badanie na choroby przenoszone drogą płciową**
> bah-<u>dah</u>-n'yeh nah hoh-<u>roh</u>-byh psheh-noh-<u>shoh</u>-neh <u>droh</u>-gohm <u>pwch'yoh</u>-vohm

Pharmacy

Where's the nearest (24-hour) pharmacy?
Gdzie jest najbliższa apteka (całodobowa)?
gdj'yeh yehst nahy-<u>bleezh</u>-shah ahp-<u>teh</u>-kah
(tsah-woh-doh-<u>boh</u>-vah)

What time does the pharmacy open/close?
O której otwierają/zamykają aptekę?
oh <u>ktuh</u>-rehy oht-fyeh-<u>rah</u>-yohm/zah-myh-<u>kah</u>-yohm ahp-<u>teh</u>-keh

Can you fill this prescription?
Czy możecie zrealizować tę receptę?
chyh moh-<u>zheh</u>-ch'yeh zreh-ah-lee-<u>zoh</u>-vahch' teh reh-<u>tsehp</u>-teh

How long is the wait?
Ile trzeba czekać?
<u>ee</u>-leh <u>tzheh</u>-bah <u>cheh</u>-kahch'

I'll come back for it.
Wrócę po nią.
<u>vruh</u>-tseh poh n'yohm

What do you recommend for …?
Co może pan/pani polecić na …
tsoh <u>moh</u>-zheh pahn/<u>pah</u>-n'ee poh-<u>leh</u>-ch'eech' nah …

allergies
alergie
ah-<u>lehr</u>-gyeh

a cold
przeziębienie
pzheh-zh'yehm-<u>byeh</u>-n'yeh

a cough
kaszel
<u>kah</u>-shehl

diarrhea
biegunkę
byeh-<u>guhn</u>-keh

a hangover
kaca
<u>kah</u>-tsah

motion sickness
chorobę lokomocyjną
hoh-<u>roh</u>-beh loh-koh-moh-<u>tsyhy</u>-nohm

post-nasal drip
spływ wydzieliny z nozdrzy (do gardła)
spwyhv vyh-dj'yeh-<u>lee</u>-nyh <u>znohz</u>-dzhyh (doh <u>gahr</u>-dwah)

a sore throat
ból gardła
buhl <u>gahr</u>-dwah

an upset stomach
rozstrój żołądka
<u>rohz</u>-truhy zhoh-<u>wohn</u>-tkah

Do I need a prescription?
Czy potrzebna mi będzie recepta?
chyh poh-<u>tsheh</u>-bnah mee <u>behn</u>-dj'yeh
reh-<u>tsehp</u>-tah

Do you have ...?
Czy mają państwo ...?
chyh <u>mah</u>-yohm <u>pahn'</u>-stfoh ...

anti-diarrheal
jakiś środek przeciwbiegunkowy
<u>yah</u>-keesh' <u>sh'roh</u>-dehk psheh-ch'eev-
byeh-guhn-<u>koh</u>-vyh

antiseptic rinse
środek antyseptyczny do płukania
<u>sh'roh</u>-dehk ahn-tyh-sehp-<u>tyh</u>-chnyh
doh pwuh-<u>kah</u>-n'yah

asprin
aspirynę
ahs-pee-<u>ryh</u>-neh

bandages
bandaże
bahn-<u>dah</u>-zheh

cold medicine
jakieś lekarstwo na przeziębienie
<u>yah</u>-kyehsh' leh-<u>kahr</u>-stfoh nah pzheh-
zh'yehm-<u>byeh</u>-n'yeh

condoms
prezerwatywy
preh-zehr-vah-<u>tyh</u>-vyh

---

cotton balls
waciki
vah-<u>ch'yee</u>-kee

gauze
gazę
<u>gah</u>-zeh

ibuprofen
ibuprofen
ee-buh-<u>proh</u>-fehn

insect repellant
środek na owady
<u>sh'roh</u>-dehk nah oh-<u>vah</u>-dyh

a thermometer
termometr
tehr-<u>moh</u>-mehtr

throat lozenges
tabletki do ssania od bólu gardła
tah-<u>bleh</u>-tkee doh <u>ssah</u>-n'yah ohd <u>buh</u>-luh <u>gahr</u>-dwah

vitamins
witaminy
vee-tah-<u>mee</u>-nyh

I'm looking for …
Szukam …
<u>shuh</u>-kahm …

aftershave
płynu po goleniu
<u>pwyh</u>-nuh poh goh-<u>leh</u>-n'yuh

baby wipes
chusteczek pielęgnacyjnych dla niemowląt
huh-<u>steh</u>-chehk pyeh-lehn-gnah-<u>tsyhy</u>-nyhh dlah n'yeh-<u>mohv</u>-lohnt

a comb
grzebienia
gzheh-<u>byeh</u>-n'yah

conditioner
odżywki do włosów
ohd-<u>zhyhf</u>-kee doh <u>vwoh</u>-suhf

dental floss
nici dentystycznej
<u>n'ee</u>-ch'ee dehn-tyh-<u>styh</u>-chnehy

deodorant
dezodorantu
deh-zoh-doh-<u>rahn</u>-tuh

diapers
pieluch
<u>pyeh</u>-luhh

a hair brush
szczotki do włosów
<u>shchoh</u>-tkee doh <u>vwoh</u>-suhf

hair spray
lakieru do włosów
lah-<u>kyeh</u>-ruh doh <u>vwoh</u>-suhf

hand lotion
balsamu do rąk
bahl-<u>sah</u>-muh doh rohnk

moisturizer
kremu nawilżającego
<u>kreh</u>-muh nah-veel-zhah-yohn-<u>tseh</u>-goh

mousse
pianki do włosów
<u>pyahn</u>-kee doh <u>vwoh</u>-suhf

mouthwash
płynu do płukania ust
<u>pwyh</u>-nuh doh pwuh-<u>kah</u>-n'yah uhst

razor blades
żyletek
zhyh-<u>leh</u>-tehk

rubbing alcohol
spirytus salicylowy
spee-<u>ryh</u>-tuhs sah-lee-tsyh-<u>loh</u>-vyh

shampoo
szamponu
shahm-<u>poh</u>-nuh

shaving cream
kremu do golenia
<u>kreh</u>-muh doh goh-<u>leh</u>-n'yah

soap
mydła
<u>myh</u>-dwah

sunblock
kremu z filtrem przeciwsłonecznym
<u>kreh</u>-muh <u>sfeel</u>-trehm

tampons
tamponów
tahm-<u>poh</u>-nuhf

tissues
chusteczek higienicznych
huh-<u>steh</u>-chehk hee-gyeh-<u>n'eech</u>-nyhh

toilet paper
papieru toaletowego
pah-<u>pyeh</u>-ruh toh-ah-leh-toh-<u>veh</u>-goh

a toothbrush
szczoteczki do zębów
shchoh-<u>tehch</u>-kee doh <u>zehm</u>-buhf

toothpaste
pasty do zębów
<u>pah</u>-styh doh <u>zehm</u>-buhf

GENERAL EMERGENCIES

Essentials

Help!
Pomocy!
poh-<u>moh</u>-tsyh

Fire!
Pali się!
<u>pah</u>-lee sh'yeh

Thief!
Złodziej!
<u>zwoh</u>-dj'yehy

Police!
Policja!
poh-<u>lee</u>-tsyah

It's an emergency!
To nagły wypadek!
toh <u>nah</u>-gwyh vyh-<u>pah</u>-dehk

Stop!
Stój!
stuhy

Leave me alone!
Zostaw mnie w spokoju!
<u>zoh</u>-stahf mn'yeh fspoh-<u>koh</u>-yuh

There's been an accident/attack!
Zdarzył się wypadek/napad!
<u>zdah</u>-zhyhw sh'yeh vyh-<u>pah</u>-dehk/<u>nah</u>-paht

Call …!
Wezwijcie …
veh-<u>zveey</u>-ch'yeh …

> an ambulance
> **karetkę**
> kha-<u>reht</u>-keh

> a doctor
> **lekarza**
> leh-<u>kah</u>-zhah

> the fire department
> **straż pożarną**
> strahsh poh-<u>zhahr</u>-nohm

> the police
> **policję**
> poh-<u>lee</u>-tsyeh

Is anyone here …?
Czy jest tu …?
chyh yehst tuh …

> a doctor
> **lekarz**
> <u>leh</u>-kahsh

> trained in CPR
> **ktoś przeszkolony z udzielania**
> **pierwszej pomocy**
> ktohsh' psheh-shkoh-<u>loh</u>-nyh s uh-dj'yeh-
> <u>lah</u>-n'yah <u>pyehr</u>-vshehy poh-<u>moh</u>-tsyh

Quickly!
Szybko!
shyhp-koh

Be careful!
Bądź ostrożny!
bohndj' ohs-troh-zhnyh

Where is the …?
Gdzie jest …
gdj'yeh yehst …

American embassy
ambasada amerykańska
ahm-bah-sah-dah ah-meh-ryh-kahn'-skah

bathroom
łazienka
wah-zh'yehn-kah

hospital
szpital
shpee-tahl

police station
posterunek policji
poh-steh-ruh-nehk poh-lee-tsyee

Can you help me?
Czy może mi pan/pani pomóc?
chyh moh-zheh mee pahn/pah-nee poh-muhts

Can I use your phone?
Czy mogę skorzystać z pana/pani telefonu?
chyh moh-geh skoh-zhyh-stahch' s pah-nah/
pah-nee teh-leh-foh-nuh

I'm lost.
Zgubiłem/Zgubiłam się.
zguh-<u>bee</u>-wehm/zguh-<u>bee</u>-wahm sh'yeh

Go away!
Proszę odejść!
<u>proh</u>-sheh <u>oh</u>-deysh'ch'

Talking to Police

I've been assaulted.
Napadnięto na mnie.
nah-pah-<u>dn'yehn</u>-toh nah mn'yeh

I've been mugged.
Napadnięto na mnie.
nah-pah-<u>dn'yehn</u>-toh nah mn'yeh

I've been raped.
Zgwałcono mnie.
zgvahw-<u>tsoh</u>-noh mn'yeh

I've been robbed.
Okradziono mnie.
oh-krah-<u>dj'yoh</u>-noh mn'yeh

I've been swindled.
Oszukano mnie.
oh-shuh-<u>kah</u>-noh mn'yeh

That person tried to … me.
Tamta osoba próbowała mnie …
<u>tahm</u>-tah oh-<u>soh</u>-bah pruh-boh-<u>vah</u>-wah
mn'yeh …

>   assault
>   **napaść i pobić**
>   <u>nah</u>-pahsh'ch'

>   mug
>   **napaść i okraść**
>   <u>nah</u>-pahsh'ch'

>   rape
>   **zgwałcić**
>   <u>zgvahw</u>-ch'eech'

>   rob
>   **okraść**
>   <u>oh</u>-krahsh'ch'

I've lost my …
Zgubiłem/Zgubiłam …
zguh-<u>bee</u>-wehm/zguh-<u>bee</u>-wahm …

>   bag(s)
>   **torbę / torby**
>   <u>tohr</u>-beh / <u>tohr</u>-byh

>   credit card
>   **kartę kredytową**
>   <u>kahr</u>-teh kreh-dyh-<u>toh</u>-vohm

>   driver's license
>   **prawo jazdy**
>   <u>prah</u>-voh <u>yahz</u>-dyh

identification
dowód tożsamości
<u>doh</u>-vuht tohsh-sah-<u>mohsh</u>'-ch'ee

keys
klucze
<u>kluh</u>-cheh

laptop
laptopa
lahp-<u>toh</u>-pah

money
pieniądze
pyeh-<u>n'yohn</u>-dzeh

passport
paszport
<u>pahsh</u>-pohrt

purse
torebkę
toh-<u>rehp</u>-keh

traveler's checks
czeki podróżne
<u>cheh</u>-kee pohd-<u>ruhzh</u>-neh

visa
wizę
<u>vee</u>-zeh

wallet
portfel
<u>pohrt</u>-fehl

My … was stolen.
Ukradli mi …
uh-<u>krah</u>-dlee mee …

I need a police report.
Muszę mieć raport z policji.
<u>muh</u>-sheh myehch' <u>rah</u>-pohrt spoh-<u>lee</u>-tsyee

Please show me your badge.
Proszę mi pokazać odznakę.
<u>proh</u>-sheh mee poh-<u>kah</u>-zahch' oh-<u>dznah</u>-keh

Please take me to your superior.
Proszę zaprowadzić mnie do swojego przełożonego.
<u>proh</u>-sheh zah-proh-<u>vah</u>-dj'eech' mn'yeh doh sfoh-<u>yeh</u>-goh psheh-woh-zhoh-<u>neh</u>-goh

Please take me to the police station.
Proszę zaprowadzić mnie na posterunek policji.
<u>proh</u>-sheh zah-proh-<u>vah</u>-dj'eech' mn'yeh nah poh-steh-<u>ruh</u>-nehk poh-<u>lee</u>-tsyee

I have insurance.
Jestem ubezpieczony/ubezpieczona.
<u>yehs</u>-tehm uh-behs-pyeh-<u>choh</u>-nyh/uh-behs-pyeh-<u>choh</u>-nah

This person won't leave me alone.
Ta osoba nie chce zostawić mnie w spokoju.
tah oh-<u>soh</u>-bah n'yeh htseh zoh-<u>stah</u>-veech' mn'yeh fspoh-<u>koh</u>-yuh

My son/daughter is missing.
Mój syn zgubił się. / Moja córka zgubiła się.
muhy syhn <u>zguh</u>-beew sh'yeh / <u>moh</u>-yah
<u>tsuhr</u>-kah zguh-<u>bee</u>-wah sh'yeh

He/She is XX years old.
Ma XX lat.
mah XX laht

I last saw the culprit XX minutes/hours ago.
Ostatni raz widziałem/widziałam
sprawcę XX minut/godzin temu.
oh-<u>stah</u>-tnee rahz vee-<u>dj'yah</u>-wehm/vee-
<u>dj'yah</u>-wahm <u>sprah</u>-ftseh XX <u>mee</u>-nuht/<u>goh</u>-
dj'een <u>teh</u>-muh

What is the problem?
O co chodzi?
oh tso <u>hoh</u>-dj'ee

What am I accused of?
O co jestem oskarżony/oskarżona?
oh tso <u>yehs</u>-tehm oh-skahr-<u>zhoh</u>-nyh/
oh-skahr-<u>zhoh</u>-nah

I didn't realize that it wasn't allowed.
Nie wiedziałem/wiedziałam, że to
zabronione.
n'yeh vyeh-<u>dj'yah</u>-wehm/vyeh-<u>dj'yah</u>-wahm
zheh toh zah-broh-<u>n'yoh</u>-neh

I apologize.
Przepraszam.
psheh-<u>prah</u>-shahm

I didn't do anything.
Nic nie zrobiłem/zrobiłam.
neets n'yeh zroh-<u>bee</u>-wehm/zroh-<u>bee</u>-wahm

I'm innocent.
Jestem niewinny/niewinna.
<u>yehs</u>-tehm n'yeh-<u>veen</u>-nyh/n'yeh-<u>veen</u>-nah

I need to make a phone call.
Muszę zatelefonować.
<u>muh</u>-sheh zah-teh-leh-foh-<u>noh</u>-vahch'

I want to contact my embassy/consulate.
**Chciałbym/Chciałabym skontaktować
się z moją ambasadą / z moim konsula-
tem.**
<u>hch'yahw</u>-byhm/hch'yah-<u>wah</u>-byhm skohn-
tah-<u>ktoh</u>-vahch' sh'yeh <u>zmoh</u>-yohm ahm-
bah-<u>sah</u>-dohm/kohn-suh-<u>lah</u>-tehm

I want to speak to a lawyer.
**Chciałbym/Chciałabym porozmawiać z
prawnikiem.**
<u>hch'yahw</u>-byhm/hch'yah-<u>wah</u>-byhm poh-
roh-<u>zmah</u>-vyahch' sprah-<u>vn'ee</u>-kyehm

I speak English.
Mówię po angielsku.
<u>muh</u>-vyeh poh ahn-<u>gyehl</u>-skuh

I need an interpreter.
Potrzebuję tłumacza.
poht-sheh-<u>buh</u>-yeh twuh-<u>mah</u>-chah

You Might Hear

Gdzie to się stało?
gdj'yeh toh sh'yeh <u>stah</u>-woh
Where did this happen?

Kiedy to się stało?
<u>kyeh</u>-dyh toh sh'yeh <u>stah</u>-woh
What time did it occur?

Jak on/ona wygląda?
yahk ohn/<u>oh</u>-nah vyh-<u>glohn</u>-dah
What does he/she look like?

disturbing the peace
zakłócanie spokoju
zah-kwuh-<u>tsah</u>-n'yeh spoh-<u>koh</u>-yuh

traffic violation
wykroczenie drogowe
vyh-kroh-<u>cheh</u>-n'yeh droh-<u>goh</u>-veh

parking fine
mandat za nieprawidłowe parkowanie
<u>mahn</u>-daht zah n'yeh-prah-vee-<u>dwoh</u>-veh
pahr-koh-<u>vah</u>-n'yeh

speeding ticket
mandat za przekroczenie prędkości
<u>mahn</u>-daht zah psheh-kroh-<u>cheh</u>-n'yeh
prehnt-<u>koh</u>-sh'ch'ee

overstaying your visa
przekroczenie terminu ważności wizy
psheh-kroh-<u>cheh</u>-n'yeh tehr-<u>mee</u>-nuh
vahzh-<u>noh</u>-sh'ch'ee <u>vee</u>-zyh

theft
kradzież
<u>krah</u>-dj'yehsh

You Might See

Pogotowie
poh-goh-<u>toh</u>-vyeh
Emergency

Szpital
<u>shpee</u>-tahl
Hospital

Policja
poh-<u>lee</u>-tsyah
Police

Posterunek Policji
poh-steh-<u>ruh</u>-nehk poh-<u>lee</u>-tsyee
Police Station

NUMBERS AND MEASUREMENT

Cardinal Number

1	9
jeden	**dziewięć**
<u>yeh</u>-dehn	<u>dj'yeh</u>-vyehn'ch'
2	10
dwa	**dziesięć**
dvah	<u>dj'yeh</u>-sh'yehn'ch'
3	11
trzy	**jedenaście**
tshyh	yeh-deh-<u>nahsh'</u>-ch'yeh
4	12
cztery	**dwanaście**
<u>chteh</u>-ryh	dvah-<u>nahsh'</u>-ch'yeh
5	13
pięć	**trzynaście**
pyehn'ch'	tshyh-<u>nahsh'</u>-ch'yeh
6	14
sześć	**czternaście**
shehsh'ch'	chtehr-<u>nahsh'</u>-ch'yeh
7	15
siedem	**piętnaście**
<u>sh'yeh</u>-dehm	pyeht-<u>nahsh'</u>-ch'yeh
8	16
osiem	**szesnaście**
<u>oh</u>-sh'yehm	shehs-<u>nahsh'</u>-ch'yeh

17
siedemnaście
sh'yehdehm-<u>nahsh'</u>-ch'yeh

18
osiemnaście
oh-sh'yehm-<u>nahsh'</u>-ch'yeh

19
dziewiętnaście
dj'yeh-vyeht-<u>nahsh'</u>-ch'yeh

20
dwadzieścia
dvah-<u>dj'yehsh'</u>-ch'yah

21
dwadzieścia jeden
dvah-<u>dj'yehsh'</u>-ch'yah <u>yeh</u>-dehn

22
dwadzieścia dwa
dvah-<u>dj'yehsh'</u>-ch'yah dvah

30
trzydzieści
tshyh-<u>dj'yehsh'</u>-ch'ee

31
trzydzieści jeden
tshyh-<u>dj'yehsh'</u>-ch'ee <u>yeh</u>-dehn

32
trzydzieści dwa
tshyh-<u>dj'yehsh'</u>-ch'ee dvah

40
czterdzieści
chtehr-<u>dj'yehsh'</u>-ch'ee

50
pięćdziesiąt
pyehn'-<u>dj'yeh</u>-sh'yohnt

60
sześćdziesiąt
shehsh'-<u>dj'yeh</u>-sh'yohnt

70
siedemdziesiąt
sh'yeh-dehm-<u>dj'yeh</u>-sh'yohnt

80
osiemdziesiąt
oh-sh'yehm-<u>dj'yeh</u>-sh'yohnt

90
dziewięćdziesiąt
dj'eh-vyen'-<u>dj'yeh</u>-
sh'yohnt

100
sto
stoh

101
sto jeden
stoh-<u>yeh</u>-dehn

200
dwieście
<u>dvyehsh'</u>-ch'yeh

500
pięćset
<u>pyehn'</u>-seht

1,000
tysiąc
<u>tyh</u>-sh'yohnts

10,000
dziesięć tysięcy
<u>dj'yeh</u>-sh'yehn'ch'
tyh-<u>sh'yehn</u>-tsyh

100,000
sto tysięcy
stoh tyh-<u>sh'yehn</u>-tsyh

1,000,000
milion
<u>meel</u>-yohn

Fractions

one-quarter
jedna czwarta
<u>yeh</u>-dnah <u>chfahr</u>-tah

one-third
jedna trzecia
<u>yeh</u>-dnah <u>tsheh</u>-ch'yah

one-half
jedna druga
<u>yeh</u>-dnah <u>druh</u>-gah

two-thirds
dwie trzecie
dvyeh <u>tsheh</u>-ch'yeh

three-quarters
trzy czwarte
tshyh <u>chfahr</u>-teh

all
wszystko / cały
<u>fshyh</u>-stkoh / <u>tsah</u>-wyh

none
nic / ani trochę / żaden / żadna
neets / <u>ah</u>-nee <u>troh</u>-heh / <u>zhah</u>-dehn /
<u>zhah</u>-dnah

Ordinal Numbers

first
pierwszy
<u>pyehr</u>-vshyh

fifth
piąty
<u>pyohn</u>-tyh

second
drugi
<u>druh</u>-gee

sixth
szósty
<u>shuhs</u>-tyh

third
trzeci
<u>tsheh</u>-ch'ee

seventh
siódmy
<u>sh'yuhd</u>-myh

fourth
czwarty
<u>chfahr</u>-tyh

eighth
ósmy
<u>uhs</u>-myh

ninth	tenth
dziewiąty	**dziesiąty**
dj'yeh-<u>vyohn</u>-tyh	dj'yeh-<u>sh'yohn</u>-tyh

Quantity and Size

one dozen	half a dozen
tuzin	**pół tuzina**
<u>tuh</u>-zh'een	puhw tuh-<u>zh'ee</u>-nah

a pair of ...
para ...
<u>pah</u>-rah ...

a couple of ...	
dwa/dwie ...	**kilka/parę ...**
dvah/dvyeh ...	<u>keel</u>-kah/<u>pah</u>-reh ...

some (of) ...	
kilka ...	**trochę ...**
<u>keel</u>-kah	<u>troh</u>-heh ...

a half
połowa
poh-<u>woh</u>-vah

a little	a lot
trochę	**dużo**
<u>troh</u>-heh	<u>duh</u>-zhoh

more	less
więcej	**mniej**
<u>vyeh</u>-tsehy	mnyehy

enough
dość / wystarczająco
dohsh'ch' / vyh-stahr-chah-<u>yohn</u>-tsoh

not enough
nie dość / nie wystarczająco
n'yeh dohsh'ch' / n'yeh vyh-stahr-chah-<u>yohn</u>-
tsoh

too many/much
za dużo
zah <u>duh</u>-zhoh

extra small (XS)
bardzo mały (XS)
<u>bahr</u>-dzoh <u>mah</u>-wyh (eeks ehs)

small (S)
mały (S)
<u>mah</u>-wyh (ehs)

medium (M)
średni (M)
<u>sh'reh</u>-dn'ee (ehm)

large (L)
duży (L)
<u>duh</u>-zhyh (ehl)

extra-large (XL)
bardzo duży (XL)
<u>bahr</u>-dzoh <u>duh</u>-zhyh (eeks ehl)

NUMBERS & MEASUREMENTS

big	bigger	biggest
duży	**większy**	**największy**
duh-zhyh	vyeh-kshyh	nahy-vyeh-kshyh

small	smaller	smallest
mały	**mniejszy**	**najmniejszy**
mah-wyh	mnyehy-shyh	nahy-mnyehy-shyh

fat	skinny
gruby	**chudy**
gruh-byh	huh-dyh

wide	narrow
szeroki	**wąski**
sheh-roh-kee	vohn-skee

tall	short
wysoki	**niski** (*person*)
vyh-soh-kee	nees-kee
	krótki (*object*)
long	kruht-kee
długi	
dwuh-gee	

Weights and Measurements

inch	mile
cal	**mila**
tsahl	mee-lah

foot	millimeter
stopa	**milimetr**
stoh-pah	mee-lee-mehtr

centimeter
centymetr
tsehn-<u>tyh</u>-mehtr

meter
metr
mehtr

kilometer
kilometr
kee-<u>loh</u>-mehtr

milliliter
mililitr
mee-<u>lee</u>-leetr

liter
litr
leetr

kilogram
kilogram
kee-<u>loh</u>-grahm

ounce
uncja
<u>uhn</u>-tsyah

cup
filiżanka
fee-lee-<u>zhahn</u>-kah

pint
pół kwarty
puhw <u>kfahr</u>-tyh
or
pół litra
puhw <u>lee</u>-trah

quart
kwarta
<u>kfahr</u>-tah

gallon
galon
<u>gah</u>-lohn

squared
(podniesione) do kwadratu
(pohd-n'yeh-<u>sh'yoh</u>-neh) doh kvah-<u>drah</u>-tuh

cubed
(podniesione) do trzeciej potęgi
(pohd-n'yeh-<u>sh'yoh</u>-neh) doh <u>tsheh</u>-ch'yehy
poh-<u>tehn</u>-gee

TIMES & DATES

Telling Time

What time is it?
Przepraszam, która jest godzina?
psheh-<u>prah</u>-shahm <u>ktuh</u>-rah yehst goh-<u>dj'ee</u>-nah

It's 5 A.M./P.M.
Jest piąta rano/po południu.
yehst <u>pyohn</u>-tah <u>rah</u>-noh/poh poh-<u>wuh</u>-dn'yuh

It's 6 o'clock
Szósta. (*6am/pm*) / **Osiemnasta.** (*6pm*)
<u>shuh</u>-stah

It's 6:30.
Szósta trzydzieści. (*6:30am/pm*) /
Osiemnasta trzydzieści. (*6:30pm*)
<u>shuh</u>-stah tshyh-<u>dj'yehsh</u>'-ch'ee

Five past (three).
Pięć po (trzeciej).
pyehn'ch' poh (<u>tsheh</u>-ch'yehy)

Half past (two).
(druga) trzydzieści. / (w) pół do (trzeciej).
(<u>druh</u>-gah) tshyh-<u>dj'yehsh</u>'-ch'ee / (f) puhw doh (<u>tsheh</u>-ch'yehy)

Quarter to (eight)
Za piętnaście (ósma)
zah pyeht-<u>nahsh</u>'-ch'yeh (<u>uhs</u>-mah)

Twenty to (four)
Za dwadzieścia (czwarta)
zah dvah-<u>dj'yehsh'</u>-ch'yah (<u>chfahr</u>-tah)

noon	midnight
południe	**północ**
poh-<u>wuhd</u>-n'yeh	<u>puhw</u>-nohts

in the morning	in the afternoon
rano	**po południu**
<u>rah</u>-noh	poh poh-<u>wuh</u>-dn'yuh

in the evening	at night
wieczorem	**w nocy**
vyeh-<u>choh</u>-rehm	<u>fnoh</u>-tsyh

early	late
wcześnie	**późno**
<u>vcheh</u>-sh'n'yeh	<u>puhzh'</u>-noh

At 1 P.M.
o pierwszej po południu / o trzynastej
oh <u>pyehr</u>-vshehy po poh-<u>wuh</u>-dn'yuh /
oh tshyh-<u>nahs</u>-tehy

At 3:28
o trzeciej dwadzieścia osiem
oh <u>tsheh</u>-ch'yehy dvah-<u>dj'yehsh'</u>-ch'yah <u>oh</u>-sh'yehm

A.M.	P.M.
rano	**po południu**
<u>rah</u>-noh	poh poh-<u>wuh</u>-dn'yuh

Duration

one month
miesiąc
<u>myeh</u>-sh'ohnts

two months
dwa miesiące
dvah myeh-<u>sh'ohn</u>-tseh

one week
tydzień
<u>tyh</u>-dj'yehn'

three weeks
trzy tygodnie
tshyh tyh-<u>goh</u>-dn'yeh

one day
jeden dzień
<u>yeh</u>-dehn dj'yehn'

four days
cztery dni
<u>chteh</u>-ryh dn'ee

one hour
jedna godzine
<u>yeh</u>-dnah goh-<u>dj'ee</u>-nah

a half hour
pół godziny
puhw goh-<u>dj'ee</u>-nyh

one minute
jedna minuta
<u>yeh</u>-dnah mee-<u>nuh</u>-tah

five minutes
pięć minut
pyehn'ch' <u>mee</u>-nuht

one second
jedna sekunda
<u>yeh</u>-dnah seh-<u>kuhn</u>-dah

five seconds
pięć sekund
pyehn'ch' <u>seh</u>-kuhnt

since
od
ohd

during
podczas, w trakcie
<u>pohd</u>-chahs, <u>ftrahk</u>-ch'yeh

before	after
przed	**po**
pshehd	poh

one year ago
rok temu
rohk <u>teh</u>-muh

five years ago
pięć lat temu
pyehn'ch' laht <u>teh</u>-muh

six months ago
sześć miesięcy temu / pół roku temu
shehsh'ch' myeh-<u>sh'yehn</u>-tsyh <u>teh</u>-muh /
puhw <u>roh</u>-kuh <u>teh</u>-muh

in two years
za dwa lata
zah dvah <u>lah</u>-tah

in five months
za pięć miesięcy
zah pyehn'ch' myeh-<u>sh'yehn</u>-tsyh

in two weeks
za dwa tygodnie
zah dvah tyh-<u>goh</u>-dn'yeh

in twelve days
za dwanaście dni
zah dvah-<u>nahsh'</u>-ch'yeh dnee

in three hours
za trzy godziny
zah tshyh goh-<u>dj'ee</u>-nyh

in five minutes
za pięć minut
zah pyehn'ch' <u>mee</u>-nuht

in ten seconds
za dziesięć sekund
zah <u>dj'yeh</u>-sh'yehn'ch' <u>seh</u>-kuhnd

Stating the Date

Relative Dates

yesterday	today	tomorrow
wczoraj	**dzisiaj**	**jutro**
<u>fchoh</u>-rahy	<u>dj'ee</u>-sh'yahy	<u>yuht</u>-roh

week	month	year
tydzień	**miesiąc**	**rok**
<u>tyh</u>-dj'yehn'	<u>myeh</u>-sh'ohnts	rohk

this week
ten tydzień
tehn <u>tyh</u>-dj'yehn'

next week
przyszły tydzień
<u>pshyh</u>-shwyh <u>tyh</u>-dj'yehn'

last week
ubiegły tydzień
uh-<u>byeh</u>-gwyh <u>tyh</u>-dj'yehn'

this month
ten miesiąc
tehn <u>myeh</u>-sh'ohnts

next month
przyszły miesiąc
<u>pshyh</u>-shwyh <u>myeh</u>-sh'ohnts

last month
ubiegły miesiąc
uh-<u>byeh</u>-gwyh <u>myeh</u>-sh'ohnts

this year
ten rok
tehn rohk

next year
przyszły rok
<u>pshyh</u>-shwyh rohk

last year
ubiegły rok
uh-<u>byeh</u>-gwyh rohk

Days of the Week

Monday **poniedziałek** poh-n'yeh-<u>dj'yah</u>-wehk
Tuesday **wtorek** <u>ftoh</u>-rehk
Wednesday **środa** <u>sh'roh</u>-dah
Thursday **czwartek** <u>chfahr</u>-tehk
Friday **piątek** <u>pyohn</u>-tehk
Saturday **sobota** soh-<u>boh</u>-tah
Sunday **niedziela** n'yeh-<u>dj'yeh</u>-lah

Months of the Year

January **styczeń** <u>styh</u>-chehn'
February **luty** <u>luh</u>-tyh
March **marzec** <u>mah</u>-zhehts
April **kwiecień** <u>kfyeh</u>-ch'yehn'
May **maj** mahy
June **czerwiec** <u>chehr</u>-vyehts
July **lipiec** <u>lee</u>-pyehts
August **sierpień** <u>sh'yehr</u>-pyehn'
September **wrzesień** <u>vzheh</u>-sh'yehn'
October **październik** pahzh'-<u>dj'yehr</u>-n'eek
November **listopad** lees-<u>toh</u>-paht
December **grudzień** <u>gruh</u>-dj'yehn'

Seasons

Winter **zima** <u>zh'ee</u>-mah
Spring **wiosna** <u>vyohs</u>-nah
Summer **lato** <u>lah</u>-toh
Fall/Autumn **jesień** <u>yeh</u>-sh'yehn'

PLACE NAMES

Countries

United States of America
Stany Zjednoczone Ameryki
<u>stah</u>-nyh zyeh-dnoh-<u>choh</u>-neh ah-meh-<u>ryh</u>-kee

(Note: This is the most formal usage. The United
States is most commonly referred to as just **Stany
Zjednoczone**.)

Canada
Kanada
kah-<u>nah</u>-dah

Great Britain
Wielka Brytania
<u>vyehl</u>-kah bryh-<u>tah</u>-n'yah

England
Anglia
<u>ahn</u>-glyah

Ireland
Irlandia
eer-<u>lahn</u>-dyah

Australia
Australia
ahw-<u>strah</u>-lyah

Cities

New York
Nowy Jork
<u>noh</u>-vyh yohrk

London
Londyn
<u>lohn</u>-dyhn

Chicago
Chicago
shee-<u>kah</u>-goh

Toronto
Toronto
toh-<u>rohn</u>-toh

Los Angeles
Los Angeles
lohs ahn-<u>djeh</u>-lehs

Vancouver
Vancouver
vahn-<u>kuh</u>-vehr

Dallas
Dallas
<u>dahl</u>-lahs

Paris
Paryż
<u>pah</u>-ryhzh

Boston
Boston
<u>bohs</u>-tohn

www.ingramcontent.com/pod-product-compliance
Lightning Source LLC
Jackson TN
JSHW011352130125
77033JS00023B/653

* 9 7 8 0 7 8 1 8 1 2 5 9 7 *